New Directions in Behavior Development

New Directions in Behavior Development

Edited by

Sidney W. Bijou
Emilio Ribes

Publisher's Note

Care has been taken to confirm the accuracy of the information presented and to describe generally accepted practices. However, the authors, editors, and publisher are not responsible for errors or omissions or for any consequences from application of the information in this book and make no warranty, express or implied, with respect to the contents of the publication.

The authors, editors, and publisher have exerted every effort to ensure that any drug selection and dosage set forth in this text are in accordance with current recommendations and practice at the time of publication. However, in view of ongoing research, changes in government regulations, and the constant flow of information relating to drug therapy and drug reactions, the reader is urged to check the package insert for each drug for any change in indications and dosage and for added warnings and precautions. This is particularly important when the recommended agent is a new or infrequently employed drug.

Some drugs and medical devices presented in this publication may have Food and Drug Administration (FDA) clearance for limited use in restricted research settings. It is the responsibility of the health care provider to ascertain the FDA status of each drug or device planned for use in their clinical practice.

Distributed in Canada by Raincoast Books

Copyright © 1996 Context Press

an imprint of New Harbinger Publications, Inc.
5674 Shattuck Avenue
Oakland, CA 94609
www.newharbinger.com

New Directions in Behavior Development / edited by Sidney W. Bijou and Emilio Ribes

A hardcover edition of this book was published by Context Press in 1996 (ISBN 1-87897-824-1).

Paperback edition by Context Press, an imprint of New Harbinger Publication, Inc. 2010
ISBN 978-1-60882-035-1

12 11 10

10 9 8 7 6 5 1 4 3 1

Contributors

Donald M. Baer is Roy A. Roberts Distinguished Professor of Human Development and Family Life, University of Kansas.

Sidney W. Bijou is Professor Emeritus, University of Illinios and Professor of Psychology at the University of Nevada.

Barbara C. Etzel is Professor Emerita, Department of Human Development and Family Life, University of Kansas.

Jacob L. Gewirtz is Professor of Psychology, Florida International University and Professor of Pediatrics, the University of Miami Medical School.

Peter Harzem is Hudson Professor of Psychology, Auburn University.

Effie Kymissis is a staff psychologist, Alpine Learning Group, River Edge, New Jersey.

Gerard Malcuit is Professor-Researcher, Laboratoire d'Etude du Nourrisson, Departement du Psychologie of the Universite du Quebec a Montreal.

Susan R. Milla is a graduate student, Department of Human Development and Family Life, University of Kansas.

N. Diane Nicholas is a graduate student, Department of Human Development and Family Life, University of Kansas.

Martha Palaez-Nogueras is Assistant Professor of Educational Psychology and Special Education, Florida International University.

Andree Pomerleau is Professor-Researcher, Laboratoire d'Etude du Psychologie, Universite du Quebec a Montreal.

Claire L. Poulson is Associate Professor of Psychology, Queens College and the Graduate School of the City University of New York.

Emilio Ribes is Professor of Psychology and Director of the Centro de Estudios e Investigaciones en Psicologia, Universidad de Guadalajara.

Josep Roca i Balasch is Doctor of Psychology, Lecturer in doctoral and post-degree courses at the Autonomores Universitat de Barcelona and the National Institute for the Physical Education and Sport in Barcelona.

Jesus Rosales-Ruiz is Assistant Professor of Psychology, University of North Texas.

Table of Contents

Chapter 1

Introduction

Sidney W. Bijou
University of Nevada
Emilio Ribes
University of Guadalajara

The first comprehensive behavioral theory of child development and personality was introduced in the 1950's with the name of social learning theory. An offshoot of Clark L. Hull's behavior theory (Hull, 1943), the new developmental theory, spearheaded by Robert R. Sears and his colleagues, soon lost its momentum mainly because of the difficulties created by Hull's concepts of drive and drive reduction. In the words of Sears (1975):

> In the sixties, one major change in the theory was the elimination of drive. As learning theory began to be applied in detail to motivational development, especially in the context of child rearing as a training process, the inexactness and lack of independent operational definition of drive made the notion more and more useless. Skinner (1938) had found it possible to conceptualize the learning process without drive or drive reduction, limiting the active agency to reinforcement (p. 48).

The two general developmental theories that emerged in the sixties were the socio-behavioristic theory of Bandura and Walters (1963) and the empirical behavior theory of Bijou and Baer (1961). The socio-behavioristic theory gradually evolved into the social cognitive theory in the hands of Bandura (1989); the empirical behavior theory became the behavior analysis theory through a series of revisions by Bijou and Baer (1978) and Bijou (1989, 1993). The behavior analysis theory was supported and supplemented with a volume of readings in child development (Bijou & Baer, 1967) and two other books, one applying the theory to behavior in infancy (Bijou & Baer, 1965) and the other to behavior in early childhood (Bijou, 1976).

Although the behavior analysis theory has been discussed in numerous journal articles and chapters (e.g., Baer, 1970, 1973; Bijou, 1979; Dixon and Lerner, 1988; Morris, Hursh, Winston, Gelfand, Hartmann, Reese & Baer, 1982; Reese, 1980 and Thomas, 1979), it has never been the sole subject of a national or international conference. It was not until 1992 that nine psychologists from four countries—Canada, Mexico, Spain and the United States—came together in Guadalajara, Mexico, at the invitation of Professor Emilio Ribes to participate in the symposium of the Science of Behavior: The Development of Behavior. They were to think through some of the conceptual issues in behavior development and to present data from programmatic research on infant and early childhood behavior. The resulting nine papers, which have undergone several revisions in preparation for publication, make up the content of this volume.

In Chapter 2 Jacob L. Gewirtz and Martha Palaez-Nogueras outline what they believe to be the features of a behavior-analytic approach to human development and discuss some of the major issues in developmental psychology. They also contrast details of the behavior-analytic approach with those in the traditional approach (behavior as a function of age) as well as with those in the organismic (Werner) and cognitive (Piaget) views. Finally, they consider some of the recurring problems associated with any theory of development, such as continuity versus discontinuity, and qualitative versus quantitative changes in the course of development.

In the next chapter, Emilio Ribes reflects on the nature of behavior development and its applications. He posits that a behavior theory of development is not complete unless it takes into account non-action behavioral categories, such as listening, qualitative as well as quantitative changes in behavior, and the hierarchical organization of behavioral changes. He furthermore examines some of the issues in a theory of behavior development, such as the distinction between individualization and development and the criteria for the stages of development. He concludes that behavior development represents the convergence of the basic principles of behavior analysis and the salient characteristics of the culture in which it is embedded.

The husband and wife team of Gerard Malcuit and Andree Pomerleau summarize, in Chapter 4, the literature of operant behavior in infants from a promising beginning to its present utilitarian state. Their review is followed by a discussion of the conceptual and methodological impasses that have befallen operant research with infants. They suggest a method that departs from that developed in animal laboratories and demonstrate this method in two studies, one on infant habituation and one on attention. Their findings reveal forms of operant behavior which up until now have been taken to demonstrate only early cognitive information processing.

The operant language-acquisition paradigm, according to the presentation in Chapter 5 by Claire L. Poulson and Effie Kymisses has been highly successful as a treatment paradigm for the enhancement of language in children and adults who have been diagnosed as mentally retarded, autistic, or otherwise developmentally delayed. They believe that normally developing children acquire language in the normal environment through a similar learning process. The operant language-acquisition paradigm consists of (a) establishing reinforcers for maintaining some level of motivation, (b) bringing that level to a rate at which the response can be brought under discriminative control, (c) bringing that response under the topographical control of models produced by an adult by training sufficient members, kinds, or combinations of exemplars to produce generalized imitation, and (d) transferring stimulus control of a given sound or work from imitative to nonimitative stimuli, such as graphemes, pictures, people, and the abstract relations among them. Their comprehensive review of the literature shows that basic and applied research support the operant language-acquisition paradigm and therefore deserves the serious attention of the psychological community.

In Chapter 6 Barbara C. Etzel, Susan R. Milla, and M. Diane Nicholas compare and contrast two theoretical approaches to the study of the acquisition of knowledge: the behavior-analytic and the cognitive. Simple discrimination and abstraction processes are discussed from both perspectives. They use error-reduction technology to illustrate how the learning environment can be arranged for the successful development of conceptual behavior. They follow this discussion with two studies as examples of more complex conditioned discriminations where stimulus-stimulus relations are trained. And, finally, they point out the implications of their programmatic research for teaching, particularly in the elementary grades.

Josep Roca i Balasch lays out in Chapter 7, some principles and general ideas about human development. He makes a distinction between descriptive and functional or causal science, and focuses on the latter, which consists of changes in (a) qualitative, or the different types of behavior, (b) quantitative, or changes in each type of behavior, and (c) developmental, or changes that integrate both qualitative and quantitative changes in behavior. The statement that "psychology is the study of adjustment of the organism as a whole to the physio-chemical, biological, and social condition of the environment" is an expression of three kinds of qualititative causes. Quantitative causes, which are the "laws" of a science, refer to changes in the formal organization of a behavior that produces increases and decreases in behavior. He goes on to say that development, or the integration of both qualitative and quantitative changes, involves one behavior affecting another behavior. A teacher teaching a child a specific subject, such as arithmetic, is an example of one person's behavior affecting another person's behavior producing both qualitative and quantitative changes. He presents three studies to document his point of view.

In Chapter 8, Sidney W. Bijou focuses on the concept of motivation in human behavior development. He appeals to developmental psychologists to consider the concepts of setting factors as a term referring to the conditions that influence the strength and "selection" of a class of behavior. He reviews some of the concepts in psychology that refer to the same phenomenon as setting factors, such as Skinner's "third variables" and Michael's "establishing operations". He then describes and discusses the three sources of setting factors: (a) operations and events that affect the physiological state of a person, (b) physical circumstances, and (c) socio-cultural conditions. He closes his discussion with a description of how these classes of events interact with other events in the daily life of a person.

Jesus Rosales-Ruiz and Donald M. Baer, University of Kansas, open their discussion in Chapter 9 with the question: What is the essence of developmental psychology? To seek an answer, they examine the various developmental theories grouped according to time, structure, and progression. They then discuss the behavior analysis view of development in terms of progressive changes, stages, interaction between behavior and the environment, and explanation of development, and come to the conclusion that the experimental analysis of behavior and progressive, orderly changes in behavior, or developmental psychology, are the same.

There are many ways of understanding human behavior, and scientific understanding is just one of these ways according to Peter Harzem in Chapter 10. Over the years, scientific understanding has proven valuable in controlling our environment and society has turned to science for an understanding of human behavior. In its development, the science of human behavior has created many overlapping concepts. Child psychology, developmental psychology, and life-span development are examples. All three are concerned with changes in behavior over time. But time, of course, is not a variable, and research involving time can only create problems, not provide answers to problems. Although it is a Herculean task, science must discover the conditions under which new patterns of actions develop, how they are sustained, and in what ways are they transmitted, i.e., science must study the phenomena involved in the development of behavior that cut across all subdivisions of psychology.

References

Bandura, A. (1989). Social cognitive theory. *Annals of Child Development*, vol.6, 1-60. R. Vasta (Ed.). London: Jessica Kingsley Publishers.

Bandura, A. & Walters, R. H. (1963). *Social learning and personality development*. New York: Holt, Rinehart & Winston.

Baer, D. M., (1970). An age–irrelevant concept of development. *Merrill-Palmer Quarterly of Behavior and Development, 16*, 238-245.

Baer, D. M. (1973). The control of developmental process: Why wait? In J.R. Nessebroade & H. W. Reese (Eds.) *Life-span developmental psychology: Methodological issues*. New York: Academic Press.

Bijou, S. W. (1976). *Child development: The basic stage of early childhood*. Englewood Cliffs, NJ: Prentice-Hall.

Bijou, S. W. (1979). Some clarification on the meaning of behavior analysis of child development. *Psychological Record, 29*, 3-13.

Bijou, S. W. (1989). Behavior analysis. *Annals of Child Development, 6*, 61-83. R. Vasta (Ed.) London: Jessica Kingsley Publishers.

Bijou, S. W. (1993). *Behavior analysis of child development*. Reno, NV: Context Press.

Bijou, S. W. & Baer, D. M. (1961). *Child development: A systematic and empirical theory*. Vol. 1. Englewood Cliffs, NJ: Prentice-Hall.

Bijou, S. W. & Baer, D. M. (1965). *Child development: Universal stage of infancy*. Vol. 2. Englewood Cliffs, NJ: Prentice-Hall.

Bijou, S.W. & Baer, D.M. (Eds.) (1967). *Child development: Readings in experimental analysis*. Englewood Cliffs, NJ: Prentice-Hall.

Bijou, S.W. & Baer, D.M. (1978). *Behavior analysis of child development*. Englewood Cliffs, NJ: Prentice-Hall.

Dixon, R. A. & Lerner, R. M. (1988). A history of systems in developmental psychology. In M. H. Bornstein & M. E. Lamb (Eds.) *Developmental psychology: An advanced textbook.* Hillsdale, NJ: Lawrence Erlbaum Associates.

Hull, C. L. (1943). *Principles of behavior.* New York: Appleton-Century Co.

Morris, E. K., Hursh, D. E., Winston, A. S., Gelfand, D. M., Hartmann, D.P., Reese, H. W. & Baer, D. M. (1982). Behavior analysis and developmental psychology. *Human Development, 25,* 340-364.

Reese, H. W. (1980). A learning theory critique of the operant approach to life span development. In W. J. Hoyer (Chair), Conceptions of learning and the study of life span development: A symposium. *Human Development, 23,* 361-399.

Sears, R. R. (1975). Your ancients revisited: A history of child development. In E. M. Hetherington (Ed.) *Review of child development research,* Vol. 5, 1-73. Chicago: University of Chicago Press.

Skinner, B. F. (1938). *The behavior of organisms.* Englewood Cliffs, NJ: Prentice-Hall.

Thomas, R. M. (1979). *Comparing theories of child development.* Belmont, CA: Wadsworth Publishing Co.

Chapter 2

In the Context of Gross Environmental and Organismic Changes, Learning Provides the Main Basis for Behavioral Development

Jacob L. Gewirtz
Martha Pelaez-Nogueras
Florida International University

In this paper, we outline the features of a behavior analytic approach to development and discuss some associated issues in developmental psychology. Wherever possible, we also contrast details of the behavior-analytic approach with those of the modal, we shall here term it "traditional," approach to development as well as to other approaches. In the traditional approach, the conception of development depends entirely on identifying the behavior changes that vary with gross units of chronological age. With Werner (1926, 1957) and Piaget (1952, 1964, 1983) as exceptions to the rule, the traditional behavior-change-with-age approach does not specify how to deal with the gross sequential changes in behavior systems that they take to comprise the corpus of behavioral data denoting development. Further, the traditional approach, and Piaget-based approaches like Bjorkland's (1989), have considered relevant *neither* the search for changes in the controlling environment that might be associated with the behavior changes that denote development to them nor the ways of changing the course (or rate) of behavioral development by environmental manipulations that facilitate or inhibit that course.

The Nature of Development

The behavior-analytic approach to the study of behavioral development has differed dramatically from approaches to development that have defined relevant developmental changes to be those associated with gross changes in *age*. At times, this fundamental difference has led to behavior analysis, with its emphasis on development-as-learning, being put beyond the pale as "nondevelopmental," as has been the frequent fate also of other nontraditional approaches to development like that of Heinz Werner (1926, 1957). (In Werner's theory, development is not an area of study but a way of studying phenomena. Thus, development is comprised of a set of issues or questions that researchers raise about the phenomena they study.) Behavior analysis has also considered development differently from the mainstream approaches that have focused on gross age differences. Its way of studying developmental phenomena is via the use of learning paradigms (primarily that of operant learning) with their derivative and associated principles and processes.

The focus of the behavior-analytic approach has been termed "merely learning, not development" by those who favor the age-correlated mainstream or other traditional approaches. Thus, some traditional child-development theorists have contrasted *development* with *learning*, arguing that while both development and learning are reflected in changes in behavior over time, *development* unfolds spontaneously, occurs over a broad range of behavior, and typically occurs over relatively long time segments, with response-contingency stimulation playing no role or a minimal role; whereas *learning* is not spontaneous but environmentally determined, involves narrowly-focused behaviors and specific stimulus conditions, and typically occurs over very short time segments. Based on these arguments, the traditionalists have concluded that the operant-learning approach is not a legitimate method for the study of organismic development. This conclusion is, to say the least, paradoxical, for few would deny that environmental factors play some role in development and, it is clear, that the operant-learning paradigm can focus the systematic effects of environmental factors on the developing-organism's behaviors more efficiently than any other approach to behavioral development.

It is recalled that, under the more traditional views, normative, often large, age units are employed to facilitate identifying the behaviors that comprise "development." A corollary of this age-validating logic is that behavioral development must necessarily be slow. This is because the major behavior changes that qualify as developmental change would be more likely to be detected in terms of long rather than short units of time. Another corollary of this usage is to delegitimize the potential-relevance of the results of process-oriented conditioning paradigms that organize behavior change efficiently in very short time segments. This is paradoxical, for the behavior changes involved can be analogous, or very similar, to those behavior changes validated against the gross-time-unit metric that is conventionally taken to denote development. At other times, the argument is that learning provides problematic leverage on development insofar as, being a function of specific experiences, it is difficult to predict what a particular child will learn and when that learning would occur without knowing individual details (e.g., Bjorkland, 1989). In other words, by ignoring potentially relevant idiosyncratic environmental influences, such theorists necessarily emphasize the gross understanding of behavioral development. In contrast, taking such experiential factors into account would permit the developmental picture to be organized more precisely and completely.

As will be seen in this paper, principles based on age as the sole index of the passage of time (e.g., critical and sensitive periods) must inevitably be weak in accounting for development, as reflections of the reality that process theories in psychology have had no place for age as such, except as a "space," as it were, in which process variables can operate sequentially to produce their effects in behavior. In general, behavior theorists also have a position regarding development. The behavior-theory idea is that development is comprised of changes in behavior effected by consequences that combine and build on each other to become "hierarchically organized." As has been indicated, in practice the methods of research under the behavioral conception of development typically reduce to the use of learning procedures. In the laboratory, rapid sequential changes in behavior have been demonstrated in very short time spans—behavior changes that are analogous to those that are validated against relatively gross-time-unit changes that conventionally denote development for the traditional developmental approach. That such rapid behavior changes can be implemented in itself, however, falls short of explaining the organization of the systematic behavior changes (behavioral skills—motor, social and cognitive) that encompass "development" for behavior analysts.

For the most part behavior analysts have focused on the principles and processes underlying behavior, and not on either the organization and content of progressive behavior changes or the increasing complexity of the patterns of controlling stimuli (Gewirtz & Pelaez-Nogueras, 1992c; Schlinger, 1992). Although at present no contemporary approach deals with development in an ideal fashion, the case is made in this paper that behavior analysis handles the matter as well as, or better than, the existing heterogeneous array of approaches to development. Behavior analysts have approached development as derivative from the principles of operant learning in the context of gross environmental and organismic changes, the main vehicle used by behavior approaches to relate environmental (stimulus) determinants to systematic behavior change. This behavior-analytic focus is analogous to the extra-developmental focus of Heinz Werner's approach to organismic development (mentioned earlier and to be discussed in a subsequent section).

Directional Criteria for Development

The directional criteria usually employed for development, such as increasing behavioral adaptiveness and complexity, are arbitrary. Relevant indices of these criteria will vary with contextual variables, and the segment of the life span being considered. For example, behavior changes in infants may be scored in a different, even opposite, way from behavior changes in the elderly. In addition, measures of adaptiveness and complexity of behavior may not intercorrelate. Moreover, implicit in the concept of development as it has often been used is the assumption that behavior change is *irreversible*.

The assumption that advances in developmental level with age are reflected only in the direction of increased complexity of behavior systems is in error. For instance, holding stimulus level constant, some members of response classes that are complex (containing undifferentiated and many response components) may be shaped into differentiated, and simple, efficient response classes by consequences. Thus, the direction of systematic developmental change often may be from the "complex" to the "simple" and not from the "simple" to the "complex" and, thus, may run counter to what is conventionally considered to be a developmental advance. Similarly, holding the response level constant, a child's repeated exposure to a gross stimulus complex may result often in the child selecting out the salient stimulus elements. Hence, while the child's response classes steadily increase in efficiency by coming to be controlled by fewer and simpler stimulus elements, s/he will attend decreasingly to irrelevant elements of that stimulus complex. Here, too, what is often termed development may reflect changes in the direction of simplifying (rather than making more complex) the stimuli controlling a behavior system.

A Behavior-Analytic Approach to Development

Due to the operational-research conception and the variegated body of research of B.F. Skinner (1935, 1938, 1953), the work of Keller and Schoenfeld (1950), and numerous others, a massive body of conceptional and research literature on operant learning has accrued involving the behavior of many species. Pioneering developmental psychology within the behavioral approach, Bijou (1976, 1979), Bijou and Baer (1961, 1965, 1978) and Gewirtz (1956, 1961, 1969, 1978, 1992) have employed operant principles and methods to organize and investigate infant learning and development. These researchers have approached infant behavioral development as the result of progressive interactions between the behavior of the infant and the sequences of discriminative and contingent stimuli produced by the environmental events comprising its functional environment. A substantial sub-body of this research literature has accrued on the operant conditioning of diverse behaviors of human neonates, infants, and children, involving numerous types of environmental contingencies (Gewirtz & Pelaez-Nogueras, 1992c). This literature on human young has demonstrated that response*learning* can: (1) occur efficiently and rapidly (in brief time segments); (2) reflect efficiently moment-to-moment changes in environmental units; (3) be facilitated or inhibited by contextual/setting factors; and (4) provide an effective basis for organizing discriminated operants and their controlling conditions under a number of headings, some metaphoric like "attachment" (see, e.g., Gewirtz & Pelaez-Nogueras, 1991).

The power and efficiency of the operant-learning paradigm can provide a clear model for the study of human development, if only to provide a basis for determining which of the behavior changes denoting development are, and which are not, susceptible to learning effected by environmental contingencies. In addition, learning operations can put into focus those contextual/environmental factors that can raise or lower the efficacy of stimuli for behavior and, in that way, inflect the course of human behavioral development.

Conventional theorists of development have used complex, sometimes unparsimonious, constructs to order the overlapping developmental areas of cognitive, social, and personality psychology. They have often used such global concepts as behavior "traits" (e.g., introvertive/extrovertive, inhibited/uninhibited) to summarize behavior patterns through lengthy time spans while ignoring environmental-context variables (e.g., Bates, 1980; Kagan, Reznick, & Snidman, 1986). In contrast, a behavior-analytic approach to development calls for a finer-grained analysis of stimulus structure and function, response structure and function, their interchange at particular moments, and the sequences of *interactions* across successive moments of time. A behavior analysis of development interests itself not only in the principles and processes responsible for the changes observed in behavior, but also in the different directions, speeds, and contingency arrangements that result from the organism's behavior-environment interactions.

The laws governing infant development should in no way differ either in general flavor or detail from the laws governing other psychological sectors in which behavior change provides the dependent variable. In behavior analysis, the term "development" is an abstraction for systematic sequential changes among responses and stimulus functions for an individual, specifically between behavior and environmental contingencies in interaction. More particularly, "development" refers to those progressive, orderly changes in the organization of stimulus-behavior relations. In this frame, it is noted that much of what looks like spontaneous development might depend on teaching practices arranged in an order by a society or culture (Baer & Rosales-Ruiz, this Volume).

To understand the behavior-change processes denoting development, analyses are required for: (1) changes in the complexity of the controlling environment, including the origins and changes in discriminative and reinforcing stimuli for infant/child behavior; (2) early experiences as potential determinants of later behavior systems; and (3) contextual variables that affect the functional relations among stimuli and responses.

Analyzing Changes in the Controlling Environment

By focusing on the environmental events, namely those providing discriminative and reinforcing stimuli that have a functional relation to behavior, a functional approach to development can indicate ways in which environment is capable of shaping the changing capacities of the infant and child and thus maximize or optimize development of behavior classes in such important traditional areas as the cognitive, the emotional, and the social. Likewise, behavior analysis can describe the way in which the organism affects its environment (for instance, its mother's behavior), taking into account the ever-changing interaction between the two.

Behavior changes often can be accounted for by the increasing complexity of the stimulus patterns that acquire control over behavior. For example, upon hearing a sound, an infant may initially orient its head in the sound's general direction (in which its mother is usually found), but eventually the infant will respond this way only to particular sounds appearing at certain times and/or in conjunction with a variety of other stimuli. Thus, the discriminative stimulus for the infant head-turning response has changed, while the unitary head-turning response it controls remains unchanged. And, systematic increases in the behavioral complexity of a more experienced child (one more advanced developmentally or operating at a "higher stage") may be due primarily to systematic increases in the complexity of stimulus-control features of the environment. In this way, the developmental level of a child's response systems is determined, in part, by the range or complexity of the functional stimuli experienced (cf., e.g., Vince, 1961). An illustration of this type of analysis is the work of Etzel (this Volume) on the hierarchies of elements in the learning of complex visual-auditory stimuli in the development of conceptual behavior.

In addition, an analysis is necessary of the origins and changes in reinforcing stimuli as a function of the role those stimuli play in behavior. At successive points in development, it remains an empirical question which of the myriad potential stimuli function as unconditioned or conditioned reinforcers for infant behavior. It appears that a very large variety of events can function as positive reinforcers of behavior. These include sensory stimuli provided through diverse tactile, olfactory, taste, auditory and visual receptors, including those consumables that are thought to meet organismic needs (food, water). Further, a variety of contingent removals of aversive events such as of those conditions that produce pain, cold, and wetness, those that are very bright or very loud, and those that involve strong cutaneous stimulation, can function as negative reinforcers of diverse responses in early life. Moreover, some of these events can support the occurrence of avoidance or escape responses. Whether physical (occurring naturally, like thunder or rain), chemical (acting at a distance, like odor), or organismic (biological, like those associated with puberty) in nature, occurring alone or in combination, such stimulus events are directly involved in the processes of behavioral development.

As the child's behavior repertoire increases and comes under more differentiated stimulus control, some of these potential reinforcing stimuli may drop out functionally to be superseded by others, or their capacity to function as discriminative or reinforcing stimuli may change. The nature of the event patterns constituting the reinforcing properties of certain stimuli may change, sometimes drastically, as the child moves from one capacity "level" to a more advanced one. For example, the social-reinforcing stimulus of attention produced by the parent may be superseded in salience for the child's responses by that of verbal or facial-cue-provided approval from the parent for successively more complex or mature child performances. This can occur in restricted settings in which the parent's approval mediates the delivery of most of the important reinforcing stimuli for the child. Thus, a developmental analysis would benefit from an examination of changes in the efficacy of reinforcing stimuli for different child behaviors in the context of changes in the receptor and effector capacities of the child due to sequences of early experiences.

Analyzing Early Experiences as Determinants of Later Behavior Systems

Development results from the changing organization of behaviors in the individual's repertory into new ones. Let us define relevant experience as environmental contingencies for particular behaviors. The assumption that later experience builds upon the results of early experience does not apply uniquely to the young child. It may hold for *any* time segment in the life of an individual. There are several reasons why early experience may influence the development of behavior systems later in the life course:

First, some structural biological systems underlying behavior systems appear to require stimulus input to become or remain functional. Physiological development depends also on the interaction between the individual's physiological systems and its environment. For example, a physically-developed eye may not be functional until it has been exposed to the light (Hinde, 1966). There is a valid place for diverse research strategies and tactics directed to the biological substrate of molar receptor and effector functions, and to coordinating such variables with molar behavior. Because changes in physiological systems and in behavior systems occur both in early and in later segments of the life span, the principles governing early behavioral development should be no different from the principles governing later behavioral development. Further, while certain kinds of stimulation may be required early in life to make functional certain physiological systems, routine stimulation may also be required throughout life to maintain the functioning of these and other systems.

Second, many behavior systems of an individual depend directly upon the previous acquisition of component response systems during infancy. There is a dependence of later-developing skills on those acquired earlier. For example, all forms of ambulatory behavior require the earlier acquisition of the ability to stand while maintaining balance. Also, to be able to divide in arithmetic, a child must learn first how to add, subtract, and multiply. An infant in the first phase of life has had relatively little cumulative commerce with the environment. Thus the context for the impact of experience on the younger child's behavioral development will be different from that of a later phase of development in which s/he has had both more cumulative experience and the necessary skills for new learning.

Third, certain more advanced, later-appearing behavior systems should be established better when supported by behavior systems learned and maintained in early life (such as involve eye contact, visual following/orienting, smiling, and vocalizing). Subsequently, these behaviors can become the elements that comprise the basis of diverse response complexes and sequences. The individual's behavior changes continuously due to experiential and organismic factors, and therefore learning processes may vary throughout the life span. Later development, with all its complexities, is necessarily related to these early experiences and existing behavior. These processes underpin the notion of continuity or consistency of environmental input over time (that is addressed in a later section).

Analyzing the Contextual Determinants of Behavioral Development

Contextual setting factors inflect various antecedent and concurrent stimuli affecting behavior (e.g., as would inhibitory or facilitory processes). They also affect the interplay between stimuli and response functions. Indeed, the probability of learning at any given moment, even within a narrow segment of the life span, may vary with any of the contextual setting factors that are operating. Various researchers have dealt with these variables under different headings, for instance: "third variables" (Skinner, 1931), "setting factors" (Kantor, 1946), "setting events" (Bijou & Baer, 1961; Bijou, this Volume), "state" and "potentiating" variables (Goldiamond & Dyrud, 1967), "historical context" and "current context" (Morris 1988; 1992); "contextual determinants" (Gewirtz, 1972), "establishing operations" (Michael, 1982), and "initial and boundary conditions" (Marr, 1993).

Rather than take context as a source of variation and hold it constant—which has been a frequent operation within behavior analysis—Morris (1988) has proposed that historical and contemporaneous context should be a subject matter for experimental analysis. Knowledge of phylogenic history (i.e., species-typic boundaries and preparedness in biological structure/vulnerability and behavioral function) and ontogenic historical causation (individual-typic boundaries and preparedness in biological and behavioral form and function, and variability in both) is fundamental for a complete understanding of behavior. The *structure* of the current context involves the biological organism (i.e., the child's anatomy and physiology), the environment (physical ecology), and the changes and variability in both. The *function* of the current context potentiates or actualizes the functions of stimuli and responses for behavior. The function of stimuli for responses involves the analysis of variables such as deprivation, fatigue, and drug effects—conditions that alter functional relations within the three-term contingency (Morris, in press).

Problems with Maturation, Critical/Sensitive Periods, and Demographic and Chronological-Age Variables

Age: The "Empty" Variable

It was noted earlier that a salient aspect of traditional developmental psychology is that many researchers have oriented primarily to identifying those behavioral changes in the child that vary with gross changes in its chronological age, and have termed their area of interest "developmental." As a descriptive, classificatory, or summary variable, with large enough time-segment units, the age of an individual in fact can index average levels or sets of responses to be found in groups of individuals who share age, and in that way could provide summary information. Thus, researchers may sometimes find it practical to use age units as efficient proxies for individual repertoires containing particular behaviors or skills that are preconditions for individuals serving as subjects in a study. Further, there are times when chronological age can order changes in behavioral development reasonably well in *preliminary* analyses under process theories (Gewirtz, 1992), as when:

(a) cultural rules dictate rigidity that certain contingencies for specific behaviors be provided at particular age points;

(b) age groups representing wide life-span segments may appear to be associated with very different portions of an independent-variable dimension so that using such groups in early work could constitute a tactic to increase the range of instances along the independent-variable dimension, thereby facilitating finding functional relations in which the independent variables could, in principle, account for increased dependent-variable variance;

(c) a phenomenon of interest may seem to occur differentially in a particular life-span segment, and work with individuals in that segment would hold the promise of leading to the identification of the underlying process(es) operating across life-span segments; and/or

(d) stimuli provided by, or associated with, gross segments of the life span function as cues for the behavior of others (e.g., in some societies the aged are venerated and/or the very young thought charming).

In this frame, Skinner (1953) has made useful observations about the uses of chronological age as independent variables:

> When changes in behavior extend over long periods, we speak of the independent variable as the age of the organism. A response may appear at a given age and later disappear. The increase in probability as a function of age is often spoken of as maturation. We achieve some degree of prediction by discovering these developmental schedules...[But] individual differences may be great; we cannot predict accurately when an individual will engage in certain kinds of sexual behavior by establishing the average age onset in a population. Usually, therefore, practical problems of this kind are not solved by appeal to schedules of maturation...chronological age may be of little value in determining readiness. The presence or absence of the relevant behavior may have to be determined by direct observation of each child (p. 156).

Principles based on the simple passage of time, i.e., chronological age, inevitably must be weak in accounting for development, as simple reflections of the reality that such process theories as we have had in psychology that are oriented to process (e.g., Freud, 1905/1938; Piaget, 1936/1952, 1983; Werner, 1948), in addition to that of Skinner (1938, 1953), have had no place for age as such. (An exception is the stimulus value of gender for Freud and of gross life-span segment category membership for some others.) The lack of focus by such process theories on chronological age results from the fact that, by its nature, chronological age is unable to provide the conceptual leverage required for detailing the processes that can account for behavior, behavioral development, and/or individual differences in behavior. For instance, whichever process theory is employed, identifying the underlying process variables would require a detailed analysis of the sequential features of environment-behavior (organism) interaction (i.e., relevant experience). This point would hold even for tests of genetic hypotheses, for the effects of genotype must be manifested in environmental contexts.

Age does not provide the relevant information, as the paucity of its usage by process theories attests. To detail this point, *age-as-time* can be seen as an *empty variable* insofar as it constitutes merely the "space" in which features of the environment and of the genome can interact with the individual's behavior, with the resulting process variables operating to produce their effects in differential behavior outcomes (phenotypes). Thus, age as such has no explanatory value for the behavior of an individual (Baer, 1970; Gewirtz, 1969, 1978; Schaie & Hertzog, 1985).

This point can be illustrated in two ways. *First*, let us examine those studies in which operant-conditioning procedures have been employed with target responses for which age norms have been available in the developmental literature. Typically, the behavior criterion levels for such target responses are reached many months *earlier* than the normative age levels for those behavioral skills found in that literature. For example, in the work of Gewirtz & Pelaez-Nogueras (1991, 1992a), the operant training of infant protests during maternal departures and separations was implemented by mothers orienting and otherwise responding contingent on those protests. As a result of such positive reinforcement, six-month-old infants exhibited cued-protest rates as high as, or higher than, rates that Schaffer and Emerson (1964) identified in infants at 11 to 12 months. The same phenomenon was observed in an experiment on infant social referencing (Pelaez-Nogueras, 1992). Infant referencing behavior attained criterion levels at 4 months of age, many months earlier than the age-norm levels found in the child-development literature.

And, *second*, let us consider how parents have received precious little help from the way age serves as "cause" in the popular and professional literature for parents on the management of their children's problem behaviors. Age-associated behavior problems tend to be listed in that literature with the advice that the child will "grow out of them," meaning that, with time, the problem behaviors will be reversed. Typically, in that literature little or no account is taken of how caregiver responding can cause, i.e., shape and maintain, children's problem behaviors, such as in the case of attachment and infant separation protests (Gewirtz & Pelaez-Nogueras, 1987 1992a, 1993).

These examples flesh out the point that it is not chronological age/time as such but the *processes* that can occur within time, wherein environmental variables affect the orderly, progressive, and increasingly complex behavior changes that imply development. We have contrasted this view with the traditional notion in developmental psychology that it is the behavior changes associated with conventionally-employed age units that comprise the content of child development. A case in point is the publication on the development of children's thinking by Bjorkland (1989). He declared that: "all children go through development in approximately the same way at approximately the same time" (p. 4). It is seen that traditional developmental theorists like Bjorkland deemphasize not only behavior consequences but even intrasubject and intersubject variation.

Demographic Variables Other than Age

In the same frame, non-age *demographic-variable* categories have been, and can be, employed as causal variables in analyses of development. Almost identical arguments to those that have been applied to the hollow-variable character of chronological age would impeach the use of such demographic categories as independent, process variables in the analysis of organismic development. For instance, let us assume that a process theory is the basis of an empirical analysis. A problem is posed when, instead of direct assessments of putative causal variables (that typically would involve cumulative features of behavior-environment inter-change), demographic categories are employed as independent-variable proxies. Then, ad hoc speculative assumptions are advanced about the implications of those demographic categories for the proximal causes, in advance of doing the research as well as in *ad hoc* explanation of the research results, to compensate for the failure directly to assess those putative causes.

No matter how sophisticated the statistical designs used in such studies carried out under the aegis of a process theory, when demographic categories are employed as independent variables scientific resources and opportunities are squandered. Finally, reports based on demographic "treatment" variables do not qualify as adequate and proper and should be labeled as the *essays* that they are (Gewirtz, 1992, October).

Maturation

Traditional theorists have stressed the study of sequential, often rapid, behavior changes comprising infant development because they assume a unique dependence of those changes upon gross changes in body structure, while often failing to note that gross biological changes can also occur during other life-span segments (e.g., Munn, 1965). Typically, those traditional theorists do not assess, much less have theories about, the biological changes to which they have attributed causal power over the overt behavior changes. Thus, when topographically-complete behavior or even a primitive approximation of a response appears *suddenly* in the child's repertory, with or without an identified stimulus basis, that change is often attributed to a process termed "maturation." Maturation is seen as the innately-determined unfolding with age-as-time of a gradual plan of development based on *unindexed* biology and (seemingly) independent of experience.

Indeed, some behavioral changes in the infant may appear to the untrained observer to be so rapid as to seem unlearned. Such sudden appearances of responses in the infant repertoire that seem not obviously to have been taught or learned are often attributed to maturation as cause (and given as evidence against environmental factors playing a role or of the behaviors in question having a learned basis). But the sudden appearance of "novel" behavior may often be due to very rapid learning processes or to other factors underlying the behavior change, like a rapid increase or decrease in the child's stimulus threshold ("capacity"). These and other bases for change are often unnoticed by the observer. The premature labeling of effects unexplainable under a given posture as due to maturation is unwarranted, because it explains little and may obscure much. The introduction of the maturation concept to account for behavior variations not readily explained may preclude the search for causal explanations in the principles and processes responsible for the observed change. The specification of the interrelation between stimulus and response functions in context is often omitted, especially when *un*accompanied by a systematic focus on environmental contingencies that may affect the behavior.

Critical Periods

A similar age-qua-time problem presents itself when the concepts critical period and sensitive period are invoked to justify age-related learning/training or intervention. A critical period refers to a time span in the individual's early life during which the capacity to acquire certain behavior systems is assumed irreversibly lost if relevant experience (i.e., stimulation) is not provided. It has been assumed also that, during critical and sensitive periods, relatively large or rapidly-occurring behavioral effects can be produced by *less* environmental stimulation or fewer stimuli than would be required to produce such effects in other time segments, if such effects could be produced at all in those time segments. These time segments are often specified imprecisely ("around six months") or broadly ("the last quarter of the first year"). For instance, the attachment process starts "around 6 months" (Schaffer & Emerson, 1964); there have been casually-documented notions that infants cannot acquire attachments to an adult after "about 9 mos." if they had not acquired one earlier, and/or that they display an "8-mos. anxiety" (e.g., Spitz, 1950); and responses denoting the infant social-referencing process begin "at 8 to 9 months of age" (Campos, Barrett, Lamb, Goldsmith & Stenberg, 1983).

Researchers who employ conceptions like maturation, or critical period or sensitive period may attend only casually to potential experiential learning factors. A critical period may reflect merely the failure of researchers to note the appearance of the behavior outside the age limits within which it earlier appeared. One reason may be that such age-linked notions depend on the samples of individuals and conditions that just happen to be surveyed, and may index merely sampling limitations. Another reason may be the lack of systematic longitudinal observations of the developing response within each individual subject across lengthy time spans.

The important message is that *any* age-defined concept is limited because it ignores the underlying process variables that require a detailed analysis of the sequential features of environment-behavior (organism) interaction. Once the processes through which cumulative experience can affect behavior systems are analyzed, we expect that age-linked critical and sensitive periods would lose even the modest precision that, at first glance, their time limits might suggest. Finally, the specification of environmental contingencies and contextual variables that either prevent the acquisition of a behavior system or give it the appearance of "irreversibility" (an issue discussed earlier) would impeach further the utility of a critical- or sensitive-period concept.

Some Issues in Development

Continuity vs. Discontinuity in Behavioral Development

Cognitive-developmental theorists such as Piaget (e.g., 1952, 1983), have conceived development to be discontinuous, an emergent, unfolding process. In contrast, a strong assumption underlying behavior-analytic approaches to development is that, with discriminative and reinforcing-stimulus continuity, there will be behavioral continuity (subject to topographic changes in behavior resulting from skill development). Behavioral continuity should be the case even while there may be times when topographic changes in responses due to such factors as skill enhancement may interact with ongoing contingencies to produce what, at first glance, may give the appearance of discontinuous changes. As in fields like embryology, large changes may occur relatively rapidly but it is always possible to demonstrate the continuity of the process, say of caterpillar to butterfly. Apart from this point, continuity or discontinuity of behavior should be detected depending on the metric of the units of observation employed. The more gross or large the units of observation, the more likely would be a finding of behavior discontinuity; the more fine or small the observation units, the more likely would be a finding of behavior continuity (Gewirtz, 1979, July).

In the context of behavior analysis, therefore, it is not constructive to make much of the issue of whether developmental change should be characterized as continuous or discontinuous. Where continuity refers to different levels of development being regulated or resulting from the same fundamental behavioral principles or contingencies, it is expected that there be continuity across behavioral development. In passing, it is noted that Morris (1988) has viewed behavioral development as a discontinuous process, but only in the technical sense that the behavioral structure of functional relationships undergoes qualitative (novel, discontinuous) reorganization with *each* interaction.

Qualitative vs. Quantitative Behavior Change

An issue overlapping the issue of the continuity versus discontinuity of behavior is that of quantitative versus qualitative behavior change. The distinction between qualitative and quantitative changes is often difficult to detect because it is also at least in part a function of the metric employed. To talk about qualitative changes, there must be clear criteria of what is meant by changes in "kind" or "type" (Marr, personal communication, March 17, 1992). An observer may not be able to detect step-by-step changes in quantity and topography of response and, thus, any observation made of a suddenly-appearing "new behavior" may lead the observer to conclude that a novel response has emerged, when in reality that "new" response is just one step forward in a continuous sequence of responses linked to one another. It is often difficult, and for many purposes irrelevant, to specify if this change has been qualitative or quantitative, as shaping and chaining procedures may be responsible to a large degree for apparent quantitative changes, and also for so-called "qualitative changes" in behavior. Because the child's behaviors are continually being shaped as the child's changing capacities permit, discrete behaviors become linked and organized to form complex, even elaborate, developmental systems.

We now summarize the two preceding themes of continuity vs. discontinuity and of qualitative vs. quantitative behavior change. In traditional developmental psychology, whether behavior patterns are found to be continuous or discontinuous across time, should depend on the metric of observation used. The more micro analytic the observation and time units, the more likely a continuity conclusion; and the more macro analytic those units, the more likely a discontinuity conclusion. Thus when development is studied by comparing behavior patterns at distant time points, one may note only *qualitative* behavior changes; on the other hand, if the unit (metric) of observation is sufficiently detailed in time to permit a fine-grained analysis of the functional relation of the behavior unit and its discriminative and reinforcing controlling stimuli, one may detect only *quantitative* behavior changes.

Behavior Irreversibility in Life Settings

A major source of variation in development among individuals results from differences in their reinforcement histories of their behaviors that led to the organization of different behavior systems. More advanced developmental systems can be maintained by the same or similar stimuli that maintained the earlier acquired responses. That is one reason why behavior(s) (systems/patterns) acquired early in life may become pervasive and may often appear "permanent" and "irreversible."

The problem is that the assumption that behavior changes are "irreversible" is implicit in the traditional concepts of development. This notion is, of course, incompatible with routine behavior-change findings in such areas as learning, memory, and perception. Further, behaviors that often appear irreversible should eventually extinguish if the contingencies maintaining them were removed. Thus, the "strength" of a behavior is due characteristically *not* to its "irreversibility,' but rather to the *locking in* of the environmental contingencies that maintain the individual's behavior. The result is that, to the untrained observer, from the earliest acquisition point onward these maintaining contingencies might not even appear to be operating. Further, in this locking-in process, the appearance of irreversibility of some behavior systems could result simply from the transfer of stimulus control from the initial sets of maintaining stimuli to different sets of stimuli. To the untrained observer, this transfer of stimulus control might not appear to be operating (Etzel & Gewirtz, 1967; Gewirtz, 1967).

A Note on Piaget's Approach to Development, Environment, and Predictability

Piaget's approach is clearly the basis of Bjorkland's (1989) conceptualization of development:

Development refers to changes in structure or function over time...has its roots in biology, and its course is relatively predictable...[and] changes between stages of development are said to be *qualitative*...of type or kind...[and not] *quantitative*...of amount or speed. Shifts from one stage to another are theorized to occur abruptly, reflecting *discontinuity* rather than *continuity* in development...Stages require that children's abilities be highly integrated within a stage (p. 14).

Piaget's (1936/1952, 1964, 1983) constructivist theory has not often been classified with environmental-control (like learning) theories, and Bjorkland very likely would not see it as one. Yet, Piaget's theory can be seen as an environmentally-oriented developmental theory. This grouping is possible even while Piaget characterized attempts to focus environmental manipulations for behavior (via training operations) with the goal of speeding up development as "the American disease." Piaget's comment was directed to demonstrations that conservation and similar tasks can be conditioned rapidly, earlier than when they would appear naturally. Even so, what is involved in such demonstrations are pockets of development/behavior change rather than the across-the-board change in an array of diverse various behaviors called for by Piaget's stage approach to development.

Independent of his stage approach, Piaget provided principles underlying developmental change and emphasized the hierarchical order in which behavior skills are organized. Using "structural"-environmental interaction concepts like *assimilation* and *accommodation* to inflect his theory's mental "structures" (that he termed "schemas"), Piaget has provided rough ways of organizing behavior changes denoting development to be the outcome of interactions between behavior and the environment. Thus, in an important sense Piaget's approach did take environmental factors into account. However, the approach was only loosely addressed to environmentally-induced behavior change. In this frame, his emergentist-constructivist approach can not deal with the prediction and control that a routine learning analysis handles readily with its focus on behavior and maintaining antecedent and consequent stimuli in context.

Thus, Piaget's general theory can not effectively predict behavior at any given point. At the same time, his stage approach cannot predict individual behavior change at all. But it can specify at which stage the individual's behavior patterns can be said to be. And his emergentist stage theory cannot predict, for instance, whether or not a child said to be in the sensory-motor stage would progress to the preoperational stage of cognitive development, or whether or not the child in the latter stage would progress to the concrete operational stage. Even so, Piaget's approach may provide useful information, such as which cognitive-developmental skills the child has acquired. And, in the ways discussed, it can be classified as an environmentally-oriented theory.

A Note on Werner's Approach to Development

To compare the behavior-analytic heuristic approach with that of Heinz Werner (1926, 1957; see also Glick, 1992) will be instructive. In Werner's approach, *development* is not an area of study but a way of studying phenomena. Development is comprised of a set of issues or questions that researchers raise about the phenomena they study. Thus, instead of targeting, as such, cognitive, language, or other development in humans (as routine developmental analyses have done), Werner would observe children's behavior in context and ask systematically if a separable and differentiated cognitive, language, or other "function" (Werner's term) existed (i.e., characterized child behavior patterns in environmental contexts). Werner's interest extended also to the levels of differentiation of particular functions from other functions, their independence, and the levels of intrafunctional organization at varying levels of interfunctional organization. Thus, for Werner *development* was not simply a history of a particular function at different levels of organization, and certainly did not involve a search for relationships between age levels and the "functions" on which he focused.

As a way of studying developmental phenomena, Werner's approach has differed dramatically from the routine approaches to development, in particular those that have defined relevant developmental changes to be those that are associated with gross age changes. This fundamental conceptual feature of Werner's approach has led also to his theory sometimes being put beyond the pale as "nondevelopmental" (as has sometimes also been the fate of the behavior-analytic approach to development). Like Werner's nontraditional approach to development, behavior analysis also approaches development differently. That way is to study developmental phenomena objectively via learning paradigms.

Summary

A functional behavioral approach to development has been emphasized here with a systematic focus upon antecedent and consequent stimuli that control behavior, contextual factors, and behavior-interchange sequences. These concepts with their underpinnings in well-established principles of behavior provide an efficient basis for organizing information in life settings about behavioral development (cognitive and social), and for interventions. The case was made that human behavior and development have shown themselves to be amenable to an operant-learning analysis, and that operant analysis has made it possible to move beyond the level of simple description of behavior to the level of identifying key processes that account for much of development. Further, operant analysis can be used to determine which behaviors denoting development could, and which could not, be susceptible to change via learning operations as well as to examine the learning basis, if any, of behaviors identified in descriptive accounts of child behavioral development. In this context, the laws characterizing or governing development should in no way be different either in general flavor or detail from the laws governing other psychological areas in which behavior change constitutes the dependent variable.

In behavior analysis, the term "development" refers to progressive, orderly changes in the organization of environment-behavior relations in the context of gross environmental and organismic changes. A functional analysis of infant behavior focuses on the many variables likely to be directly responsible for behavior change patterns denoting development. Thus, to understand behavioral development, analyses are required for: 1) changes in the complexity of the controlling environment (including the origins and changes in reinforcing stimuli for behavior); 2) early experiences as potential determinants of later behavior systems; and 3) the contextual variables involved, and their interplay in interactions among stimulus and response functions.

Because many studies have shown that operant procedures could produce rapid behavior changes in the child, they have become—for behavioral and nonbehavioral researchers alike—the preferred methods for studying processes that, otherwise, have been inaccessible by the traditional methodologies of nonbehavioral psychology. In this manner, the use of operant procedures and derivative methodologies has progressed enormously in the last four decades leading to an impressive advance in our knowledge of child behavior.

We have noted that the traditional and the behavioral approaches to development may differ more as value systems about what must be included or excluded than in terms of scientific issues. Hence, the pessimistic view is that these approaches may never be reconciled. The optimistic view is that traditional approaches to development would someday appreciate the power of a behavior-analytic approach to development and reconcile that focus with their own approaches to development.

References

Baer, D. M. (1970). An age-irrelevant concept of development. *Merrill-Palmer Quarterly of Behavior and Development, 16*, 238-246.

Baer, D. M., & Rosales-Ruiz, J. (In press). A behavior-analytic view of development. In S. W. Bijou & E. Ribes (Eds.), *New directions in behavioral development.* Guadalajara, Mexico: Editorial Universidad de Guadalajara.

Bates, J. E. (1980). The concept of difficult temperament. *Merrill-Palmer Quarterly, 26*, 299-319.

Bijou, S. W. (1976). *Child Development: The basic stage of early childhood.* Englewood Cliffs, NJ: Prentice Hall.

Bijou, S. W. (1979). Some clarifications on the meaning of a behavior analysis of child development. *Psychological Record, 29*, 3-13.

Bijou, S. W. (In press). The role of setting factors in the behavior analysis of development. In S. W. Bijou & E. Ribes (Eds.), *New directions in behavioral development.* Guadalajara, Mexico: Editorial Universidad de Guadalajara.

Bijou, S. W., & Baer, D. M. (1961). *Child development: Vol 1. A systematic and empirical theory.* New York: Appleton-Century-Crofts.

Bijou, S. W., & Baer, D. M. (1965). *Child development: Vol 2. Universal stage of infancy.* New York: Appleton-Century-Crofts.

Bijou, S. W., & Baer, D. M. (1978). *Behavior analysis of child development.* Englewood Cliffs, NJ: Prentice-Hall.

Bjorkland, D.F. (1989). *Children's thinking: Developmental function and individual differences.* Pacific Grove, CA: Brooks/Cole Publishing Co.

Campos, J. J., Barrett, K. C., Lamb, M. E., Goldsmith, H. H., & Stenberg, C. (1983). Socio-emotional development. In M. M. Haith & J. J. Campos (Eds.), *Handbook of child psychology: Vol. 2. Infancy and developmental psychobiology* (pp. 783-916). New York: Wiley.

Etzel, B. C. (In press). The development of conceptual behavior: Hierarchies of elements in learning complex visual-auditory stimuli. In E. Ribes & S. W. Bijou (Eds.), *New directions in behavioral development*. Guadalajara, Mexico: Editorial Universidad de Guadalajara.

Etzel, B. C., & Gewirtz, J. L. (1967). Experimental modification of caretaker-maintained high-rate operant crying in a 6- and a 20-week-old infant (*Infans tyrannotearus*): Extinction of crying with reinforcement of eye contact and smiling. *Journal of Experimental Child Psychology, 5*, 303-317.

Freud, S. (1938). Three contributions to the theory of sex. In A.A. Brill (Trans.). *The basic writings of Sigmund Freud* (pp. 553-629). NY: Modern Library, 1938. (Original published in 1905.)

Gewirtz, J. L. (1956). A program of research on the dimensions and antecedents of emotional dependence. *Child Development, 27*, 205-221.

Gewirtz, J.L. (1961). A learning analysis of the effects of normal stimulation privation and deprivation on the acquisition of social motivation and attachment. In B. M. Foss (Ed.), *Determinants of infant behavior* (pp. 213-299). London: Methuen (New York: Wiley).

Gewirtz, J. L. (1969). Mechanisms of social learning: Some roles of stimulation and behavior in early human development. In D. A. Goslin (Ed.), *Handbook of socialization theory and research* (pp. 57-212). Chicago: Rand-McNally.

Gewirtz, J. L. (1972). Some contextual determinants of stimulus potency. In R. D. Parke (Ed.), *Recent trends in social learning theory* (pp. 7-33). New York: Academic Press.

Gewirtz, J. L. (1978). Social learning in early human development. In A. C. Catania & T. Brigham (Eds.), *Handbook of applied behavior-research: Social and instructional processes* (pp. 105-141). New York: Irvington Press.

Gewirtz, J. L. (1979, July). *Continuity vs. discontinuity in development*. Paper presented at the biennial meeting of the International Society for Behavioral Development, Lund, Sweden.

Gewirtz, J. L. (1991). Social influence on child and parent via stimulation and operant-learning mechanisms. In M. Lewis & S. Feinman (Eds.), *Social influences and socialization in infancy* (pp. 137-163). NY: Plenum.

Gewirtz, J. L. (1992, October). Essays masquerading as proper research designs: On the uses of demographic independent variables in process analyses in psychology [summary]. *Proceedings of the First International Congress of Behaviorism and the Sciences of Behavior, 1*, 173-174. Guadalajara, Mexico: Universidad de Guadalajara.

Gewirtz, J. L., & Pelaez-Nogueras, M. (1987). Social-conditioning theory applied to metaphors like "attachment": The conditioning of infant separation protests by mothers. *Revista Mexicana de Analisis de la Conducta, 13*, 87-103.

Gewirtz, J. L., & Pelaez-Nogueras, M. (1991). The attachment metaphor and the conditioning of infant separation protests. In J. L. Gewirtz & W. M. Kurtines (Eds.), *Intersections with attachment* (pp. 123-144). Hillsdale, NJ: Erlbaum.

Gewirtz, J. L., & Pelaez-Nogueras, M. (1992a). Infants' separation difficulties and distress due to misplaced maternal contingencies. In T. Field, P. McCabe, & N. Schneiderman (Eds.), *Stress and coping in infancy and childhood* (pp. 1946). Hillsdale, NJ: Erlbaum.

Gewirtz, J. L., & Pelaez-Nogueras, M. (1992b). Infant social referencing as a learned process. In S. Feinman (Ed.), *Social referencing and the social construction of reality in infancy* (pp. 151-173). New York: Plenum Publishing Co.

Gewirtz, J. L. & Pelaez-Nogueras, M. (1992c). B. F. Skinner's legacy to human infant behavior and development. *American Psychologist, 47*, 1411-1422.

Gewirtz, J. L., & Pelaez-Nogueras, M. (1993). Leaving without tears: Parents inadvertently train their children to protest separation. *The Brown University Child and Adolescent Behavior Letter.*

Glick, J. A. (1992). Werner's relevance to contemporary developmental psychology. *Developmental Psychology, 28*, 558-565.

Goldiamond, I., & Dyrud, J. (1967). Behavioral analysis for psychotherapy. In J. Schlien (Ed.), *Research in psychotherapy* (Vol. 3, pp. 58-89). Washington, DC: American Psychological Association.

Hinde, R. A. (1966). *Animal behavior: A synthesis of ethology and comparative psychology.* New York: McGraw-Hill.

Kagan, J., Reznick, J. S., & Snidman, N. (1986). Temperamental inhibition in early childhood. In R. Plomin & J. Dunn (Eds.), *The study of temperament: Changes, continuities, and challenges.* Hillsdale, NJ: Erlbaum.

Kantor, J. R. (1946). The aim and progress of psychology. *American Scientist, 34*, 251-263.

Keller, F. S., & Schoenfeld, W. N. (1950). *Principles of Psychology*, New York: Appleton-Century-Crofts.

Marr, M. J. (1993) Contextualistic mechanism or mechanistic contextualism?: The straw machine as tar baby. *The Behavior Analyst, 16*, 59-65.

Michael, J. L. (1982). Distinguishing between discriminative and motivational functions of stimuli. *Journal of Experimental Analysis of Behavior, 37*, 149-155.

Morris, E. K. (1988). Contextualism: The world view of behavior analysis. *Journal of Experimental Child Psychology, 46*, 289-323.

Morris, E. K. (1992). The aim, progress, and evolution of behavior analysis. *The Behavior Analyst, 15*, 3-29.

Morris, E. K. (In press). Mechanism and contextualism in behavior analysis: Just some observations. *The Behavior Analyst.*

Munn, N. L. (1965). *The evolution and growth of human behavior* (2nd Ed.). New York: Houghton Mifflin.

Pelaez-Nogueras, M. (1992). *Infant learning to reference maternal emotional cues.* Unpublished doctoral dissertation, Florida International University, Miami.

Piaget, J. (1952). *The origins of intelligence in children.* (2nd. Ed.). New York: International University Press, 1952. (Original published in 1936).

Piaget, J. (1964). Cognitive development in children: Development and learning. *Journal of Research in Science Teaching, 2*, 176-186.

Piaget, J. (1983). Piaget's theory. In P. Mussen (Ed.), *Handbook of child psychology* (Vol 1, pp. 103-128). New York: Wiley.

Schaffer, H. R., & Emerson, P. E. (1964). The development of social attachments in infancy. *Monographs of the Society for Research in Child Development, 29*, (3, Serial No. 94).

Schaie, K. W., & Hertzog, C. (1985). Measurements in the psychology of adulthood and aging. In J. E. Birren & K. W. Schaie (Eds.). *Handbook of the psychology of aging* (2nd Ed.).

91). NY: Van Nostrand.

Schlinger, H. D. (1992). Theory in behavior analysis. *American Psychologist, 47*, 1396-1410.

Skinner, B. F (1931). The concept of the reflex in the description of behavior. *Journal of Genetic Psychology, 5*, 427-458.

Skinner, B. F. (1935). The generic nature of the concepts of stimulus and response. *Journal of General Psychology, 12*, 40-65.

Skinner, B.F. (1938). *The behavior of organisms.* New York: Appleton-Century-Crofts.

Skinner, B.F. (1945). The operational analysis of psychological terms. *Psychological Review, 52*, 270-277.

Skinner, B.F. (1953). *Science and human behavior.* New York: Macmillan.

Spitz, R. A. (1950). Anxiety in infancy: A study of its manifestations in the first year of life. *International Journal of Psychoanalysis, 21*, 138-143.

Vince, M. A. (1961). Developmental changes in learning capacity. In W. H. Thorpe & O. L. Zangwill (Eds.), *Current problems in animal behavior,* (pp. 225-247). Cambridge: Cambridge University Press.

Werner, H. (1926). *Comparative psychology of mental development* (2nd ed. 1948). New York: International Universities Press.

Werner, H. (1957). The concept of development from a comparative and organismic point of view. In D.B. Harris (Ed.), *The concept of development.* Minneapolis: University of Minnesota Press.

Chapter 3

Some Thoughts on the Nature of a Theory of Behavior Development and Its Application

Emilio Ribes
University of Guadalajara[1]

Although behavior analysts have dealt with developmental problems, it is difficult to say that there is a theory about the development of behavior. The only significant effort, that by Bijou and Baer (1961, 1965) in the sixties, consisted of a hermeneutic exercise combining categories formulated by Kantor (1924-1926) with the available knowledge about the "principles", or better said, the procedures related to the change of behavior. The absence of systematic thinking on the issue of the ontogenic evolution of behavior and the formation of individuality has been evident. It is surprising that a theory such as Skinner's (1953), based on operant conditioning and devoted to the analysis of behavioral change, never formally addressed the problems of the development of behavior in its own right. Although Skinner in *Verbal Behavior* (1957) presented the first-order verbal operants in a sequence suggesting a developmental course, including the concept of the minimal-unit repertoire, he never explicitly formulated an evolutive relationship among them.

As I have mentioned in my earlier writings (Ribes, 1985; 1986a), the operant conditioning theory has been accepted as a non-hierarchical taxonomy of behavioral processes. Two basic processes make up the classification of behavior: those related to the procedures of both respondent and operant conditioning (Skinner, 1938). Although it has been recognized that emitted behavior derives from respondent sources (Skinner, 1937; Segal, 1972), both respondent and operant conditioning framed processes supposedly take place in a common empirical domain, sharing the same logical geography regarding the conceptual levels of the theory. Operant and respondent behaviors are considered to be not totally incompatible, so their simultaneous occurrence is thought to take place in the form of an additive or multiplicative algebraic interaction (Estes & Skinner, 1941; Hearst, Besley & Farthing, 1970; Davis & Hurwitz, 1977).

In any case, from a developmental point of view, the relationship between respondent and operant behavior has been analyzed in two ways: (a) Respondent behavior is seen as the raw material from which operant behavior is shaped and differentiated in terms of topographies and stimulus control; and (b) Respondent behavior, through a process of causal stimulus displacement, is thought to change to forms of operant behavior controlled by stimulus consequences.

These two relationships among respondent and operant behaviors seem to close any developmental link between the two classes of behavioral processes. The simultaneous interactions between respondents and operants during development do not seem to require a special treatment different from those that account for their interaction in traditional experimental process analysis. On the other hand, development has been conceived as a quantitative process along time in which behavioral repertoires increase in amount and differentiate themselves. This means that development is tantamount to more behaviors and to progressively differentiated response morphologies.

From this perspective, development consists of a cumulative process in which behaviors change, increasing in number and in the variability of morphology, displacing most of respondent stimulus control to operant stimulus control contingencies. This informal account of development is unsatisfactory. Ordinary observation of behavior development seems to point to three aspects that have not been dealt with in behavior analytic terms, and that probably can not be dealt with according to the logic of operant conditioning theory:

1) Although the development of behavior necessarily involves the occurrence of observable responses, there are many situations in which the process of "acquisition" (to be consistent with the cumulative metaphor in use) takes place without apparent changes in the observable morphology of behavior, e.g., movements and sounds. A case in point is that of listening, which is correlated but not identical, as Skinner (1957) assumed, to responding and or reinforcing to a speaker. Both common sense and experimental data (Ribes, 1986b) seem to support the contention that in order to speak according to the standards and style of a given verbal community it is necessary to listen. But listening - as reading and many other kinds of competencies- can not be restricted to the emission of articulated sounds or movements. Listening is something other than doing something. Sometimes listening is not observable as a particular doing. In general terms, listening has to do with the functional organization of a variety of actions and reactions in order to interact with the conventional properties of human environment. This is not a return to mentalism or to the postulation of inner cognitive actions. The organization of functional behavior is something more complex than the mere identification of particular responses taking place in relation to particular stimulating conditions. When listening, the individual reacts in special ways, but listening is not only reacting in special says. Listening as a special class of functional behavior involves particular morphologies and actions, which are not identical to listening. It is senseless to discuss the observability or non-observability of listening, or of thinking or imagining, for that matter. They are not action categories (Ribes, 1990).

2) A notion of development that involves only quantitative and, to some extent, cumulative changes in behavior seems to be incomplete. It lacks *qualitative* changes. The concept of quality is not foreign to science. Physics, chemistry and biology, just to cite the hard sciences, recognize quality as an analytic dimension of their theories. Unfortunately, in psychology, quality is historically related to mental elements or faculties, and more recently, to changes in morphological patterns. The mere appearance of "new" behaviors is not sufficient to account for or to describe development as a process. These changes might more accurately be referred to as learning. Development is identified not only by the passage of time and the changes in variety and number of potential behaviors, but especially by the *kind* of behaviors manifested and their ontogenic transformation. To refer to the quality of behavior is to refer to the *functional organization* of behavior. To understand a chemical formula requires knowing how to read, but you may read the formula in textual terms or you may read it knowing what it is about, or even more, how to transform that formula into different ones. In the three cases, reading as spelling a text is the observable component of behavior, but in the three cases we are dealing with different qualitative types of behavior. In order to account for them as a progressive outcome, a theory of development is needed that recognizes quality as a crucial dimension of behavior, and henceforth, would be able to resort to process categories that allow for such a recognition.

3) The recognition of qualitative differences in the functional organization of behavior entails the formulation of a hierarchical theory of behavior processes. Behavior processes should be thought of as interacting in a vertical functional axis. According to this perspective, development becomes a matter of changes in the quality of behavior along a hierarchical axis of qualitative complexity, in which particular behaviors may be included at any qualitative level of interaction. Behaviors as actions and responses do not change much during development. What changes is the way in which behaviors are functionally organized. The postulation of a hierarchical organization of behavior implies a twofold course of development. On one hand, complex processes or types of functional organization- must emerge from simple processes. On the other hand, simple processes, according to the particular situation, may be functionally subordinated to complex processes or may work independently. Which of these two cases takes place depends not only upon the external situation but also upon the behavioral biography of the individual interacting with it. Let me refer to listening again. It is obvious that the kind of hearing that is necessary to recognize a melody is quite different from that involved in the identification of the musical structure of that song. Hearing in the first case is reacting to a known sound pattern, and hearing in the second case implies reconstructing the sound pattern from the analytical fragmentation of the song. In the second kind of listening to a song, hearing the sound patterns does not follow the same parameters as in the first case, yet some kind of hearing is still involved, at least in the beginning!

The Logical Role Of A Theory Of Behavior Development

A theory about the development of behavior is equivalent to the historical branches of other sciences such as physics, chemistry, biology and even linguistics and sociology. Sciences deal with both synchronic and dyachronic approaches to events.

Synchronic analysis is concerned with process type theory, that is, with the analysis of a general empirical domain just as it is here and now. On the other hand, dyachronic analysis focuses on the historical evolution of that empirical domain. Astrophysics, geology, paleontology, philology, the history of social formations, and many other disciplines are examples of the dyachronic analyses of science. In this context, a theory of behavior development must deal with the history of psychological events as they evolve, and must represent the branch of psychology that accounts for the ontogenesis of behavior.

There are some issues specific to a theory of development of the evolution of individual behavior, namely:

1) The distinction between individuation and development, that is, between biographical and process-related evolution;

2) The problem of continuity and discontinuity as raised by the emergence of new *kinds* of behavioral organization and the progressive-cumulative nature of development;

3) The criteria for determining stages or periods of development and its direction; and

4) The logical dimensions of developmental categories as contrasted to those of causal-type process theory.

Individuation refers to how processes and conditions unique to a single subject interact and converge in order to produce within-individual consistencies that, when compared with other subjects, are labeled as individual differences. Individuation is an outcome of development, and development has to be analyzed in terms of generic processes interaction along *and* across time, as related to social and ecologically significant behaviors, circumstances, and criteria. Nevertheless, it is important to point out that although individuation takes place during development, the concepts are not equivalent. Individuation refers to a unique outcome of development in terms of particular competencies and interactive styles (Ribes & Sanchez, 1992). Individuation has to do with contingencies and interactions that typify the peculiar and unique behavioral development of each individual. Consequently, a theory of individuation has to do with the description and prediction of this particular synthesis of content and process in single subjects. Extrapolation from process and development theories should allow for synthesizing individuality. The theoretical route consists of reconstructing—or experimentally synthesizing—the actual behavior of an individual as the peculiar achievement or outcome of the incidental interactions of contingencies during his/her development.

On the other hand, development is related not to biographies, but to the generic conditions which allow for the sequential and coordinated interaction of processes along *real-time* and in *real-ecological and cultural settings*. Development does not refer to any particular individual or setting, but its content is related to *typical* settings and *typical* abstract individuals in those settings. To this extent, developmental theory is both descriptive and predictive as related to the outcomes of processes-interaction in different kinds of settings. Nevertheless, its foundation, which is based on processes, allows developmental *theory* -but not developmental concepts *per se*- to have a *restricted* explanatory role, one having to do with transitions as the outcome of sequences and coordination of processes. To the extent that development is concerned with abstract individuals in typical settings, the theoretical emphasis is on how, in the *general* conditions of a *particular* culture or environment, contingencies operate in shaping up the intermingling of behavioral processes in a temporal sequence and according to prescribed outcome criteria. Developmental theory is interested in the interaction of processes in abstract individual members of a particular environmental organization. Its explanatory power derives from its emphasis in processes interaction. Nevertheless, to the extent that development depends upon the identification of cultural and ecological criteria of effectiveness, its course is always reconstructed from the terminal outcome set up or prescribed by such criteria. Dependence on achievement or outcome criteria restricts the explanatory generality of developmental categories as compared with "pure" process categories. This may help to understand why cultural approaches to psychological development have correctly criticized inferring "primitive minds" from primitive societies, and have emphasized development as specific to culture. Unfortunately, these approaches seem to have overlooked the importance of **general** processes in behavioral development (Le Vine, 1982).

The issue of continuity and discontinuity pertains to quantitative and qualitative change. Although some quantitative change is needed to produce qualitative change, quantitative change in and of itself does not explain qualitative change. It is only under particular conditions of organization that quantitative changes do transform themselves into a qualitative change. Discontinuity refers to the qualitative change observed in the organization of a phenomenon under *continuous* quantitative changes. Quality is not a matter of form or morphology, nor is complexity restricted to the mere number of variables, elements, or factors involved. Quality, as an index of complexity, deals with the increasing *differentiation* and *specialization* in the organization of behavior *and*, in the case of human behavior, with the progressive displacement of so-called control (which I prefer to call *functional regulation*) from behavior-independent physiochemical factors and contingencies to behavior-produced and conventional ones (Ribes, 1986b). Writing and reading provide an example. Both reading and writing are acquired as behaviors regulated by the morphological properties of textual stimuli. In the case of reading, the individual has to utter certain sounds in correspondence with the symbols and spaces being spelled in the text. In writing, the individual has to copy through his/her own handwriting or through a machine the symbols and spaces being first merely observed and afterwards being spelled in the text.

Reading and writing become more skillful behaviors with time to the extent that they increase in speed, amount, and variety of performance. Nevertheless, reading and writing, conceived as spelling a text, referential reading, copying, or transcribing are qualitatively different from the behavior of reading stylistic or poetic relations between words while writing. The morphologies may be the same -or almost the same- but the quality of behavior thought as its differentiation and functional organization is *obviously* different. It may require a high diversity of reading and writing behaviors to become engaged with creative literary writing and reading, but the mere "amount" of behavior does not allow for understanding the emergence of more complex behaviors than the one being examined.

Stages seem to be a critical and, sometimes, a questionable issue. I would like to point out two aspects that seem to require a stage-like conception in the description and explanation of behavior development.

First, stages are necessary to deal with qualitative changes in behavior organization because of the fulfillment of interactive *sequential* conditions. Stages do not necessarily have to be thought of as being massive and homogenous changes, but rather they can be conceived of as asymmetric sequential changes in the organization of some behavioral competencies, changes that although they may facilitate generalized changes, may not necessarily be automatic outcomes. The observations by Vigotsky as reported by Luria (1980, Spanish translation), provide an illustration of what it is being discussed. Vigotsky observed that peasants in Central Asian Republics of the Soviet Union who were illiterate could not detach themselves from the particular circumstances in which their behavior had taken place. When asked how much time it took them to go from their homes to the place where they were being taught to read, they were able to tell the time and distance traveled. But when asked to calculate how much time it would take to go to Moscow, telling them the distance to that city, they replied that they did not know since they had never before gone to Moscow. After learning how to read, the peasants were able to answer the second kind of question. Reading did not produce the automatic emergence of the calculation of distance and time regarding unfamiliar places, but it seemed to be a requirement to be able to do so.

Secondly, stages should not be thought of as all-or-none exclusive forms of behavioral organization. Following the Aristotelian conception of the soul and modern biological thinking, stages may instead be conceived of as progressive inclusions, which under certain conditions work as alterations of functional parameters typical of less complex forms of organization. They nonetheless still allow for previous functions to be exercised when circumstances make them relevant. In operant conditioning theory, respondent and operant processes are thought of as working on the same level. When both are called for according to experimental manipulations, operant and respondent processes have to interact in the same empirical space, and they do so by facilitating or inhibiting each other. The mathematical description always consists of an algebraic operation. Nevertheless, processes may be thought of as *emerging* one from the other, with the more complex process *containing* the simpler one. For example, an infant learns to discriminate the circumstances in which his/her mother approaches and pays some kind of attention to him (cleaning, hugging, feeding, etc.). Since the mother's approaches depend on certain schedules, and her behavior correlates with systematic environmental changes such as talking, making some sound, putting lights on, etc., the infant learns to react differentially to these stimuli and may vocalize utterances such as "ma...", which could be conceived of as respondent utterances in terms of their stimulus control.

Nevertheless, the utterances themselves may appear in the absence of the environmental changes correlated with the mother's approach, and their progressive increase in intensity may result in "calling for" the mother. The utterance becomes an operant, according to classical terms. But the operant "ma..." does not exclude the environmental control and differential reactivity involved in the previously considered respondent utterance. In fact the operant "ma..." is emitted and progressively increased in intensity according to the presence or absence of differential environmental stimuli. The change is not only in the dynamic properties of the utterance, but in the functional mother-infant interaction. Initially, the mother's behavior regulated the presence or absence of utterances by the infant. Later, the infant's utterance regulated the presence of the mother. The operant utterance did not exclude the respondent utterance. It emerged from it, and their properties were regulated according to the scheduling of the mother's approaches according to the new functional properties of the infant's "calling" behavior.

Although categories for accounting for development consist of process categories thought to be in a dyachronic interactive relation, they are not explanatory as process-categories in synchronic analyses are. Two major reasons seem to apply:

1) Development consists of a theoretical reconstruction of behavior along ecological and/or social time, and accordingly, is conceptualized as a general trend in the change and organization of behavior. Popper (1961) stated that historical categories are not causal in the sense that they fulfill the conditions of generality for factual statements to which they relate. Therefore, behavioral processes, as processes related to trends in the organization of behavior, can not be considered causal categories. The trend of changes in the organization of behavior, consisting of dyachronic relations of processes, cannot be explained by the same processes involved in such a trend. Development, as a trend, is significant only from the perspective of ultimate stages of behavior organization which vary according to cultural and ecological criteria. As a trend, development is always constructed by the culture (or nurture), and therefore, cannot be thought of in causal terms. Development, as a concept, has suffered the same kind of logical mistreatment as memory (Ribes, 1991). Memory has been viewed as a special process or activity directed to the past, that is, retroaction, whereas development has been seen as a process evolving from a beginning toward a preconstructed end. Neither of these conceptions is acceptable. Memory may be better understood as projective behavior, development as a reconstructed trend.

2) Developmental categories are time-related, behavior availability concepts. Thus, they can be seen only as dispositional statements having to do with modal and capacity categories, using Ryle's terminology (1949). According to such a view, developmental categories are process categories which, to the extent that they are framed in the history of interactions of the individual, work as setting factors; in other words, as concepts dealing with the historical facilitation or interference of new forms of behavior organization or the acquisition of particular competencies. In this limited sense, development may be conceived of as the historical interaction of behavioral capacities along time, in which the behavioral competencies progressively acquired become the necessary condition for the further development of new behavioral competencies.

The Domain of Developmental Theory

A theory concerning the development of behavior should be thought of in terms of an empirical domain different from that assigned to a basic-process explanatory theory. The specificity of development as a subject-matter relates to: (a) the transition between processes involving progressively more complex behavioral organization, and (b) the sequential and coordinated acquisition of skills and competencies as an implicit outcome of cultural contingencies, without the intervention of formal training conditions.

In regard to the first issue, if development is seen as something different than a mere narration of changes of behavior in time, it is necessary to look at development as an abstracted generic transitional relation between those processes known to regulate behavior interactions. The conception of development as a sequence of transitions leads to three fundamental issues:

1) Development is not related to the identification of patterns of behavior in cultural and ecological contingencies, but to the identification, description, and experimental study of the transitional periods in which new behavioral processes emerge from previous ones. Learning refers to the analysis of transitions related to changes in contingencies when the same response classes are maintained, or in a very restricted sense, to the establishment of new response morphologies as behavior patterns. In contrast to learning, development is concerned not with new response patterns or response functions as such, but rather with the emergence of new kinds of behavioral organization as the outcome of transitional sequences from previous conditions.

2) The analysis of transitions in terms of the emergence of new processes from previous ones deserves special attention. As has already been mentioned, a process is understood as a general form of organization of behavioral interactions. Therefore, it refers not only to a particular course of quantitative changes taking place during the interaction but also to a qualitative relation among those changes. Looking for developmental changes means looking for transitions from one kind of behavioral organization and its quantitative features *to* a new kind of behavioral organization. The experimental analysis of how the variables and parameters involved in the

existing behavioral organization change into a new kind of organization overcomes the conceptual boundaries of a development theory. But the analysis of how the existing conditions of behavioral organization interact with new contingencies in the cultural and ecological environment so as to allow for the transition to new forms of behavioral organization is the substantial subject-matter of a theory of behavior development.

Behavioral processes as identified in particular competencies become the setting factors, defined as *developmental capacities*, facilitating the emergence of new kinds of interaction organization. Developmental transitions, from this viewpoint, are conceived of as the interaction of new contingencies with enabling available processes. Behavior interactions are seen as samples of behavioral processes displaying dispositional properties in relation to potential forms of organization facing new contingencies.

3) Development as the analysis of transitions must be thought of as having direction. Although this characteristic is not intrinsic to the biological or psychological individual, it does consist of a set of criteria, demands, and interventions built up by the culture. If culture is understood to mean the shared conventional practices of the reference group, it imposes a direction to behavioral organization in terms of the kinds of interactions and morphology and patterning of behavior that are relevant. Complexity of behavioral organization does not grow irrespective of the direction imposed by the culture. Moreover, progressive complexity of behavioral organization viewed as *development* reflects the progressive complexity of contingencies, kinds of behavioral interactions, and response (and stimulus) patterning and morphologies set up by the culture as differential requirements to be fulfilled by the social practices of individuals in a vast array of situations. If complexity, as a progressive qualitative and quantitative change in behavioral organization, could not be *observed* as the natural outcome of differential participation of the individual in social life, then the concept of *behavioral development* itself would be completely meaningless. The comparative analysis of different cultures at the same time and a same culture in different historical stages may provide empirical support to the idea that development is not a naturally "predetermined", universal process, but a process driven by cultural and ecological criteria that change in history and between societies.

The second issue relative to the logical domain of a behavior development theory also deserves special consideration. Development has traditionally been accepted as a longitudinal, and hence, a sequential course of changes in behavior, but it is also essential to include horizontal-synchronic changes as a central issue of developmental changes. As was mentioned above, transitions in development are considered sequential relations between *processes* along a progressive continuum of complexity in the organization of behavior. Nevertheless, there is an additional analysis of sequential relations in development, that although it is logically included in the first kind of analysis in terms of transitions, it demands special attention for its own sake. The first kind of analysis -transition analysis- might be called a molar analysis of development; the second type, both in terms of sequences *and* synchronic coordinations, might be considered a molecular analysis of development.

A molecular analysis of development involves the description of the *content* of behavior, which may be accounted for in terms of three concepts (Ribes, 1989): a) responses; b) skills; and, c) competencies. Responses are defined as morphological units, varying in size and composition, that can be measured according to of duration, magnitude or amplitude, latency, frequency, precision, or any other direct or indirect measure selected. Skills are functional groupings of responses, defined in terms of the fulfillment of *outcome* criteria, in such a way that the morphology of the responses being grouped depends upon the morphological and functional properties of the events and objects to which they relate. From this viewpoint, the responses comprising skill must have functional correspondence with objects and events based upon their morphology. Otherwise, it would not be possible to fulfill the outcome criteria required by the concept of skill itself. Competencies have to do with the *qualitative* organization of skills. A skill like reading, for instance, may be performed at different levels of complexity. A different kind of competence is needed to spell a text (in Skinner's sense, 1957) consisting of a paragraph on the law of gravity than to read it in terms of an abstract formula. In both cases, reading is the skill but the competence of reading is quite different. Not only is the interaction qualitatively different but the morphological composition and functional correspondence of the skill(s) involved are also different.

In a molecular analysis of development, the central phenomenon to be analyzed is traditionally labeled as *transference*. Transference, in functional terms, deals with the "acquisition" or "emergence" of new behavioral functions under two different conditions:

(a) when the same response is emitted to a new stimulus that shares some cross-modal properties with stimuli under which the response was previously trained, as when the utterance "water" is acquired in presence of the liquid and later is emitted to the printed word "water"; and

(b) when the new response shares some morphological properties with a previous response trained under a different stimulus, as, for example, when calling from a public-pay phone requires a response that is similar to buying cigarettes from a vending machine.

This usage of the concept of transference may be extended to conditions that involve not only morphological changes under similar contingencies -or functional levels- but that also deal with changes in the functional organization of behavior as capacities, as in the previous example about reading. Framed in this way, transference may be conceived of in a horizontal perspective as *coordination*, or in a vertical perspective as *sequence*. While coordinations have to do with the traditional sense of transference, sequences involve a new meaning, that is, the change of the functional organization of a given skill performance: changes in competence. Both kinds of analyses are fundamental for a functional analysis of behavioral development content.

Some Final Remarks

The logical justification of a theory of behavior development rests upon a fundamental consideration: although processes that take place during development are generic to any individual, they have a constrained generality imposed by the content prescribed both by the availability of biological reaction and action systems, and by the tacit and explicit competence criteria dictated by the culture.

Behavioral development represents the convergence or inter-section of the generality of basic processes (functions) with the specificity of cultural -and ecological- content forms. For this reason, and in contrast to basic experimental analysis and similarly to applied and technological analyses, the behaviors and environments studied in the context of a theory of the development of behavior cannot be arbitrary.

References

Bijou, S. W. & Baer, D. M. (1961). *Child Development: A Systematic and empirical theory*. New York: Appleton-Century-Crofts.

Bijou, S. W. & Baer, D. M. (1965). *Child Development II: Universal Stage of Infancy*. New York: Appleton-Century-Crofts.

Davis, H. & Hurwitz, H. (1977). *Operant-Pavlovian Interactions*. Hillsdale, N.J.: Lawrence Erlbaum.

Estes, W. K. & Skinner, B. F. (1941). Some quantitative properties of anxiety. *Journal of Experimental Psychology, 29,* 390-400.

Hearst, E., Besley, S. & Farthing, G. W. (1970). Inhibition and the stimulus control of operant behavior. *Journal of the Experimental Analysis of Behavior, 14,* 373-409.

Kantor, J. R. (1924-1926). *Principles of Psychology*. New York: Alfred Knopf.

Le Vine, R. (1982). Culture, context and the concept of development. In W. A. Collins (Ed.), *The Concept of Development. The Minnesota Simposia on Child Psychology. Volume 15.* Hillsdale, N.J.: Lawrence Erlbaum.

Luria, A. R. (1980). (Spanish translation) *Los Procesos Cognitivos: Análisis socio-histórico*. Barcelona: Fontanella.

Popper, K. (1961).(Spanish translation) *La miseria del historicismo*. Madrid: Taurus.

Ribes, E. (1985). Human behavior as operant behavior: an empirical or conceptual issue? In C.F. Lowe, M. Richelle, D.E. Blackman & C. M. Bradshaw (Eds.) *Behavior Analysis and Contemporary Psychology*. Hillsdale, N.J.: Lawrence Erlbaum.

Ribes, E. (1986a). Is Operant Conditioning sufficient to cope with human behavior? In P. Chase & L. Parrot (Eds.) *Psychological Aspects of Language: The West Virginia Lectures on Psychology*. Springfield, II.: Charles Thomas.

Ribes, E. (1986b). Language as Behavior: Functional mediation vs. morphological description. In H. Reese & L. Parrot (Eds.) *Behavior Science: Philosophical, Methodological and Empirical Advances*. Hillsdale, N.J.: Lawrence Erlbaum.

Ribes, E. (1990). *Psicología General*. México: Trillas.

Ribes, E. (1991). Pseudotechnical language and conceptual confusion in psychology: the cases of learning and memory. *The Psychological Record, 41,* 361-369.

Ribes, E. (1989). La inteligencia como comportamiento: un análisis conceptual. *Mexican Journal of Behavior Analysis, 15,*51-68.

Ryle, G. (1949). *The Concept of Mind.* New York: Barnes & Noble.

Segal, E. (1972). Induction and the provenance of operants. In R. M. Gilbert and J. R. Millenson (Eds.), *Reinforcement: Behavioral Analyses.* New York: Academic Press.

Skinner, B. F. (1937). Two types of conditioned reflex: a reply to Konorski and Miller. *Journal of General Psychology, 16,* 272-279.

Skinner, B. F. (1938). *The Behavior of Organism.* New York: Appleton-Century-Crofts.

Skinner, B. F. (1953). *Science and Human Behavior.* New York: MacMillan.

Skinner, B. F. (1957). *Verbal Behavior.* New York: Appleton-Century-Crofts.

Footnote

[1] On leave of absence from the National University of Mexico.

Chapter 4

Operant Learning and Habituation in Infants

Gérard Malcuit and Andrée Pomerleau
University of Québec at Montréal[1]

The Evolution Of Operant Research

Fundamental research on operant learning with humans, as well as its many applications in clinics, institutions, schools, and business organizations, has been the object of remarkable development and achievement in the sixties and seventies. Basic and applied researches covered the entire life-span and all domains of human activity. In human infants, studies revealed their great behavioral plasticity to meet changing environmental contingencies. These experimental demonstrations tended to confirm the generality of the principles and the practical efficacy of the techniques of operant learning. In the meantime, there appeared what has been called the "cognitive revolution" (Newell & Simon, 1972), leaving no area totally immune from its influence. We witnessed the intrusion of cognitive concepts in many strongholds of behavior analysis. In parallel, one gets the impression that the upsurge of progress in human behavior analysis is fading out. Such an assertion could appear exaggerated, especially when we take into consideration the quantity and the variety of researches that rely on operant procedures. As a matter of fact, the resort to operant contingency procedures is growing in many domains of fundamental research (with infant as well as with adult humans), and most interventions in the clinical and educational worlds integrate operant contingencies as part of their tools. However, this reliance on operant *procedures* might overshadow the fact that less research efforts aim at expanding our knowledge on learning processes as such. While most psychologists admit it is possible to establish operant control on certain *simple* human behaviors, they also consider that an operant analysis level of conceptualization is limited to explain the complex and higher-order activities that constitute the core of human behaviors. Cognitive concepts are introduced to make up for the seeming limitation of an operant account of human action. Despite a widespread utilization of operant procedures in the study of basic human processes, and most obviously in the case of infancy research, our understanding of how humans learn does not grow in a commensurable way. Two explanations can be called upon for this apparent stagnation.

Firstly, many behavior analysts spend a great part of their research effort to demonstrate with humans the generality and applicability of the basic principles governing behaviors that have been established in the laboratory with animals. This is not a futile endeavour. Behavior analysts have excelled in "exercises in interpretation" (Skinner, 1953), identifying instances of naturally occurring human behaviors in which the related events (stimuli and behaviors)—because they appeared to parallel analogous relations studied under the controlled conditions of the animal laboratory—were given an operant account (Baron, Perone, & Galizio, 1991). Although these exercises are considered ingenuous and enlightening by psychologists of behavioristic orientations, they do not succeed in thoroughly convincing people outside the field of their relevance. More importantly, they have not led to a new wave of original experiments, nor to an enrichment of our conceptual tools. Speculation alone is not sufficient. In the human laboratory, efforts have been largely concentrated on the effects of reinforcement schedules on behavior distribution and patterning. Because discrepancies in the performances of humans and animals under intermittent schedules are the norm more than the exception (Perone, Galizio, & Baron, 1988), this phenomenon seems to have monopolized behavior analysts up to the neglect of other problems. The second explanation is probably more a characteristic of researches with human infants. Operant procedures are dominantly used as tools to investigate early cognitive abilities, like discrimination, memory and information processing. Infants' sensitivity to operant contingencies, documented in a series of provocative studies, has proven to be a powerful means to question organisms who, because of their immatury, possess a restricted behavioral repertoire. However, operant procedures in these researches fulfil mainly a utilitarian function, giving limited and indirect gains in our knowledge of operant learning *per se*.

This presentation has three goals. First, we will describe what we know of operant learning in infants, from a promising start to its present utilitarian state. Second, we will discuss the conceptual and methodological impasses whereby operant research with infants appears to stumble. We will put forward other means to study operant behaviors that extend beyond behavior analysis' traditional methods. Finally, we will present two recent studies from our laboratory on infant habituation and attention. In these studies, we attempted at an operant account of activities which, up until now, have served to demonstrate early cognitive information processing.

Operant Research With Infants

Following the demonstrations of Papousek (1959), Siqueland (Siqueland & DeLucia, 1969; Siqueland & Lipsitt, 1966), Rheingold, Gewirtz and Ross (1959), and the series of studies they initiated, we know that from the beginning of their extrauterine life—and probably even before (Papousek & Papousek, 1979) —, infants can act on their environments and are affected in return by the effects their actions bring about. The selective action of the environment retains in the infants' repertoire the

functional behaviors which allow them to meet the various and complex requirements of experimental situations, and of their natural milieu as well. These first
studies revealed unsuspected learning capacities in infants (Reese & Lipsitt, 1970).

The experimental procedures of these pioneer studies relied on behaviors
belonging to behavioral systems already present in infants. Sucking, for example, is
a well-coordinated behavioral system apparent even before birth (Papousek &
Papousek, 1979). From the status of a response unconditionally elicited by a limited
set of events, this behavior can readily be transformed into an operant behavior. In
other words, behaviors, like sucking, that are biologically preprogrammed (but with
a sufficient level of plasticity to adjust to environmental variations) are modifiable
via contact with external contingencies. One of the first demonstrations of operant
learning came through the mixed procedure elaborated by Papousek (1959). When
we stroke an infant's cheek close to the mouth, we elicit a rooting reflex: the infant
turns his or her head towards the source of stimulation, with mouth opening and
sucking activity. The full reflex occurs after approximately 25% of the stimulations
when no consequent event other than meeting the stroking finger is programmed.
Papousek modified the frequency of this reflex by having each of its occurrence
followed with the ingestion of milk. Siqueland and Lipsitt (1966) later established
stimulus control in newborns by reinforcing with sucrose water head-turns preceded
by an auditory discriminative stimulus and a stroke. Head turns following stroking
of the cheek preceded by another stimulus were not reinforced. After a few trials,
head turns were emitted only when the proper discriminative stimulus signaled the
reinforcement contingency. This research showed that shortly after birth infants are
capable of learning a discriminative operant. In this instance, the behavior was an
elicited response, whose occurrence was modified by an operant contingency.
Siqueland and DeLucia (1969) modified the topography of 4-month-old infant
sucking activity by reinforcing particular aspects of this behavior. They monitored
sucking on a non-nutrive nipple and presented visual stimuli only when high-
amplitude movements occurred. This dimension of sucking increased its rate of
emission when reinforced that way. Departing from food-intake related behaviors,
Rheingold et al. (1959) modified the rate of 3-month-old infants' spontaneous
vocalisations by presenting contingent social stimuli after each burst of their vocal
production.

These first demonstrations of operant reinforcement's control on some infant
behaviors were important for two reasons. They showed the generality of the operant
reinforcement principle in infants. They established that operant reinforcement is
active very early in the life of humans, thus confirming its pre-eminence as a basic
process in the biology of organisms. Secondly, and perhaps of greater significance,
these results revealed that infant behaviors could also be reinforced by the changes
these behaviors bring about in the environment, and not only by nutritive
consequences. This was a major demonstration. Babies manage to modify certain
behaviors of their early repertoire not solely to satisfy primary biological needs, or
to maintain a homeostatic equilibrium, as shown in animal researches, but also for

the sake of stimulating their sensory systems, of making the world move (Skinner, 1953). Manifestly, their behaviors are reinforced because they allow them to act upon and to control their physical and social environments. Reciprocally, results of these experiments also indicated the effectiveness of certain classes of stimuli as reinforcing events. Visual and auditory transformations of the immediate surroundings (ecological reinforcers), as well as stimuli from a human source (social reinforcers) could differentially reinforce a vast array of behaviors. Benefiting from the contribution of Jacob Gewirtz and Claire Poulson in this book, we will focus our arguments on nonsocial behaviors and stimuli, although we consider our arguments also apply to social behaviors and stimuli. After these demonstrations, infancy researchers resorted to studying many other behavioral units (leg, arm or head movements, visual fixations on a target, object manipulations, etc.) as operants, followed by various types of visual, auditory or tactile stimuli as reinforcers (for reviews, see Fagen & Ohr, 1990; Pomerleau & Malcuit, 1983; Rovee-Collier, 1987). All studies tended to confirm the importance of operant processes in the analysis of infant development.

The shift from biological reinforcers to what Bijou and Baer (1965) and Bijou (1980) have called "ecological reinforcers" in studying operant reinforcement control on behaviors was a major turning point. Research evidenced particularities of this type of stimuli and their nontraditional effects on behavior. Contrary to the so-called primary reinforcers (ie: the provision of food and water, or the removal of nociceptive stimuli) classically used with animals, or the secondary reinforcers (i.e.: delivery of tokens and points subsequently exchangeable for back-up reinforcers) utilized with human adults, ecological reinforcers used with infants have a short life. That is, the reinforcement effect of any ecological stimulus fades out more or less rapidly. After some repetitions of this behavior-stimulus contingency, infants cease to emit the behavior followed by the appearance of the stimulus, as if they had attained a satiation level. But, unlike the case with primary reinforcers, the intake of ecological stimuli does not bring about a *general* state of satiation. While it still remains possible to temporarily satiate infants with ever-changing ecological stimuli, there is nothing equivalent to a general "drive-reduction" as with the ingestion of food or water. Only the specific ecological stimulus has *temporarily* lost its capacity to reinforce the repetition or the maintenance of the operant. A modification of this stimulus or the presentation of a novel stimulus bring back the previous rate of responding. In other words, high-amplitude sucking movements contingently followed by a given visual stimulation will progressively decrease in rate. A change in the stimulus content will very likely reinforce anew the emission of high-amplitude sucking. As conceived by Bijou (1980), the presentation of new stimuli or the modification of the surroundings contingent on an operant behavior may well have a reinforcing effect on the emission rate of this behavior in a given context, and also on the probability of its future emission in subsequent similar situations. Ecological reinforcement appears to be a potent means to study behaviors of developing children. As well, it enlarges our analysis of behaviors beyond the gathering of food and the escape-avoidance of aversive events to which, according to Timberlake (1984), learning studies were mainly confined.

With ecological reinforcers, infant activities categorized under the general concept of exploration—such as visual scanning and fixation of a display, tactile manipulation of three-dimensional objects, displacement to new parts of their environment—could be analyzed as operant behaviors reinforced by the natural consequences or transformations these behaviors bring about in the environment. Everyday play contexts, as well as experimental situations, could serve to investigate how infants learn to explore, make contact, and take advantage of environmental events. As well, the types of sensory events to which infants are most sensitive and preferentially allocate their attention could be determined. A behavior analysis account of infant development from birth on was emerging. Despite these possibilities, infancy research took another stand, mainly cognitivist. Two correlated factors can explain this evolution. First, the principal characteristics of ecological reinforcers showed up as convenient qualities for studying cognitive processes. The rapid modifications induced by ecological operant procedures, and their even more rapid evolution over time, were seen as *indicators* of the functioning of processes inaccessible by the traditional questioning methods of cognitive psychology. One must readily acknowledge that the use of operant procedures in this manner has led to impressive advances in our understanding of young infants' discrimination capacities. The fact that operant procedures became useful in exploring other processes and theoretical issues outside those around which concern was centered at their inception can be seen as indicative of their value. However, relegating operant learning to the status of an instrument is an impoverishment. This prevents from obtaining information on the learning process itself, such as its proper conditions, its adaptive functions, the factors apt to facilitate the acquisition of new behaviors, and the evolution of learning during this crucial phase of child development. It may also preclude the integration of data collected in such a utilitarian fashion within the general study of operant learning. The second factor put forward to explain the cognitive drift of operant procedures in infancy research can be paradoxically attributed to the operant approach itself. The relative easiness of implementing certain operant procedures, and the variety of questions on early cognitive processes their utilization apparently permitted to answer, contrasted with the conceptual limitations resulting from the adoption of a strict model of behavior analysis in infancy research.

Operant Learning In Infancy: A Research Tool

The many studies based on ecological operant contingencies with infants can be conveniently grouped under three headings: researches resorting to sucking behaviors, to head and limb movements, and to visual fixations.

Following the first experiments of Siqueland and Lipsitt (see Malcuit, Pomerleau, & Lamarre, 1988a) demonstrating that sucking could be modified by contingent presentations of visual stimuli, and that the repetition of this contingent coupling reduced the reinforcing effect of the visual stimuli on sucking rate, the procedure was successfully adapted with auditory stimuli as reinforcers (Eimas, Siqueland, Juszyck & Vigorito, 1971). When the fading of the reinforcing value of a particular auditory stimulus brought about a diminishing rate of sucking, the contingent presentation of a novel sound reinstated the high rate of emission of the target behavior. The immediate differential effect of these two auditory stimuli on infants' behavior allowed to infer that infants did indeed discriminate the two events. Conversely, no change of stimulus or the presentation of a nondiscriminable stimulus should not affect sucking rate. Because of this characteristic of ecological reinforcers, the high-amplitude sucking procedure became *the* preferred tool for assessing infants' capabilities for discrimination of speech phonemes (Jusczyk, 1985). However, even though a modification in the sucking rate concomitant to the introduction of a novel contingent stimulus permits conclusions about the infant's discriminative competence for this phonemic contrast, one cannot assert that no-change in sucking rate means the infant does not discriminate the new stimulus from the first. A discontinuity in the reinforcing value of sounds, more than a discontinuity in the infant's discriminative capacities might explain this result (Trehub, 1973). Some sensory events that can be shown with other procedures to be discriminated, might be insufficiently reinforcing to have a noticeable impact on the infant's operant behavior. The rate and maintenance of sucking behaviors are more efficiently reinforced by some stimuli than by others. The differential efficacy of ecological stimuli to reinforce behaviors and to maintain their reinforcing value for an extended duration was used in another procedure to study sound discrimination in infants. DeCasper and colleagues, in investigations on the relative reinforcing value of stimuli in the newborn's auditory environment, found that human voice stimuli, and particularly the infant's mother's voice, were potent reinforcers of sucking (e.g., DeCasper & Fifer, 1980). Researchers used this effect in an operant discrimination learning procedure. In this task, the phonemic stimuli to be discriminated had an insufficient reinforcing value to increase or maintain the emission of sucking. Thus, they were used as discriminative stimuli signaling the contingent availability of another event sufficiently reinforcing to result in differential sucking (Bertoncini, Bijeljac-Babic, Kennedy, Jusczyk, & Mehler, 1988; Moon & Fifer, 1990). For instance, in the Moon and Fifer study (1990), the discriminative stimuli were alternated strings of 4-second repeated speech syllables (/pæt/and/pst/,or/a/ and / i/). One stimulus of a pair was the S^{D+}. If the infant sucked while the S^{D+} string was presented, the string ceased and the infant then heard contingent recording of the mother's voice for the duration of the sucking burst. Sucking emitted during the S^{D-} string interrupted the string and was followed by silence. At the end of any sucking burst, the 4-s syllable strings resumed alternation. The authors reported differential probabilities of sucking to S^{D+} and S^{D-} during the second 6-minute period of the experiment, indicating that their 2-day-old newborns learned over time to begin a burst of sucking more frequently during the presentation of the syllable stimulus that signalled the availability of the mother's voice as a consequence of sucking.

Durations of these bursts were also longer during contingent mother's voice presentations than during quiet periods. Thus, as conclusions, the utilitarian one: Newborns appear to possess precocious speech discrimination competence; and the behavior analysis counterpart: Newborns can learn very early a finely-tuned discriminative operant behavior when this discriminative behavior is reinforced by the presentation of a highly (apparently!) salient stimulus.

The second group of researches includes head and limb movements. Head-turning responses to an eliciting stimulus, as in a habituation procedure, will be examined later. Here, we take into consideration discrete head movements comparable to limb movements, for instance, head-rotations reinforced by the illumination of a display (see Hulsebus, 1973; Papousek, 1977) or discriminative head-turning towards a sound source reinforced by a highly attractive stimulation (Meltzoff & Kuhl, 1989). This last procedure, used in speech sound discrimination with infants over 4 months of age, is analogous to the discriminative operant sucking procedure described above. Infants learn to turn their heads toward a specific area only when they hear a change in a sound sequence. The turns emitted at the change of stimuli are reinforced by the presentation of a puppet show. When discriminative control is established with easy-to-detect changes, test stimuli are presented, and discrimination is assessed. In other researches, infants' arm movements, hand contacts with a manipulandum or an object, or kicks on a pressure-sensitive pillow were brought under the control of an operant contingency (Millar, 1985; Pomerleau, Malcuit, Chamberland, Laurendeau, & Lamarre, in press). Actually, the dominant infant operant procedure during the last two decades consists of a context where leg movements activate a mobile suspended over the infant's crib (Amabile & Rovee-Collier, 1991; Rovee-Collier, 1987; Rovee-Collier & Gekoski, 1979). Repetitive infants' kicks make this mobile move at a rate and with an intensity proportional to the rate and intensity of kicking (conjugate reinforcement, see Rovee-Collier & Gekoski, 1979). The dependent variable consists of counting the minute-by-minute vertical and horizontal movements of the leg with the ankle ribbon attached to it (response rate) in the various phases of the experiment, while the mobile is moving contingently or noncontingently, or remaining stable regardless of the infants' movement (e.g., Rovee-Collier & DuFault, 1991). In a recent chapter on infant conditioning and memory, Fagen and Ohr (1990) reported 27 published empirical studies on these related topics: Half of these studies were based on the mobile conjugate reinforcement procedure. This procedure emerged over the others as *the* procedure to study learning and memory in infants. A first factor for its popularity may be its simplicity and ease of implementation. Infants can be tested in their own crib at home; there is no complicated nor expensive devices for measuring behaviors. Secondly, kicking has a high probability of occurrence with awake infants supine in a crib. This class of behavior possesses a high rate of spontaneous as well as elicited appearance. The mobile movements are potent events to catch the infant's interest and can readily become a reinforcing event under an operant contingency. Thus, each of these elements—a high probability of behavior occurrence, the noteworthy reinforcing value of the contingent stimulus, a behavior-reinforcer dependency that is far from arbitrary (the infant may have previously experienced that by making jerky movements, objects move around: the secondary circular reaction, see Piaget, 1952)–contributes to the rapid operant reinforcement control over kicking. This is not a lame advantage considering the difficulty involved in maintaining infants' state and interest at an optimal level for long periods of time. High attrition rates plague infancy research (Pomerleau et al., in press). Thus, a recurrent obligation of infancy research is to devise short sessions with simple behaviors readily amenable to contingency control. These practical reasons converge with a conceptual argument to explain the popularity of the mobile procedure. Its methodological structure appears to fulfil the requirements of the operant chamber model. There is a baseline phase (usually 3 minutes) during which infant kicking rate in face of a suspended nonmoving mobile is calculated. Then, the acquisition phase begins: every kick makes the mobile contingently move. The acquisition phase usually lasts around 9 minutes, and the kicking rate must exceed the mean baseline rate by at least 1.5 times (this is a learning criterion) in 2 of any 3 consecutive minutes of the acquisition phase. At the end of this phase, the contingency is withdrawn, and there is a 3-minute extinction phase (now preferably called "immediate retention test", after zero delay). The kicking rate shall diminish during the extinction phase (but preferably shall remain high if the intent is to assess short-term memory during this immediate retention phase). To evaluate longer term memory, this three-phase session is repeated 24 hours or a few days later. The operant baseline or nonreinforcement phase right at the outset of this subsequent session is called a long-term retention test. It is worth noticing that all measures of retention are taken during "nonreinforcement periods", either during an immediate or a delayed extinction phase.

With this procedure, one can demonstrate, in an apparently traditional manner, the establishment of operant control over a behavior by examining modifications in the kick *rate* that coincide with the three phases. This demonstration has been made many times, proving that reinforcement works, that infant behavior is sensitive to reinforcement-nonreinforcement contingencies, and that response strength of the conditioned behavior can be seen in spaced extinction phases. But the scope of these conclusions is limited. Research activities with the mobile procedure were oriented towards other goals, like the study of factors influencing memory encoding and retrieval (Hayne, Greco, Earley, Griesler, & Rovee-Collier, 1986; Rovee-Collier, Earley, & Stafford, 1989), retention (Enright, Rovee-Collier, Fagen, & Caniglia, 1983), the context of memory (Boller, Rovee-Collier, Borovsky, O'Connor, & Shyi, 1990; Borovsky & Rovee-Collier, 1990), and the reactivation of memory (Amabile & Rovee-Collier, 1991; Rovee-Collier & Hayne, 1987). The object of these researches is memory, and the operant procedures serve as convenient tools to gain access to the structure and content of infant memory. They represent today's main trend in learning researches with infants.

The third group of experiments concerns gaze orientation and visual fixations as operants. A number of these researches have a clear and stated objective to study operant control over these visual behaviors (e.g., Julien, Pomerleau, Feider, & Malcuit, 1983; Watson, Hayes, Dorman, & Vietze, 1980). However, the majority of them are run to assess early information processing in infants. In the first case, eye orientation and fixation on a specific target is synchronously reinforced by the addition of auditory or visual stimuli to the infant's sensory environment. In the second case, the visual exploration of slides or of three-dimensional objects is synchronously reinforced by the content of the stimuli itself. Looking and visual exploration is maintained by a synchronous reinforcement contingency whose control bears upon the duration rather than the rate of behavior. The reinforcing consequence is present for as long as the behavior that brings it about persists (Rovee-Collier & Gekoski, 1979). In infancy research, these studies are better known as infant-control habituation studies (Horowitz, Paden, Bhana, & Self, 1972). The infant "controls", via his or her gaze orientation and maintenance on the stimulus, the length of stimulus presentations. The infant's gaze is first attracted by the projection of a stimulus that remains in place for as long as the infant looks at it. When the infant looks away for more than (usually) one second, the stimulus disappears, and his or her gaze is attracted–by means of a blinking light–to another location. Once the infant's gaze is turned toward this light, the original stimulus is projected again. The sequence is repeated up until fixation times reach a proportion of those observed on the first trials. The infant-control situation extends beyond the usual procedures of habituation, which consists of presenting repeatedly a short duration stimulus that elicits an orienting response. The orienting response will progressively disappear with its repeated elicitation. The infant learns to inhibit nonessential responding to an initially response-eliciting stimulus which has been experienced as having no particular function for the organism's ongoing activity. The adaptive role of this process permits the infant's activity not to be constantly disrupted by all incoming stimuli. As a result, the infant will be free to allocate his or her attention towards the functional environmental events for the ongoing activity or for the reorganization of activity towards new objects. But when we consider the infant-control procedure, we leap from the habituation of an orientation response (a respondent process) to operant exploration behaviors, and the fading out of the reinforcement value of ecological stimuli. The stimulus is looked at for as long as it remains more "attractive" than other stimuli present in the situation. As its differential reinforcing value becomes reduced, infants' looking will be directed towards other stimuli in the environment.

The domain of investigation in infant "habituation" is presently thriving (Bornstein, 1989). It also became a cognitivist private territory. Although basic and important learning processes are called upon in either habituation of orienting responses or visual exploration of stimuli, "habituation" experiments are conceived as assessing the earliest manifestation of an underlying information processing activity in infants that is in continuity with, and thus predictive of, later cognitive abilites (Bornstein & Sigman, 1986). The cumulative duration of visual fixation on a particular stimulus before reaching the criterion is seen as representing the time taken to process the information contained in the stimulus, to build up an internal template, and to compare the incoming stimulus with this schema (Dunham 1990). As a consequence, the shorter the duration, the more efficient the information processing is conceived to be. Because there is important variability in looking time during these infant-control habituation (visual exploration) tasks, the speed of reaching the criterion becomes an index of a superior trait-like cognitive characteristic that differentiates infants (Colombo & Mitchell, 1990). As a confirmation, researchers have reported moderate correlations between shorter looking time in the infant-control procedure during infancy and measures of intellectual performance later in childhood (Bornstein & Sigman, 1986).

To summarize, we appear to be immersed in cognitive interpretations of infant development. After a promising start by operant learning studies that revealed important findings on infants' early learning capacities and sensitivity to operant contingencies, as well as findings on the differential reinforcing value of ecological stimuli, behavior analysts are presently absent (or temporarily silent, letting the cognitive tidal wave pass over) except through their methodological improvements borrowed by others. Operant procedures, sometimes overly extended, fulfil a utilitarian function, from which we need to depart. The present state of affairs, as we shall argue, depends in part upon a relative rigidity in our experimental settings with humans, and upon a distorted reliance on the animal laboratory model. As a corollary, we may have lacked sufficient imagination to create new concepts and new methodologies to study infants, and, shall we dare, humans in general.

The Operant Model and Human Infant Behavior

Laboratory-based accounts of human operants have predominantly been quests to establish the generality of principles identified in the laboratory with animals. These accounts reflect more an interspecies replication of results than the extension of operant analysis to human action. Although it might be relatively easy to demonstrate the impact of an operant reinforcement contingency on behaviors, results with humans often do not resemble those typical of animals (Baron et al., 1991). The problem of discrepancies in the performance of humans and animals is a highly debated topic in behavior analysis literature (see Davey & Cullen, 1988). Many factors were called upon to explain the recurrent difficulty of validating these animal-based principles with humans. Among these, the rich, but intrusive, extra-experimental variables of humans when they enter the operant laboratory (Branch, 1991). Extra-experimental variables, like history and individual characteristics, are to be considered also with infants, even though one may peremptorily assert they have a very short history and less strongly defined characteristics. Extra-experimental variables cannot be readily amenable to control as is routinely done with animals. A second factor concerns the presence of humans' verbal abilities which may mediate or intervene in all external contingency control, via explicit rules elaborated by subjects while in the experiment, or induced by pre-experimental instructions (Hayes, Brownstein, Hass, & Greenway, 1986). Without question, these factors may *partly* explain why results derived from human studies appear less orderly than results derived from animals studies. However, we might have overestimated the impact of these factors because they are too promptly associated with what is traditionally seen as specific of the human condition. As a direct consequence, we have often overlooked the analysis of other important variables that make animal and human studies hardly comparable.

Operant procedures with animals are characterized by steady-state performances after a prolonged exposure to the experimental contingency. Animals learn the implemented contingency between a brief, discrete behavior and a brief, discrete subsequent stimulus, after having arranged an appropriate deprivation level. Also, procedures with animals are especially constraining. Reinforcers are virtually always primary reinforcers linked with basic biological needs and survival pressures. Because of these experimental constraints, animals are compelled to execute repeatedly what is planned in the experimental setting, in a persisting motivational state. The operant chamber is specifically designed to collect frequency or rate measures. Skinner's choice (1938) of adopting rate of responding as the primary datum of response strength and cumulative recording of response rate allowed for the study of performances that vary in orderly ways as a function of reinforcement schedule parameters. Changes in response rate thus became *the* measure of operant contingency control over behavior, and the operant chamber became the model of experimental procedures to provoke and observe changes in response rate. Within this model, the qualifying characteristic of the reinforcement process evolved from an increase in the probability of occurrence of the operant under subsequent similar circumstances to an *emphasis* on the increase of response *rate* under the present contingency conditions. Learning becomes deduced from the increase in response rate of a particular behavior under a reinforcement contingency over a preceding operant base level.

Researchers in human operant learning have tended to follow the methodological prescriptions of the operant chamber model, and to select appropriate experimental counterparts. But, are the essential conditions actually implemented in procedures with humans? Although they appear to mimic many aspects commonly used in the animal operant chamber, it is far from certain that the relevant factors have been effectively isolated (Shull & Lawrence, 1991). As analogs to the brief, discrete and repetitive operants of animals in the operant chamber, infancy researchers relied on game-like behaviors (brief, discrete, repetitive and highly sensitive to changes in contingency conditions), such as kicking activity followed by contingent mobile movements. The variety of infant behaviors amenable to a rate analysis of that sort are not numerous and, many times, rather trivial. These behaviors are often not representative of activities infants must learn to master nor of the types of contingency learning they face in this period of their development. Kicking and mobile movements might look analogous to a lever press and the delivery of food, but the similarities are somewhat superficial and misleading (Shull & Lawrence, 1991). The current experimental contexts set up for humans are much less constraining than those with captive animals where behaviors produce the essential nutrient or subtract the painful stimulus. For their part, infants face a game-like situation which allows of a great variety of behaviors. They may act in these experiments to find the rule of the game, to explore the various possibilities of the context, and to take pleasure in that activity; in these cases, consequent stimuli can be seen as informational feedback stimuli whose function is far apart from the function of a classic primary reinforcer in the operant chamber procedure (Wearden, 1988). Because relevant conditions are different in animal and human experimental contexts, it is not surprising that different results are obtained. The attempts at replication have not been as direct as some investigators had hoped. Efforts in the search of generality should be more profitably directed towards the extension and refinement of our understanding of behavioral principles. For that purpose, alterna-tives (or modifications) to the standard operant chamber procedures are needed (Buskisk et al., 1991), even at the cost of reducing the alleged generality of *basic* principles, which could become more condition- or context-specific.

Operant research with infants gives even more reasons to challenge the operant chamber model in studying human action. On the one hand, contrary to great expectations (Branch, 1991) and limited interesting data (Bentall, Lowe, & Beasty, 1985), research on infants has not eliminated the problem of discrepant results, regardless of their nonverbal status and shorter history. On the other hand, as we have seen from our analysis of constraints and difficulties in operant researches with infants, other variables, under different conditions, need to be studied to account for operant behaviors and learning in developing infants. The techniques, procedures and methodologies derived from the animal operant chamber have limited applica-bility for studying infant behavioral repertoire. Aside from studies with nutritive reinforcers (Papousek, 1959; Siqueland & Lipsitt, 1966), the majority of experiments (and of interesting findings) are grouped under the heading of ecological reinforce-ment. As well, these ecological reinforcers reinforce classes of behaviors better conceived as exploratory, mastery or play behaviors. These behaviors and their consequent events possess specific features that need to be taken into account when devising an experiment.

Baron et al. (1991) have set forth three conditions to render human operant experiments compatible with the operant chamber model. The first two conditions are inapplicable in ecological reinforcement experiments with infants. Conse-quently, the third condition becomes obsolete. First, the authors emphasized the necessity that experimental variables are imposed long enough to manifest their effects; second, that behavior is studied as a steady state; and finally, that subjects are matched in terms of factors that cannot be easily brought under experimental control. The first two precepts are related: A steady-state performance under a specific contingency is obtained only after a sufficient exposure to that contingency. In the operant chamber model, to confirm that a behavior is under the control of a particular contingency, the response rate must change from its preceding stable level under a prior condition *and* attain a new stable level under the new contingency.

According to Sidman (1960), a stable behavior represents a "steady state", a point of equilibrium in the reciprocal interaction between the behavior and the conditions that influence it. A behavior attains a steady-state when entirely under the control of a prevailing contingency condition. All elements of this contingency condition–behavior-stimulus relations, signaling stimuli and setting-events–must also remain relatively stable or constant. A change in one of these elements, for instance, a modification in the motivational level or in the reinforcing value of the stimulus, will result in a change of behavior and in a rupture of the steady-state. Thus, the true defining characteristic of the operant chamber model is the steady-state. As is often the case in operant research with humans (infants and adults), the passage from a base-level to a reinforcement condition may rapidly trigger a change in the response rate, thus momentarily and partially reflecting the impact of the experimental variable on the behavior. But a steady-state is hardly attained because experimental sessions with infants are generally too short. Sessions are short not because we are too hurried to compute the data, but because we could hardly do otherwise. Firstly, the collaborative time-span of infants is brief, and expanding over this margin results in distress, and subject attrition. Secondly, this restricted collaboration is not solely explained by the limited capacities of our subjects. In experiments with ecological reinforcement, sessions are short and a real steady-state never (rarely) attained because of particularities of the ecological reinforcement paradigm itself. The reinforcing effects of ecological stimuli used with infants are short-lived. Consequently, short sessions are planned in order to ensure that the contingent stimuli retain their reinforcing functions, so that infants remain on task.

Infant learning studies deal mainly with the differential reinforcing effects of various stimuli on the maintenance of infant attention. This explains their popularity with cognitive developmentalists. The first appearance of the reinforcing event arouses attention and interest in the infant. With a few repetitions of the behavior-stimulus sequence, the behavior–kicks or head-turns–is brought under the control of the reinforcement contingency. The behavior is repeated until the consequent stimulus loses its reinforcing value. Even though the response rate decreases, we could still conclude with Watson (1979) that the infant "perceives the contingency" between his or her behavior and a subsequent sensory event and that the infant has learned something. The reinforcement function of ecological stimuli does not lead to the *persistence* or to the prolonged *repetition* of the operant, as a steady-state would require. The transient effect of ecological stimuli on the increase and maintenance of response rate precludes the possibility of a traditional assessment of operant learning. The rapid downward changes in rate following from this effect might be confounded with a transitory loss of operant control over the behavior, or even with the nonlearning of the operant contingency. The short life of the ecological reinforcement effect renders impossible the attainment of successive steady-states necessary for the usual demonstration that learning has taken place.

Moreover, the ecological stimulus may fulfil other functions aside from being associated with the reduction of a state of deprivation. It is difficult to identify setting factors, prior deprivation conditions, prior experiences, and specific stimulus characteristics that compose the differential reinforcement value of ecological stimuli (Malcuit & Pomerleau, in press). It seems preferable to analyse the particular functions a stimulus and a behavior entertain in a given context. Some authors have reported on the hedonic dimension of discovering the contingency between one's behavior and resultant changes in one's surroundings (DeCasper & Carstens, 1981; Lewis, Sullivan, & Brooks-Gunn, 1985; Papousek & Papousek, 1982; Watson, 1972). Under that alleged function rest two different functional possibilities which are difficult to empirically disentangle. Is the stimulus reinforcing the kicking behavior because a moving mobile is an exciting event to look at? Or, is the stimulus reinforcing the kicking behavior because the resulting mobile movement is an indication of control over the event, an informational feedback (Wearden, 1988)? In the first case, the operant will be repeated until the consequent event ceases to be interesting. The repetitive behavior may persist for a while, depending on an undetermined hypothetical ratio of response-cost and magnitude of the environmental effect, as well as on the availability or not of concurrent events. Usually, outside social games wherein an adult provides continuously varied and changing stimulations as reinforcers, the behavior will rapidly decrease. However, modifications in the rate of responding and its total cessation cannot readily be attributed to the same variables as those in the operant chamber procedure. In the second case, the behavior-subsequent event contingency will be quickly learned. As a result, the infant will cease to emit the behavior. This cessation of responding would be concomitant with the fact that the infant has learned how, for instance, to make a mobile move over his or her head. Learning, thus, can be assessed, not through a difference in rate between two steady-states, but through the re-appearance of this behavior with less trial-and-error search, in similar situations on later occasions.

Many laboratory learning contexts with infants are more adequately analyzed in terms of exploration and problem-solving contexts. Response rate changes thus does not appear as the most appropriate way to assess whether contingency learning has taken place. Infants learn the relationship between an operant and particular events occurring in their environment. Once this relationship is learned, there is no compelling reason to immediately repeat the operant. Infants may, according to conditions still undetermined, produce the sequence again to confirm that there is indeed a relationship, or because to "make the world move" once more is an interesting activity, *especially* when there is no competition with other events in the experimental context. But their operant activity will eventually cease, the consequent event being the sign, or the feedback, of a successful action. Infants have learned which behavior, in what circumstances, brings about a given event. Their behavior is reinforced in the sense that among all the behaviors they could emit, and among all those they have actually emitted, this particular one is retained because of the effect it *has* produced. Therefore, this behavior has a higher probability of being emitted in subsequent similar situations. On the other hand, if the situation still arouses their attention and interest, infants may keep on emitting behaviors until these behaviors fall under contingency control, or stated otherwise, until the contingency is clearly perceived by the infants (Watson, 1972). In this precise meaning (a response-contingent event that increases the probability of occurence of this response in subsequent similar circumstances, see Malcuit & Pomerleau, 1980), "feedback stimuli" can be conceived as reinforcers, contrary to Wearden's assertion (1988).

At this point, it is necessary to distinguish between the reinforcement of a behavior (under these circumstances, a given behavior brings about a given consequence) and the reinforcement of maintenance or persistence to the task (under the present circumstances, a given behavior is repeated [rate] or maintained [duration] because it meets the conditions of the situation). Operant behavior is interactive: By their action babies modify their environment. Following an "effective" behavior, the environment thus becomes different, as well as the particular contextual events of which this specific behavior was a function. Consequently the infant is in another context that renders other behaviors more probable. For instance, after many other unsuccessful attempts resorting to other classes of behaviors, an infant says "baby" when his or her doll is visible but unattainable, and gets the doll at a reaching distance as a consequence. With the doll at proximity, play activities become more probable. Even though the infant has learned a new behavior to make a doll come closer, there are no variables in this context favoring an immediate increase in the rate of this verbal behavior. This specific behavior will reappear with a shorter latency and less trial-and-error when a doll is unreachable and an adult is around. On the other hand, an experimental context can be set up so as to maintain a high rate of behaviors or the persistence of a behavior. Infants may have their attention and interest maintained in a task through certain arrangements and, consequently, this may result in a greater opportunity to emit the target operant behaviors. One possibility consists in making the contingency more difficult to learn, for instance, by implementing a "nonperfect" contingency condition (intermittent reinforcement combined with noncontingent presentation of the stimulus) (Pomerleau et al., in press; Watson, 1984). In these experiments where behaviors, such as handling a manipulandum, touching a specific target, and leg movements on a pressure pillow, were followed by visual or audio-visual stimuli, the nonperfect contingency condition fostered a persistent performance during a more prolonged period of time than a "perfect" contingency condition (that is, continuous reinforcement and contingent only presentations of stimuli). Watson (1984) concluded that perfect contingency "depressed learning". We can differently state that a perfect contingency relationship is more rapidly learned, and as a consequence, the infant's interest in the task is not maintained. Another possibility to maintain high rates of behavior consists in making the operant behavior bring about different or varied consequent events. For instance, leg movements produce renewed video images (Bahrick & Watson, 1983) or kicking movements, because of their variability and their conjugate relationship (although not evaluated), produce varied mobile movements (Rovee-Collier, 1987). More elaborated ecological stimuli preserve their reinforcing effect on behaviors for longer durations. However, their reinforcement value on the persistence of behaviors will eventually fade out.

In conclusion, we claim that the operant chamber model to study infant learning is not adequate with ecological reinforcers, and is not relevant within the context of a problem-solving analysis of operant behavior. Rate measures of operant behaviors do not appear as the most appropriate way to assess learning in many of these experimental contexts. The insistence on response rate may sometimes prevent detection of changes in other response parameters and, as a result, may not permit the evaluation of the learning processes that we want to study (Rovee-Collier & Lipsitt, 1982). This insistence also precludes the search for other means to assess response probability, and for other behavior-units for which rate measures are irrelevant or inappropriate. Although at this moment we have raised more problems than solutions (but hopefully constructive discussions), we urge for a fresh look in the study of operant behavior.

In the last part of our presentation, we will examine empirical attempts at a functional analysis of visual attentional behaviors in the infant. Such an analysis is largely based on synchronous reinforcement. In a synchronous reinforcement schedule, the reinforcing stimulus stays in place for as long as the infant's behavior lasts. For instance, infants get contingent synchronous auditory stimuli for as long as they look at a target (Julien et al., 1983), or contingent synchronous visual stimuli for as long as they maintain hand-contact with a manipulandum (Pomerleau et al., in press). A simpler, yet common contingency consists of having a contingent visual stimulus available for as long as the infant keeps his or her eyes on it (Malcuit et al., 1988b). In other words, looking at a stimulus is synchronously reinforced by having something (interesting) to look at. These reinforcement conditions, together with the conjugate reinforcement schedule, are considered to be representative of those encountered by infants (and adults) in their everyday experiences (Rovee-Collier & Gekoski, 1979).

Habituation and Operant Looking

In a debated article (Malcuit et al., 1988b), we have proposed a behavioral analysis account of the information processing activity alleged to be called into play during an infant-control procedure. In this procedure, a respondent and an operant processes are active. A stimulus elicits a head turn and a gaze orientation in its direction. The decrement of these elicited responses with repeated presentations of this otherwise functionally neutral stimulus is the product of the habituation process. This enables the infant to allocate behavioral resources to stimuli of greater relevance. Conversely, the infant may persist in turning his or her head toward a stimulus that has a functional value. The elicited head turn or gaze orientation is followed by a particular consequence: the appearance, within the focal visual field, of a stimulus that is attractive, at least more attractive than the drab surroundings in which it ispresented. The stimulus remains in place only if the infant attends to it. Looking is maintained by the availability of a stimulus sufficiently interesting to reinforce attention. With a synchronous reinforcement condition, the behavior will cease when the stimulus loses its reinforcing value or when another behavior becomes more probable (Malcuit et al., 1988c).

This functional analysis of infant visual attention has raised criticisms from researchers who use looking behavior measures to assess early information processing. One criticism concerns the circularity attributed to operant interpretations, and is paraphrased as "whatever attracts and maintains the infant's attention the most is the most reinforcing" (Cohen, 1988; Colombo & Mitchell, 1988). Another recurring criticism refers to the impossibility, or at least the difficulty, of experimentally contrasting the operant model's propositions with those of information processing. How can we modify the reinforcement value of a stimulus without simultaneously increasing the number of elements to be processed? (McCall, 1988; Morrongiello, 1988). In other words, by making a stimulus susceptible to reinforce prolonged looking, don't we, by the same token, add more information to the stimulus, more processing demand, thus more information processing time, all these resulting in prolonged looking? At this point, the two competing models appear to face a tautology in their capacity to explain the variables responsible for the capture and maintenance of attention. Following the illustration of this tautology by Lécuyer (1989, p. 112), for the information processing model, a complex stimulus maintains the infant's attention longer because it contains more information to be processed, while from a functional approach, this is because the stimulus has a greater reinforcement value. In short, the two models, apparently, do not explain anything and are mutually confounded. To come out of this deadlock, we need to demonstrate that a stimulus with a high reinforcement value is characterized differently from being a stimulus requiring more processing time because it is more complex. An experimental demonstration would consist in showing that an identical stimulus—hence defined by an identical number of elements to be processed and having a stable biological valence—may differ in its capacity to capture and retain attention depending on the functional values it has through the demands of the task and following the experience of the infant with this stimulus.

In a study on the habituation of orienting responses in 4-month-old infants (Malcuit, Pomerleau, & Bastien, in preparation), we manipulated the functions an eliciting stimulus may have in habituation procedures. We assessed the differential impact of these functions on head turn and gaze orientation responses with repeated presentations of the stimulus. As we have seen, in a classic infant-control procedure, the stimulus elicits an orienting response which places the infant in front of a picture more or less attractive for maintaining his or her attention. With repetition, the eliciting stimulus comes to have two confounded functions. First, it may preserve its initial function of an unconditional trigger of orienting. A stimulus lighting up all of a sudden within a context where there are few stimuli competing for attention, may maintain, for a certain time, its power to elicit an eye orientation in its direction, even after several repetitions. Second, it acquires a function of discriminative stimulus. The event seen in the periphery comes to signal that by turning in its direction, there is something to be looked at. Finally, the stimulus has a synchronous reinforcement function on looking activity. In an infant-control procedure, the stimulus for triggering head turns, and signaling and reinforcing visual exploration is the same stimulus. The stimulus can also inform the baby that she or he has mastered the situation. By turning her or his head toward and away from the stimulus, slides appear and disappear. In this experiment, we isolated the variables for the first three functions: eliciting orientation, signaling the possibility of looking at a visual pattern and synchronously reinforcing its exploration.

Three groups of 16 four-month-old infants were submitted to three conditions. In the first, the visual stimulus had only a triggering function: a stimulus of short duration (2 seconds) was presented. Half the infants saw a 4x4 checkerboard, the other an 8x8 checkerboard. In the second condition, one or the other checkerboard was presented and continued to be visible as long as the infant looked at it. In this infant-control condition, the stimulus had an eliciting function for head turning, a signaling function and a reinforcing function for visual exploration. In the third condition, one or the other checkerboard was presented for 2 seconds; then, visible only after the first orientation towards the checkerboard, another attractive stimulus (an animated cartoon) was projected in a more peripheral location for as long as the infant looked at it. In this condition, the checkerboard had an eliciting and a signaling function; the event that reinforced the maintenance of attention was different.

The orienting response, when the eliciting function was isolated in this manner, was gradually becoming habituated. The percentage of infants who turned their head in response to the stimulus (within a 5-second time frame) decreased over the 12 presentations, and was significantly lower than that of infants in the other two conditions. Interestingly, infants in the third condition showed even more orienting than those in the second condition, although the stimulus was of short duration (as in the first condition) rather than continuous (as in the second). Moreover, only in this third condition, where the function of signaling a salient stimulation was present, did we find an increase of orientations over successive presentations. The 8x8 checkerboard (considered more complex according to the number of contrasts) elicited a higher percentage of orienting responses than did the 4x4 checkerboard for infants in the first two conditions, but not for those in the third condition. It appears that the functional value of signaling is more important than the intrinsic value of complexity in a situation where one or the other type of checkerboard signals the opportunity to observe an attention maintaining event. Actually, there was no decrease in the duration of looking at the cartoons over trials. Infants kept looking at the stimulus for as long as a mean of 19 uninterrupted seconds at the last trial, confirming its high value of reinforcement.

The complexity and functional value of the stimulus induced other interesting effects at the presentations of a novel stimulus (attention recovery) and at the re-introduction of the first stimulus thereafter (dishabituation). After 12 habituation trials, there was two response-to- novelty trials during which the 8x8 checkerboard was projected to infants who had been shown the 4x4 checkerboard, and vice versa, followed by two further trials with the initial stimulus. We found the classic complexity effect in the first two conditions only. The percentage of infants orienting to the novel stimulus increased from the final two habituation trials when the new stimulus was the more complex checkerboard, but decreased in the case of a change from the complex to the simpler stimulus. Conversely, the dishabituation effect was more marked with the return of the more complex stimulus (i.e., 8x8 4x4 8x8) than the inverse (i.e., 4x4   8x8   4x4). In this procedure, the impact of "complexity" was more potent than its "novelty". Interestingly, none of these effects appeared in the third condition. There was no differential effect of habituation, of response to novelty nor of dishabituation as a function of stimulus complexity. The percentage of orienting responses remained uniformly high regardless of the complexity level of the stimulus.

We also computed the latency of head turning from the onset of stimulation to the moment when the infant's gaze reached the checkerboard (or its location, when the stimulus had already disappeared). Only the latencies of the third group showed a decrease over trials. The relation between complexity and speed of responding appeared in those infants for whom the triggering-signalizing stimulus was the same as the reinforcing stimulus. In this condition of infant-control procedure, the latencies were longer for the 4x4 as compared to the 8x8 checkerboard. But they remained uniformly rapid when both checkerboards elicited and signaled the occasion to look at a more interesting stimulation as in the third condition. Hence, the affirmation that pattern complexity has an effect on attention-getting (Cohen, DeLoache & Rissman, 1975) needs to be qualified and made more precise.

In a study still in progress we also varied the functional value of a visual stimulus (an 8x8 checkerboard) and analysed its relation to orientation and looking behavior. Our starting point was the two processes involved when infants pay attention to a stimulus: orienting their sensory apparatus towards the stimulus and looking at it. In the first case, attention can be elicited by a stimulus that appears suddenly, as in most habituation studies, or by a stimulus that is already present in the infant's sensory environment. In either case, it is by orienting their receptors focally on the stimulus that this particular stimulus may become the object of their attention. This operant aspect in habituation procedures has already been commented on (e.g., Cohen, 1976; Lécuyer, 1988), but without having isolated its first *respondent* dimension. A stimulus to which an infant orients his or her gaze needs to be present in the visual field (either through a sudden intrusion or through its constant availability). In order to separate the operant and respondent processes in operation, one can imagine a condition in which a head turn effectively *makes* the stimulus appear, brings about the addition of a stimulus to the infant's attentional universe as a direct consequence of her or his behavior (a positive reinforcement contingency). This operant may or may not be signaled. A discriminative stimulus can indicate the occasion for a head turn to be reinforced by the appearance of a stimulus. Such conditions indicate pricisely the role of operant and respondent variables in head turning responses. The following attending behavior (or visual exploration) is an operant synchronously reinforced by an ecological stimulus. It is by assigning different values to this stimulus, whose intrinsic characteristics (of complexity or processing load) remain fixed, and by observing ensuing variations in the maintenance of attention that we can depart from competing explanations. We have thus created four experimental conditions to which we have assigned four groups of 16 4-month-old infants. The first condition is a classic infant-control procedure. There is one stimulus fulfilling the three functions of eliciting head turning, signaling the occasion of reinforcement, and synchronously reinforcing visual exploration. Condition 2 is a situation in which the stimulus is constantly present: There is no sudden eliciting stimulus; the stimulus has a discriminative and a synchronous reinforcing function. Condition 3 is a situation in which the stimulus appears if and only if the infant turns her or his head towards an illuminated surface. There is no sudden eliciting stimulus, but a discriminative stimulus that is different from the reinforcing stimulus (signaled operant). The fourth condition is a free-operant situation. The checkerboard appears if and only if the infant turns her or his head in the direction of a nonsignaled point in space. There is no sudden eliciting, nor discriminative stimulus.

Preliminary results showed that a constantly present stimulus (condition 2), without sudden appearance, is looked at the least (it reinforces visual inspection for the shortest period). When the infant's behaviors make the checkerboard appear, whether these operants are signaled or not (conditions 3 and 4), the peaks of fixation are of the longest durations, as are the mean looking times at each fixation. These two duration parameters attain values more than twice as high as those observed in the situation where the checkerboard is constantly present (condition 2), while those in the classical infant-control procedure (condition 1) occupy an intermediate position. In this study, all infants were under identical time constraints: Each session lasted 4 minutes following the first visual fixation on the checkerboard. Dividing the session into three blocks of equal duration, we observed that while the number of turns remained equal and relatively stable in the three blocks for conditions 1 and 2, there was a linear increase across blocks for the two operant conditions. This is an indication of operant learning. In parallel, the peaks and the mean durations in fixation times decreased linearly over blocks of durations, as well as over blocks of equal number of trials, among all groups, yet they always remained superior in the two operant conditions.

Two observations follow from these results. First, the decrease in duration parameters of looking with repeated trials reflects the weakening of the checkerboard's reinforcement value on visual exploration. Second, the durations of looking are different according to the functional characteristics of the stimulus (in opposition to its physical characteristics which are constant in all four conditions). A stimulus that appears suddenly as a consequence of a particular behavior seems to be more potent in sustaining attention than a stimulus that is always present, or a stimulus whose sudden appearance triggers attention. There are intuitive reasons for expecting different amounts of attention to be triggered and sustained by contingent and noncontingent stimuli. According to Watson (1972), one should expect more attention to be given to contingent than to noncontingent stimuli. A stimulus which is contingent upon the infant's own activity should produce more intense and habituation-resistant orienting behavior, only to be reduced once the infant has mastered the contingency (Papousek & Papousek, 1984). In contrast, Millar (1975), and Millar and Schaffer (1972) consider that infants will more readily habituate to contingent stimuli for the likely reason that contingent stimuli become progressively redundant for them. Since these interpretations apply to data derived from different experimental contexts, it is difficult to make a clear-cut decision in favor of one or the other. Apparently, a stimulus contingent on a specific behavior may be looked at more by a baby than a stimulus already present in the context. When the experimental situation becomes a problem-solving task ("what makes it that this checkerboard appears all of a sudden?") then the presentation of the checkerboard becomes a reinforcer of head turning, providing feedback about what actions are relevant to produce the stimulus, rather than being a reinforcer of sustained attention. We might then expect an increase in the rate of head turns and a decrease in the duration of looking. Under these conditions, the stimulus comes to confirm that two events are interrelated, one being dependent upon the other; hence the stimulus no longer needs to be explored.

There still is ample room left for studying differences in orienting and attending behaviors induced by stimuli whose functional value is experimentally manipulated. These preliminary attempts are encouraging. By departing from procedures and experimental designs that mimic those developed in the animal laboratories, these attempts reveal the possibility of exploring new areas in early learning processes. Neither the many criticisms we have addressed to the "orthodox" behavior analysis (in the sense of being too close to the operant-chamber model) nor the greater flexibility or inventiveness in experimental procedures we call for should be seen as rejection of the behavior analytic approach. In concordance with Shull and Laurence's assertion (1991), nothing inherent in a functional analysis of behavior requires that procedures or data collection resembles what has been and what is done in the operant chamber. We shall keep analyzing infants' behavior in a behavior analysis perspective and hope to benefit from comments of our behavior analyst colleagues.

References

Amabile, T.A., & Rovee-Collier, C. (1991). Contextual variation and memory retrieval at six months. *Child Development, 62*, 1155-1166.

Bahrick, L.E., & Watson, J.S. (1983 April). Contingency perception as a basis for early self-perception. Paper presented at the biennal meeting of the Society for Research in Child Development, Detroit.

Baron, A., Perone, M., & Galizio, M. (1991). Analyzing the reinforcement process at the human level: Can application and behavioristic interpretation replace laboratory research? *The Behavior Analyst, 14*, 95-105.

Bentall, R.P., Lowe, C.F., & Beasty, A. (1985). The role of verbal behavior in human learning: II. Developmental differences. *Journal of the Experimental Analysis of Behavior, 43,* 165-185.

Bertoncini, J., Bijeljac-Babic, R., Kennedy, L.J., Jusczyk, P.W., & Mehler, J. (1988). An investigation of young infants' perceptual representations of speech sounds. *Journal of Experimental Psychology: General, 117,* 21-33.

Bijou, S.W. (1980). Exploratory behavior in infants and animals: a behavior analysis. *The Psychological Record, 30,* 483-495.

Bijou, S.W., & Baer, D.M. (1965). *Child development. Vol.2: Universal stage of infancy:* New York: Appleton-Century-Crofts.

Boller, K., Rovee-Collier, C., Borovsky, D., O'Connor, J., & Shyi, G. (1990). Developmental changes in the time-dependent nature of memory retrieval. *Developmental Psychology, 26,* 770-779.

Borovsky, D., & Rovee-Collier, C. (1990). Contextual constraints on memory retrieval at six months. *Child Development, 61,* 558-594.

Bornstein, M.H. (1989). Stability in early mental development: From attention and information processing in infancy to language and cognition in childhood. In M.H. Bornstein & N.A. Krasnegor (Eds.), *Stability and continuity in mental development: Behavioral and biological perspectives* (pp. 147-170). Hillsdale, NJ: Erlbaum.

Bornstein, M.H., & Sigman, M.D. (1986). Continuity in mental development from infancy. *Child Development, 57,* 251-274.

Branch, M.N. (1991). On the difficulty of studying "basic" behavioral processes in humans. *The Behavioral Analyst, 14,* 107-110.

Buskist, W., Newland, M.C., & Sherburne, T. (1991). Continuity and context. *The Behavior Analyst, 14,* 111-116.

Cohen, L.B. (1976). Habituation of infant visual attention. In T.J. Tighe & R.N. Leaton (Eds.), *Habituation: Perspectives from child development, animal behavior, and neurophysiology* (pp. 207-238). Hillsdale, NJ: Erlbaum.

Cohen, L.B. (1988). The relationship between infant habituation and infant information processing. *European Bulletin of Cognitive Psychology, 8,* 445-454.

Cohen, L.B., DeLoache, J.S., & Rissman, M.W. (1975). The effect of stimulus complexity on infant visual attention and habituation. *Child Development, 45,* 611-617.

Colombo, J., & Mitchell, D.W. (1988). Infant visual habituation: In defense of an information-processing analysis. *European Bulletin of Cognitive Psychology, 8,* 455-461.

Colombo, J., & Mitchell, D.W. (1990). Individual differences in early visual attention: Fixation time and information processing. In J. Colombo, & J. Fagen (Eds.), *Individual differences in infancy: Reliability, stability, prediction* (pp. 193-227). Hillsdale, NJ: Erlbaum.

Davey, G., & Cullen, C. (Eds.) (1988). *Human operant conditioning and behavior modification.* New York: Wiley.

DeCasper, A.J., & Carstens, A.A. (1981). Contingencies of stimulation: Effects on learning and emotions in neonates. *Infant Behavior and Development, 4*, 19-35.

DeCasper, A.J., & Fifer, W.P. (1980). Of human bonding: Newborns prefer their mother's voices. *Science, 208*, 1174-1176.

Dunham, P. (1990). Temporal structure of stimulation maintains infant attention. In J.R. Enns (Ed.), *The development of attention: Research and theory* (pp. 67-85). Amsterdam: Elsevier Science Publishers.

Eimas, P.D., Siqueland, E.R., Juszyck, P., & Vigorito, J. (1971). Speech discrimination in infant. *Science, 171*, 303-306.

Enright, M.K., Rovee-Collier, C.K., Fagen, J.W., & Caniglia, K. (1983). The effects of distributed training on retention of operant conditioning in human infants. *Journal of Experimental Child Psychology, 36*, 209-225.

Fagen, J.W., & Ohr, P.S. (1990). Individual differences in infant conditioning and memory. In J. Colombo & J. Fagen (Eds.), *Individual differences in infancy: Reliability, stability, prediction* (pp. 155-191). Hillsdale, NJ: Erlbaum.

Hayes, S.C., Brownstein, A.J., Haas, J.R., & Greenway, D.E. (1986). Instructions, multiple schedules, and extinction: Distinguishing rule-governed from schedule-controlled behavior. *Journal of the Experimental Analysis of Behavior, 46*, 137-147.

Hayne, H., Greco, C., Earley, L., Griesler, P., & Rovee-Collier, C. (1986). Ontogeny of early event memory: II. Encoding and retrieval by 2- and 3-month-olds. *Infant Behavior and Development, 9*, 461-472.

Horowitz, F.D., Paden, L., Bhana, K., & Self, P. (1972). An infant control procedure for studying infant visual fixations. *Developmental Psychology, 7*, 90.

Hulsebus, R.C. (1973). Operant conditioning of infant behavior: A review. In H.W. Reese (Ed.), *Advances in child development and behavior*. New York: Academic Press.

Julien, D., Pomerleau, A., Feider, H., & Malcuit, G. (1983). Temporal and content variations as determinants of infants' visual control of verbal stimulations. *Developmental Psychology, 19*, 366-374.

Jusczyk, P.W. (1985). The high amplitude sucking technique as a methodological tool in speech perception research. In G. Gottlieb & N.A. Krasnegor (Eds.), *Measurement of audition and vision in the first year of postnatal life: A methodological overview*. Norwood, NJ: Ablex.

Lécuyer, R. (1988). Please infant can you tell me exactly what you are doing during a habituation experiment? *European Bulletin of Cognitive Psychology, 8*, 476-480.

Lécuyer, R. (1989). *Bébés astronomes, bébés psychologues*. Liège: Mardaga.

Lewis, M., Sullivan, M.W., & Brooks-Gunn, J. (1985). Emotional behavior during the learning of a contingency in early infancy. *British Journal of Developmental Psychology, 3*, 307-316.

Malcuit, G., & Pomerleau, A. (1980). *Terminologie en conditionnement et apprentissage*. Québec: Presses de l'Université du Québec.

Malcuit, G., & Pomerleau, A. (in press). A functional analysis of visual fixation, habituation, and attention in infancy. In A. Vyt, H. Bloch, & M.H. Bornstein (Eds.),*Early mental development: Perspectives on structure and process from francophone countries*. Hillsdale, NJ: Erlbaum.

Malcuit, G., Pomerleau, A., & Bastien, C. (in preparation). Habituation of the orienting response to visual stimuli of different functional values in the infant.

Malcuit, G., Pomerleau, A., & Lamarre, G. (1988a). La recherche sur l'apprentissage opérant chez le nourrisson: un parallèle avec l'état général de la question chez l'humain. *L'Année Psychologique, 88,* 257-282.

Malcuit, G., Pomerleau, A., & Lamarre, G. (1988b). Habituation, visual fixation and cognitive activity in infants: A critical analysis and attempt at a new formulation. *European Bulletin of Cognitive Psychology, 8,* 415-440.

Malcuit, G., Pomerleau, A., & Lamarre, G. (1988c). Habituation and operant visual fixation: A comment on comments. *European Bulletin of Cognitive Psychology, 8,* 539-547.

McCall, R.B. (1988). Habituation, response to new stimuli, and information processing in human infants. *European Bulletin of Cognitive Psychology, 8,* 481-488.

Meltzoff, A.N., & Kuhl, P.K. (1989). Infants' perception of faces and speech sounds: Challenges to developmental theory. In P.R. Zelazo & R.G. Barr (Eds.), *Challenges to developmental paradigms: Implication for theory assessment and treatment* (pp. 67-91). Hillsdale, NJ: Erlbaum.

Millar, W.S. (1975). Visual attention to contingent and non-contingent stimulation in six- and nine-month-old infants. *Psychological Research, 37,* 309-319.

Millar, W.S. (1985). The effect of proximal and distal feed-back on the contingency learning of 6- and 12-month-old normal and perinatally compromised infants. *Journal of Child Psychology and Psychiatry, 26,* 789-800.

Millar, W.S., & Schaffer, H.R. (1972). The influence of spatially displaced feedback on infant operant conditioning.*Journal of Experimental Child Psychology, 14,* 442-453.

Moon, C., & Fifer, W.P. (1990). Syllables as signals for 2-day-old infants. *Infant Behavior and Development, 13,* 377-390.

Morrongiello, B.A. (1988). Habituation, visual fixation and cognitive activity: Another "look" at the evidence. *European Bulletin of Cognitive Psychology, 8,* 489-493.

Newell, A., & Simon, H.A. (1972). *Human problem solving.* Englewood Cliffs, NJ: Prentice Hall.

Papousek, H. (1959). A method of studying conditioned food reflexes in young children up to the age of 6 months. *Pavlov Journal of Higher Nervous Activity, 9,* 136-140.

Papousek, H. (1977). The development of learning ability in infancy. In G. Nissen (Ed.), *Intelligence, learning, and learning disturbances* (pp. 75-93). Berlin: Springer-Verlag.

Papousek, H., & Papousek, M. (1979). The infant's fundamental adaptive response system in social interaction. In E.B. Thoman (Ed.), *Origins of the infant's social responsiveness* (pp. 175-208). Hillsdale, NJ: Erlbaum.

Papousek, H., & Papousek, M. (1982). Integration into the social world: Survey of research. In P. Stratton (Ed.), *Psychobiology of the human newborn* (pp. 367-390). New York: Wiley.

Papousek, H., & Papousek, M. (1984). Learning and cognition in the everyday life of human infants. In J.S. Rosenblatt, C. Beer, M.-C. Busnel, & P.J.B. Slater (Eds.), *Advances in the study of behavior, Vol. 14* (pp. 27-61), New York: Academic Press.

Perone, M., Galizio, M., & Baron, A. (1988). The relevance of animal-based principles in the laboratory study of human operant conditioning. In G. Davey & C. Cullen (Eds.), *Human operant conditioning and behavior modification* (pp. 59-85). New York: Wiley.

Piaget, J. (1952). *The origins of intelligence in children.* New York: International Universities.

Pomerleau, A., & Malcuit, G. (1983). *L'enfant et son environnement. Une étude fonctionnelle de la première enfance.* Bruxelles: Mardaga.

Pomerleau, A., Malcuit, G., Chamberland, C., Laurendeau, M.-C., & Lamarre, G. (in press). Methodological problems in operant learning research with human infants. *International Journal of Psychology.*

Reese, H.W., & Lipsitt, L.P. (1970). *Experimental child psychology.* New York: Academic.

Rheingold, H.L., Gewirtz, J.L., & Ross, H.W. (1959). Social conditioning of vocalization in the infant. *Journal of Comparative and Physiological Psychology, 52,* 68-73.

Rovee-Collier, C. (1987). Learning and memory in infancy. In J.D. Osofsky (Ed.), *Handbook of infant development (2nd ed.)* (pp. 98-148). New York: Wiley.

Rovee-Collier, C., & DuFault, D. (1991). Multiple contexts and memory retrieval at three months. *Developmental Psychobiology, 24,* 39-49.

Rovee-Collier, C., & Gekoski, M.J. (1979). The economics of infancy: A review of conjugate reinforcement. In H.W. Reese & L.P. Lipsitt (Eds.), *Advances in child development and behavior* (vol. 13, pp. 195-255). New York: Academic Press.

Rovee-Collier, C., Earley, L.A., & Stafford, S. (1989). Ontogeny of early event memory: III. Attentional determinants of memory retrieval at 2 and 3 months. *Infant Behavior and Development, 12,* 147-161.

Rovee-Collier, C., & Hayne, H. (1987). Reactivation of infant memory: Implications for cognitive development. In H.W. Reese (Ed.), *Advances in child development and behavior* (Vol. 20, pp. 185-238). New York: Academic Press.

Rovee-Collier, C., & Lipsitt, L.P. (1982). Learning, adaptation, and memory in the newborn. In P. Stratton (Ed.), *Psychobiology of the human newborn* (pp. 147-190). New York: Wiley.

Shull, R.L., & Lawrence, P.S. (1991). Preparations and principles. *The Behavior Analyst, 14*, 133-138.

Sidman, M. (1960). *Tactics of scientific research.* New York: Basic Books.

Siqueland, E.R., & DeLucia, C.A. (1969). Visual reinforcement of non-nutritive sucking in human infants. *Science, 165*, 1144-1146.

Siqueland, E.R., & Lipsitt, L.R. (1966). Conditioned head-turning behavior in newborns. *Journal of Experimental Child Psychology, 3*, 356-376.

Skinner, B.F. (1938). *The behavior of organisms: An experimental analysis.* New York: Appleton-Century-Crofts.

Skinner, B.F. (1953). *Science and human behavior.* New York: MacMillan.

Timberlake, W. (1984). An ecological approach to learning. *Learning and Motivation, 15*, 321-333.

Trehub, S.E. (1973). Infants' sensitivity to vowel and tonal contrasts. *Developmental Psychology, 9*, 91-96.

Watson, J.S. (1972). Smiling, cooing, and "the game". *Merrill-Palmer Quarterly, 18*, 323-339.

Watson, J.S. (1979). Perception of contingency as a determinant of social responsiveness. In E.B. Thoman (Ed.), *Origins of the infant's social responsiveness* (pp. 33-64). Hillsdale, NJ: Erlbaum.

Watson, J.S. (1984 April). Perfect contingency depresses learning at 4 months. Paper presented at the International Conference on Infant Studies, New York City.

Watson, J.S., Hayes, L.A., Dorman, L., & Vietze, P. (1980). Infant sex differences in operant fixation with visual and auditory reinforcement. *Infant Behavior and Development, 3*, 107-114.

Wearden, J.H. (1988). Some neglected problems in the analysis of human operant behavior. In G. Davey & C. Cullen (Eds.), *Human operant conditioning and behavior modification* (pp. 197-224). New York: Wiley.

Footnote

[1] We gratefully acknowledge the support of research grants from the Natural Sciences and Engineering Research Council of Canada and from Université du Québec à Montréal. We also wish to thank Helga Feider for her comments and assistance in the English version of this paper, as well as our graduate students, Christian Bastien, Christian Carpenter, Joane Normandeau, and Michelle Sala for their stimulating contribution.

Chapter 5

The Operant Language-Acquisition Paradigm and its Empirical Support

Claire L. Poulson[1]
Queens College and the Graduate School
City University of New York
Effie Kymissis
Alpine Learning Group, River Edge, New Jersey

The operant language-acquisition paradigm, developed during the past three decades by behaviorally-oriented researchers, teachers, and clinicians, has been highly successful as a treatment paradigm for the development of language in children and adults who have been diagnosed as mentally retarded, autistic, or otherwise developmentally delayed. Skinner laid the conceptual groundwork for an operant analysis of linguistic development in his *Verbal Behavior* in 1957. Since then, many aspects of this operant learning paradigm have been empirically analyzed, and the resulting language-training procedures have been reported by Baer, Guess, and Sherman (1972), Harris (1976), Lovaas (1977, 1981), and Risley, Hart, and Doke (1972), and Schumaker and Sherman (1978).

The Paradigm

Referring to the broad outline proposed by Schumaker and Sherman (1978), the paradigmatic language-training procedures are the following: (a) establish reinforcers for maintaining some level of vocalization, (b) bring that level to a rate at which the response can be brought under discriminative stimulus control, (c) bring that responding under the topographical control of models produced by an adult by training sufficient numbers, kinds, or combinations of exemplars to produce generalized imitation, and then (d) transfer stimulus control of a given sound or word from imitative stimuli to nonimitative stimuli such as graphemes, pictures, people, objects, and abstract relations among them. If one interrupts the paradigm at this point, one will have a well-documented formula for producing single-word utterances that function as labels. This one-word stage of language development is expected to have occurred in normally developing infants by the end of the first year of life. By 18 months, the typical infant is chaining together words in what Roger Brown terms "Stage I Language Development" (Brown, 1976).

The implications of our language-training paradigm, broadly described above, for the account of normal language-acquisition processes are that if many aspects of language can be taught using these procedures, then those aspects of language can be learned according to the principles that govern these procedures. It is, therefore, possible that normally developing children acquire language through similar learning processes that occur in the natural environment. Of course, the successful use of the operant learning paradigm to deliberately teach does not justify the conclusion that operant procedures are necessary for language development; it shows merely that operant procedures might be sufficient to produce some aspects of language development. The paradigm described above specifies the processes by which an initial labeling or tacting vocabulary might be formed (Nelson, 1973). Baer, Guess, and Sherman (1972) present this argument in a more expanded form in their classic paper, "Adventures in simplistic grammar."

The operant-learning paradigm has been heuristic in generating research questions concerning both the normal course of language development and the design of specific language-intervention procedures (Schumaker & Sherman, 1978). In much of this research, these two kinds of questions go hand-in-hand; that is, the experimental treatment procedures used in the study of normal language development recommend themselves as therapeutic procedures for amelioration of language delays or deficiencies in people with mental retardation or autism, and as procedures for prevention of linguistic problems in normally developing infants (Baer, Guess, & Sherman, 1972).

At a finer level of detail within the above paradigm, different researchers have held differing views concerning the precise role of parental and societal stimulation on language in the account of normal development. For example, Fry (1966) proposed that parents directly reinforce infant vocalization rates and shape infant imitation of first adult-like sounds and words, whereas Mowrer (1960) and Risley (1977) held that parents and other caregivers directly reinforce only some rate of infant vocalization, but that similarity between the infant's and the parent's vocalizations becomes a conditioned reinforcer that automatically shapes ever-closer approximations to adult speech. A more detailed review of their positions is presented by Kymissis and Poulson, in their article, "The history of imitation in learning theory: The language-acquisition process" (1990).

Similarly, when the above paradigm is viewed primarily as an intervention strategy, different researchers have used differing tactics. For example, Lovaas, Freitas, Nelson, and Whalen (1967), Metz (1965), and Risley (1968) approached the teaching of imitation skills by teaching a motor response first, using putting-through, fading, and shaping procedures to establish a class of imitative motor responses. Sherman (1965) extended that class of motor responses to include vocal responses by fading in modeled responses that were closer approximations to vocalizations, such as mouth opening, blowing, emitting unvoiced sounds, and finally, voiced sounds. Sherman then chained the sounds together to produce whole words.

By contrast, Kerr, Meyerson, and Michael (1965), Lovaas, Berberich, Perloff, and Schaeffer (1966), and Lovaas (1977, 1981) taught imitation skills by starting directly with vocal imitation. The procedures involved (a) first reinforcing any vocal sounds made by the client, (b) then reinforcing only those vocal sounds that followed adult-modeled vocalizations within 5 seconds, (c) then reinforcing only those vocalizations that approximated the modeled responses, and, (d) finally, reinforcing only those vocalizations that are topographically close matches of the modeled responses. A thorough description of these basic language intervention procedures has been written by Lovaas (1977, 1981).

Empirical Support

Most of the behavior-analytic research relevant to the overall language-acquisition paradigm has been undertaken with older preschool children (Baer & Sherman, 1964), with children and adolescents with severe or profound mental retardation (Baer, Peterson & Sherman, 1967), with people with autism (Lovaas, 1977, 1981), with adults with psychoses (Sherman, 1965), with a wide range of people of different ages and intellectual abilities using artificial languages (Wetherby, 1978), and even with apes, using nonvocal communication (Premack, 1976; Rumbaugh, 1977; and Terrace, 1979). Although the operant language-acquisition paradigm for the establishment of one-word utterances has been extrapolated to infant prelinguistic development, infants seldom have been the subjects of systematic empirical analyses within that paradigm (Poulson & Nunes, 1988).

Step 1. Reinforcement-Schedule Control

Concerning the first step in the paradigm, obtaining reinforcement schedule control over infant vocalization, there is a substantial body of research on the establishment of reinforcer control over vocalization rates with normally developing 3-month-old infants. Research demonstrating that overall rates of infant vocalization can be changed by virtue of social reinforcement contingencies has been published by Poulson (1983, 1984), Ramey and Ourth (1971), Rheingold, Gewirtz, and Ross (1959), Sheppard (1969), and Weisberg (1963). Furthermore, change in infant vocalization rates has been demonstrated under delayed contingencies of social reinforcement (Reeve, Reeve, Brown, Brown & Poulson, 1992; and Reeve, Reeve & Poulson, in press).

Some of this work has been undertaken with infants at risk for mental retardation. Poulson has reported successful operant conditioning of vocalization rate in 3-month-old infants with Down Syndrome (1988), and Weigerink, Harris, Simeonsson, and Pearson (1974) demonstrated similar control with 11-to-22 month-old infants with developmental delays.

Step 2. Discriminative-Stimulus Control

The second step in the paradigm is the establishment of discriminative stimulus control over infant response rates or topographies. Research demonstrating operant control over specific topographies of infant vocalization has been undertaken by

Hursh and Sherman (1973), Routh (1969), and Wahler (1969). Of these, only the studies by Hursh and Sherman (1973) show the level of experimental control required of an experimental analysis of behavior (Poulson & Nunes, 1988). That is, in the Hursh and Sherman study, (a) the primary data analysis was in terms of individual subject data, (b) stability of responding for each subject was the criterion for introducing changes in experimental conditions, (c) reliable measurement of both the independent and dependent variables was reported, and (d) the relationship between the independent and dependent measures showed that the experimental procedures that were programmed to occur actually functioned as intended with respect to the behavior of the infants.

Step 3, Control by Modeled Responses

The third step in the operant language-acquisition paradigm is the establishment of stimulus control by bringing the topographies of infant responding under the topographical control of modeled responses.

The Hursh and Sherman (1973) studies represent a beginning point in the experimental analysis of the development of imitation in infants. These studies were undertaken with normally developing infants 15, 17, and 20 months of age over a 2-to-4-month period, in the living room of each child's home. Using a multiple-baseline across infant vocalizations experimental design, Hursh and Sherman systematically introduced a treatment procedure consisting of parental modeling of vocal responses, with parental presentation of descriptive praise and repetition of the infant's vocalization contingent upon the infant's producing the target vocalizations.

After it was shown that the treatment procedure was effective in producing higher frequencies of the targeted vocalizations than had been observed during non-treatment baselines, Hursh and Sherman undertook a component analysis of the treatment package to determine the relative strengths of parental modeling, praising, and repetition of the infant's vocalization. They found that the total package was the most effective in increasing the frequency of a particular infant vocalization over baseline frequencies, and that the following components of the package were effective to a lesser degree: second most effective was modeling alone, and least effective were praise alone, and praise with repetition of the infant's vocalization.

As Hursh and Sherman concluded, the two studies described above support the operant learning paradigm for language acquisition in that the results obtained show that the effects of the modeling, praising, and repetition procedures (combined, or separately) functioned to increase the frequency of the specific target vocalizations being treated, and not merely to produce a generalized arousal or elicitation of infant vocal behavior. Nevertheless, because they did not demonstrate generalized imitation, they did not claim to have demonstrated imitative responding in infants.

Generalized imitation refers to the observation that nonreinforced imitative responses occur in the presence of other reinforced imitative responses of the same functional response class. The concept of generalized imitation is critical to an operant paradigm of language development because it accounts for the relatively rapid emergence of generative, linguistic productions in infancy and early childhood. If all linguistic responses had to be modeled and reinforced directly, we would not call the products of that modeling and reinforcement "language." Only when nonreinforced members of a modeled class of responses are produced do we call those productions "language" responses.

Generalized imitation is a more robust concept than imitation, because generalized imitation refers to a learning phenomenon in which more behavior is generated than was directly taught. It is precisely this kind of rule-governed, generative, productive repertoire that appears to be so important to the teaching of functional language skills to severely developmentally delayed individuals, as pointed out by Guess, Sailor, and Baer (1974), and for which there is empirical evidence among normally developing language-speaking children (Clark & Clark, 1977). That empirical evidence for generalized imitation has been lacking in infants.

The first analyses of generalized imitation in infants have occurred in the Queens College Infant Laboratory of the City University of New York. We have been working with both motor and vocal generalized imitation. To the extent that similar procedures produce similar effects on both vocal and gestural imitative behavior, they would appear to be similar types of response classes. Such an outcome would be consistent with the finding, based on very different experimental methodology, that both vocalizations and gestures seem to be involved in enactive or symbolic naming by 9-to-13-month olds (Bates, Bretherton, Snyder, Shore & Volterra, 1980). Thus, it may be important to consider both vocal and gestural responding when examining generalized imitation as a mechanism for the acquisition of language and communication skills.

The general procedures we use in the Queens College Infant Laboratory are the following: Parents bring their infants to the Laboratory 3 to 5 times a week for 20-minute experimental sessions. During all sessions parents present prescribed models to their infants, wait 6 seconds for a response, and model another response. During model-and-praise treatment conditions, parents deliver praise following their infants' matching of their modeled responses.

Motor Imitation in Normally Developing Infants

Using these kinds of procedures, we first demonstrated generalized motor imitation in three normally developing 10-month-old infants in a study by Poulson and Kymissis (1988). During baseline the parents did not model or praise contingently on the infant's emitting the targeted motor responses, but, as in the Hursh and Sherman study, they were asked to play normally with their infants. During the subsequent model-and-praise treatment condition, parents modeled responses and praised the infants contingent on infant matching responses during training trials, but during probe trials the parents only modeled responses; they did not deliver praise for infant matching. Reinforced training trials and nonreinforced probe trials were intermixed throughout all sessions at a ratio of 3 training trials to 1 probe trial.

Percentage of trials during which the infants produced the targeted motor response was the dependent measure. In a multiple-baseline-across-infants experimental design, it was demonstrated that the model-and-praise treatment procedure was effective in increasing targeted infant motor responses, thus demonstrating that parental modeling and contingent praise was sufficient to produce generalized imitation in young infants.

Motor Imitation in Younger Infants

This study was subsequently replicated with four infants 7-to-8-months of age by Poulson, Gena, Kymissis, Andreatos, and Kyparissos (1993). In this study, parents modeled motor responses during baseline and treatment. During the model-and-praise treatment condition, parents praised the infant contingent on matching responses during training trials, but not during probe trials. The dependent measure was percentage of trials during which the infants matched the parent-modeled responses. In a multiple-baseline-across-infants experimental design, it was demonstrated that the model-and-praise treatment procedure was effective in increasing matching, but not non-matching, infant responses, over a model-alone baseline. This study demonstrated that parental praise was sufficient to produce generalized motor imitation in infants as young as 7-to-8 months of age, and that an increase in matching was not accompanied by an increase in nonmatching responses. Thus, the effect of the parental praise procedure was not merely to elicit more infant behavior in general, but to increase only matching behavior. Therefore, we can conclude that parental praise functioned as a reinforcer for generalized infant imitation.

Motor Imitation in Infants with Developmental Disabilities

A systematic replication of the above generalized motor-imitation study has been undertaken with three male infants with developmental disabilities, one with microcephaly, and two with Down Syndrome, who were between 10 and 12 months of age, by Poulson, Andreatos, Parnes, and Kymissis (1993). On the Mental Development Index of the Bayley Scales of Infant Development, in which the average score is 100, the infant with microcephaly scored 81, and the two infants with Down Syndrome scored 77 and below 50. All the infants had functional hearing and vision.

During each session parents presented 15 toys to their infants. During each trial the parent modeled a specific action with each toy. During one-third of all trials (probe trials), for one-third of the toys (probe toys), there was no praise associated with infant matching responses. Five probe trials were interspersed among 10 training trials during each session. The independent variable was contingent social praise and lollipop delivered by the parent following the infant's matching of the motor responses with toys during training trials.

With the introduction of contingent parental praise there was a systematic increase in matching above baseline percentages for all three infants during both training and probe trials. There was no systematic increase in non-matching responses with the introduction of the model-and-praise treatment procedure. By extending experimental analysis of behavior technology to produce generalized motor imitation in infants with developmental disabilities, we have developed a technology for producing generalized imitation in infants who need early intervention, because they are at risk for delayed speech and language development.

Vocal Imitation in Normally Developing Infants

The first study of generalized vocal imitation in infants was published by Poulson, Kymissis, Reeve, Andreatos, and Reeve (1991). Three normally developing female infants between 9 and 12 months of age participated over a 2-to-3 month time span. A pre-baseline assessment of each infant's vocal repertoire produced 6 vocalizations for treatment and 3 for use as nonreinforced probes. These were modeled by the parent in a controlled randomization sequence throughout each session. During baseline experimental conditions the parent modeled the training and probe vocalizations selected for each infant. During treatment the parent continued to model the probe vocalizations with no special consequences programmed, but when he or she modeled training vocalizations, infant vocal matching produced praise. Treatment was implemented in a multiple-baseline-across-subjects experimental design. With the introduction of contingent parental praise, there was a systematic increase above baseline percentages of matching for all three infants, during both training and probe trials. There was no systematic increase in percentages of nonmatching responses by infants, thus showing that the increase in matching was specific to matching, and not to any general arousal of infant responding. Thus, it was shown that generalized vocal imitation in infants can be produced by contingent social praise delivered by an infant's parent.

Vocal Imitation in Infants with Developmental Disabilities

Using similar procedures, an experimental analysis of vocal generalized imitation in infants with developmental delays has been conducted by Poulson, Parnes, Andreatos, and Kymissis (1993). Four 18-to-26-month-old infants with Down Syndrome participated in 3 to 4 20-min. experimental sessions over a three-month period. Three of the infants had Bayley Scale Mental Development Index scores in the 50's, and one had a score of 91 (100 is average). As usual, during each session a familiar adult modeled 10 training trials (to be associated with reinforcement during intervention) and 5 probe trials (never to be associated with reinforcement). During the baseline phase, there was no social praise following infant matches and nonmatches of the adult's vocal models. The model-and-praise condition was implemented in a multiple-baseline across infants experimental design. With the introduction of the model-and-praise intervention, there was a systematic increase in the percentage of training and probe models followed by infant vocal matching responses. There was no systematic increase in the percentage of training or probe models followed by infant vocal nonmatching responses, thus showing that the increase in vocal matching was a specific increase, not just an overall increase in all vocal responding following the introduction of the model-and-praise treatment condition. Thus, this study demonstrated generalized vocal imitation in a new population: infants with Down Syndrome. This is an important study, because it shows that these same generalized imitation training procedures work with infants with Down Syndrome, a group very much in need of such training (Hanson & Lynch, 1989; Mahoney, Glover, & Finger, 1981).

Step 4, Transfer of Stimulus Control from Models to Labels

There has been a wealth of published information on procedures for transferring stimulus control from imitative stimuli to nonimitative stimuli, such as graphemes, pictures, people, objects, and abstract relations among them. The reader is referred to Guess, et al. (1974), Harris (1976), and Lovaas (1977) for reviews of these procedures.

Response-Class Formation in Generalized Imitation

An important question emerging out of the above research on motor and vocal imitation is what governs the formation of the response classes of generalized imitation? Is it one large response class, such that if some members are directly taught, others will emerge without training? Or does it form a number of smaller response classes?

Children with mental retardation. The latter was suggested in research by Garcia, Baer, & Firestone (1971). They worked with mentally retarded children from 8-to-14 years of age in a study of generalized imitation within the topographically defined boundaries of small-motor, large-motor, and short-vocal responses. Although generalized imitation within each of these three response types did occur, imitation did not generalize across the three types of response, indicating that they were members of different response classes.

Normally developing infants. In the infant laboratory we have undertaken research to systematically replicate the Garcia, Baer, and Firestone study, with the important difference that normally developing 12-to-14-month-old infants, instead of older developmentally delayed children, were participants, and that different response measures more appropriate to infants were the dependent measures (Poulson, Kyparissos, Andreatos, Kymissis, & Parnes, 1993). The focus of this research, as in Garcia, et al. (1971), is on the effects of the different vocal and gestural response topographies on nonreinforced probe responding in the generalized imitation paradigm. The first study focused on generalized imitation across vocal and gestural response modalities and was designed to determine whether similar procedures would be effective in producing both vocal and gestural generalized imitation within the topographically-defined boundaries of vocal responses, motor-with-toy responses, and motor-without-toy responses. Three infants and their parents participated. There were two male and one female infant, and their ages ranged from 12 to 14 months during baseline. Their Bayley Scales Mental Development Index scores were 118, 125, and 131 (100 is average). They participated in 2 to 4 20-minute sessions over a 3- to 5- month period.

During each session there were 6 training trials and 3 nonreinforced probe trials for each of the three response types modeled by the parent. They were presented in a controlled randomization sequence of 27 models presented in an unpredictable order during each experimental session. During baseline, parents modeled all the responses, but they did not praise the infant if he or she matched the parent's model. During treatment, praise was delivered contingently upon infant matching of the training models, but not of the probe models. In this study, parental praise was accompanied by bits of an infant's favorite pudding, cookies, or crackers.

For each infant, model-and-praise training was implemented in a multiple-baseline-across-responses experimental design following baseline measures during which the parent modeled each of three types of responses. For two of the infants, the model-and-praise treatment condition was introduced first for motor-with-toy responses, second for motor-without-toy responses, and third, for vocal responses. One of the infants received the model-and-praise treatment on the same three response topographies, but in a different order, with training on vocal imitation first, motor-with-toy second, and motor-without-toy third.

For each of the three infants, generalized imitation occurred within each of those three response topographies, but generalization across response topographies did not occur. Thus, we conclude that the infant's generalized imitation occurred within topographically-defined boundaries and, therefore, that individual infant response classes can emerge within generalized imitation. These findings are consistent with those of Garcia, Baer, and Firestone (1971). That is, under these conditions, with these infants, imitation of motor-with-toy, motor-without-toy, and vocal responses was shown to consist of three independent response classes.

Young children with autism. This response-class formation research has been replicated with young children with autism at the Princeton Child Development Institute, in Princeton, New Jersey (Young, Krantz, McClannahan, & Poulson 1993). Participants were one girl and three boys between 2 1/2 and 4 years of age who were largely nonverbal and nonimitative. Using the same procedures described above for infants, we found that we can produce generalized imitation within topographically defined response modalities with children with autism as well. The three response types measured were vocal, toy play, and pantomime. These were essentially the same response types we measured in the Poulson, Kyparissos, Andreatos, Kymissis, & Parnes (1993) study with infants. The autistic children required many more trials to produce generalized imitation than the normally developing infants, but their data showed the same overall patterns as the infant data. That is, the data obtained from autistic children show that response-class formation can occur within the larger response class of generalized imitation, and that these smaller response classes can be defined by the response topographies themselves.

These findings on response-class formation within generalized imitation have direct implications for treatment. For example, these findings suggest that for some infants and children, teaching motor imitation might not necessarily facilitate vocal imitation training. Thus, it may be more efficient to teach vocal imitation first to children with speech and language delays. Nevertheless, it also points out that teaching them merely to imitate vocal sounds does not necessarily provide them with the skills to imitate the motor responses modeled in their environments, and that, those, too, may need to be directly taught. By carefully analyzing the boundaries of response-class formation within generalized imitation, it is hoped that we can learn some of the conditions under which such generalization does and does not occur.

Conditioned Reinforcement Hypothesis

Another approach to the study of response-class formation in generalized imitation is exemplified in research by Baer and Deguchi (1985). In their analysis of generalized imitation, they proposed a description of the formation of the response class of imitation that echoed Mowrer and Risley: When a response class of imitative responding is formed as a result of direct reinforcement, similarity between the stimuli produced by the model's response and the stimuli produced by the subject's matching of that response becomes a conditioned reinforcer. Furthermore, the similarity between the stimuli produced by the new model and the stimuli produced by the new imitative behavior also becomes a conditioned reinforcer through primary generalization. Thus, newly established imitative responding is maintained as long as other imitative responding is directly reinforced.

Motor imitation. In an experiment with normally developing preschool children, Baer and Deguchi (1985) demonstrated that the children systematically changed preference for pushing a button that signalled the child to imitate an adult, when the child's imitation of other adult-modeled responses produced direct reinforcement. The authors concluded that this analysis was consistent with a conditioned-reinforcement explanation of generalized imitation.

Vocal imitation. The Baer and Deguchi (1985) study was systematically replicated in a multiple-baseline-across-children experimental design by Kymissis and Poulson (1993) to determine whether the same kind of experimental control can be demonstrated over vocal, as well as motor, responding. The non-reinforced vocal activities that the children could choose from were: matching, non-matching, listening, and waiting. The results of the Kymissis and Poulson study indicated that the introduction of reinforcement for vocal matching during some trials produced a systematic increase over baseline levels of the number of non-reinforced vocal matching responses. The choice of the other three responses (non-matching, listening, and waiting) did not systematically increase along with matching, and these responses remained at lower levels than matching responses during treatment.

Both studies are consistent with the conditioned-reinforcement hypothesis regarding generalized imitation by demonstrating that, as long as imitation of some responses is directly reinforced, thereby reinforcing similarity between the child's and the model's response, similarity becomes a conditioned reinforcer for some other, never-reinforced responses of the same response class.

The Emergence of Novel Vocalizations

In all of the above studies, demonstration that the fine-grained topography of the model's response actually controls the topography of the resulting imitative response, not just the timing of the response, is important because, ultimately, the role of imitation in the language-acquisition paradigm is to account for the emergence of *new* vocalizations not previously seen in the infant's or child's repertoire. Nevertheless, there are only three published studies actually demonstrating the emergence of *novel* vocalizations in children as a function of generalized-imitation training: Brigham and Sherman (1968), Lovaas, Berberich, Perloff, and Schaeffer (1966) and Schroeder and Baer (1972). In these three studies increasing accuracy of vocal imitation was the dependent variable. There have as yet been no analyses of entirely novel generalized imitative responding with infants. In all the above studies with infants, the responses selected for study had been observed to occur at least once during pre-baseline sessions for a given infant, and, in fact, those responses were selected precisely because they had been so observed to occur. This procedure ensured that a given response was within the capabilities of the infant to begin with. Nevertheless, use of such a procedure does limit the conclusions one can draw regarding novelty of generalized responding. Although assessment of novel responding would be especially difficult with infants, future research directed toward that end would be highly desirable.

Summary

In summary, there is a large body of experimental developmental research on several aspects of the operant language-acquisition paradigm as defined at the beginning of this paper: (a) With both normally developing infants and infants with developmental delays, it has been demonstrated that infant vocalization rates can be changed systematically by the application of parental social reinforcement, either immediate (Poulson, 1983, 1988; Weigerink, et al., 1974) or delayed (Reeve, et al., 1992, and in press). (b) It has been demonstrated with normally developing infants that infant vocalization rates can be brought under the discriminative stimulus control of adult models (Hursh & Sherman, 1975; Routh, 1969; Wahler, 1969). (c) Generalized motor imitation was demonstrated in infants with normal development (Poulson & Kymissis, 1988) and in normally developing infants as young as 7 months of age (Poulson, Gena, Kymissis, Andreatos, & Kyparissos, 1993). Furthermore, generalized motor imitation has been demonstrated with infants with developmental delays (Poulson, Andreatos, Parnes, & Kymissis, 1993). Generalized vocal imitation has been demonstrated in infants with normal development (Poulson, et al., 1991) and in infants with developmental delays (Poulson, Parnes, Andreatos, & Kymissis, 1993). (d) Transfer of stimulus control from models to labels such as graphemes, pictures, people, objects, and abstract relations among them has been documented extensively (Guess et al., 1974; Harris, 1976; and Lovaas, 1977). Furthermore, studies of response-class formation within generalized imitation have been accomplished with infants (Poulson, Kyparissos, Andreatos, Kymissis, & Parnes, 1993), with young children with autism (Young, Krantz, McClannahan, & Poulson 1993) and with older children with mental retardation (Garcia, Baer & Firestone, 1971).

Experimental analyses of the mechanisms underlying response class formation in generalized imitation have been conducted with normally developing preschool children with both motor responding (Baer & Deguchi, 1985) and vocal responding (Kymissis & Poulson, 1993). In both of these studies the primary variable under study was that of conditioned reinforcement properties of behaving similarly to the behavior of a model. Both studies reported experimental control over the imitative behavior of some subjects, but not others. These findings recommend that we undertake future studies of the conditional nature of generalized imitative responding.

That generalized imitative responding can be readily established in infants as young as 7 months of age, and that both motor and vocal generalized imitative responding can be shown to occur in infants and young children underscores the power of generalized imitation as both a model for early language acquisition and for deliberate language intervention procedures. Further research on the conditions under which generalized imitation occurs is of central importance in understanding and treating language development.

Levels of Explanation

On a broader scale, it is worth noting that many developmental psychologists and psycholinguists may never regard either the research on generalized imitative response- class formation or the work on similarity as a conditioned reinforcer for generalized imitation as explanatory. They will not be satisfied by experimental analyses of the conditions under which generalized imitation does and does not occur. They will instead continue to look for an internal mechanism to explain the emergence of that imitation. In fact, Meltzoff and Moore (1989) propose "active intermodal mapping" as just such an internal mechanism in the account of early infant imitation. Nevertheless, while some continue to search for internal causal variables, behaviorists will continue to search for those directly manipulable variables controlling generalized imitation and all the subsequent developmental skills in the operant language-acquisition paradigm. If we produce enough such research, it may become less pressing for anyone to continue the search for hypothetical internal mechanisms.

Applied Research on Child-Language Intervention

We need only to examine the applied research on language intervention to see how this might come about. The applied research on language intervention procedures, also supports the operant language-acquisition paradigm. In 1991 Goldstein and Hockenberger produced a major review of the child language-intervention research published between 1978 and 1988. In it they present data to show that of the professional journals regularly reporting empirical research on the treatment of child language disorders, the largest single source (of almost a third of the articles) was the *Journal of Applied Behavior Analysis* (*JABA*).

Goldstein and Hockenberger's criterion for including articles in their review was that they reported data-based studies evaluating treatment of child language disorders. They excluded articles that focused strictly on phonology, case studies with no experimental design, and articles in which there were no reports of interobserver agreement for the dependent measures.

The journals they reviewed included the *Journal of Speech and Hearing Disorders*, the *Journal of Speech and Hearing Research*, the *Journal of Communication Disorders*, *Augmentative and Alternative Communication* and *Language, Speech, and Hearing Services in Schools*. Their review also included journals more familiar to educators: *Education and Training of the Mentally Retarded*, the *Journal of Special Education*, *Journal of Special Education Technology*, and the *Journal of the Association for Persons with Severe Handicaps*. Their review included the major journals that publish empirical research with people with developmental disabilities, for whom language and communication often represent core deficits. Those journals were the *Journal of Autism and Developmental Disorders*, the *American Journal of Mental Retardation*, the *Journal of Abnormal Child Psychology*, and *Research in Developmental Disabilities* and its predecessors. It included two developmental psychology journals: the *Journal of Experimental Child Psychology*, and *Child Development*. Their review also included the journal *Behavior Modification*. Within these 17 major journals there were 151 articles that met the authors' criteria for inclusion as research studies on language intervention with children. Fully 44 of those 151 research articles were published in *JABA*.

Conclusion

Basic experimental-analysis-of-behavior research on the operant language-acquisition paradigm continues to be produced, and it consistently supports the operant-learning paradigm for language acquisition. Applied behavioral analysis research on language-intervention procedures represents the largest single source of research on child-language intervention. That research is based on the operant language-acquisition paradigm, and it empirically supports that paradigm. Therefore, the operant language-acquisition paradigm deserves to be treated very seriously, not only by behaviorists, but by the broader scientific community. Although much more empirical research remains to be accomplished, we have advanced importantly in the extent to which we have added empirical analyses to the theoretical analyses published in Skinner's *Verbal Behavior*.

References

Baer, D. M., & Deguchi, H. (1985). Generalized imitation from a radical-behavioral viewpoint. In S. Reiss & R. R. Bootzin (Eds.), *Theoretical issues in behavior therapy* (pp. 179-217). Orlando, Fl: Academic Press.

Baer, D. M, Peterson, R. F., & Sherman, J. A. (1967). The development of imitation by reinforcing behavioral similarity to a model. *Journal of Experimental Analysis of Behavior*, *10*, 405-416. Baer, D. M., & Sherman, J. A. (1964). Reinforcement control of generalized imitation in young children. *Journal of Experimental Child Psychology*, *1*, 37-49.

Baer, D. M., Guess, D., & Sherman, J. A. (1972). Adventures in simplistic grammar. In R. L. Schiefelbusch (Ed.), *Language of the mentally retarded* (pp. 93-105). Baltimore: University Park Press.

Bates, E., Bretherton, I., Snyder, L., Shore, C., & Volterra, V. (1980). Vocal and gestural symbols at 13 months. *Merrill-Palmer Quarterly*, *26*, pp. 407-423.

Brigham, T. A., & Sherman, J. A. (1968). An experimental analysis of verbal imitation in preschool children. *Journal of Applied Behavior Analysis*, *1*, 151-158.

Brown, R. (1976). *A first language: The early stages.* Cambridge, MA: Harvard University Press.

Clark, H. H., & Clark, E. V. (1977). *Psychology and language: an introduction to psycholinguistics.* New York: Harcourt, Brace, & Jovanovich.

Fry, D. B. (1966). The development of the phonological system in the normal and deaf child. In F. Smith & G. Miller (Eds.), *The genesis of language.* Cambridge, MA: The M. I. T. Press.

Garcia, E., Baer, D. M., & Firestone, I. (1971). The development of generalized imitation within topographically determined boundaries. *The Journal of Applied Behavior Analysis*, *4*, 101-112.

Goldstein, H. & Hockenberger, E. H. (1991). Significant progress in child language intervention: An 11-year retrospective. *Research in Developmental Disabilities*, *14*, 401-424.

Guess, D., Sailor, W., & Baer, D. M. (1974). How to teach language to retarded children. In R. L. Schiefelbusch & L. L. Lloyd (Eds.) *Language perspectives, acquisition, retardation, and intervention.* Baltimore: University Park Press.

Hanson, M. L., & Lynch, E. W. (1989). *Early intervention.* Austin, Texas: Pro-ed, Inc.

Harris, S. L. (1976). Behavior modification: Teaching speech to a nonverbal child. *Managing behavior, Vol. 8.* Lawrence, KS: H & H Enterprises.

Hursh, D., & Sherman, J. A. (1973). The effects of parent presented models and praise on the vocal behavior of their children. *Journal of Experimental Child Psychology*, *15*, 328-339.

Kerr, N., Meyerson, L., & Michael, J. (1965). A procedure for shaping vocalizations in a mute child. In L. P. Ullman & L. Krasner, (Eds.), *Case studies in behavior modification.* New York: Holt, Rinehart, & Winston.

Kymissis, E., & Poulson, C. L. (1990). The history of imitation in learning theory: The language-acquisition process. *Journal of the Experimental Analysis of Behavior*,*54*, 113-127.

Kymissis, E., & Poulson C. L. (1993). Variables controlling generalized imitation in preschool children. Manuscript submitted for publication.

Lovaas, O. I. (1977). *The autistic child: Language development through behavior modification.* New York: Irvington Publishers.

Lovaas, O. I. (1981). *Teaching developmentally disabled children: The me book.* Baltimore: University Park Press.

Lovaas, O. I., Berberich, J. P., Perloff, B. F., & Schaeffer, B. (1966). Acquisition of imitative speech by schizophrenic children. *Science*, *151*, 705-707.

Lovaas, O. I., Freitas, K., Nelson, K., & Whalen, C. (1967). The establishment of imitation and its use for the development of complex behavior in schizophrenic children. *Behavior, Research, and Therapy, 5*, 171-182.

Mahoney, G., Glover, A., & Finger, I. (1981). Relationship between language and sensorimotor development of Down syndrome and nonretarded children. *American Journal of Mental Deficiency, 86*, 21-27.

Meltzoff, A. N., & Moore, M. K. (1989). Imitation in newborn infants: Exploring the range of gestures imitated and the underlying mechanisms. *Developmental Psychology, 25*, 954-962.

Metz, J. R. (1965). Conditioning generalized imitation in autistic children. *Journal of Experimental Child Psychology, 2*, 389-399.

Mowrer, O. H. (1960). Learning theory and language learning. In O. H. Mowrer (Eds.), *Learning theory and the symbolic process*. New York: John Wiley & Sons.

Nelson, K. (1973). Structure and strategy in learning to talk. *Monographs of the Society for Research in Child Development, 38*, (1 & 2).

Poulson, C. L. (1983). Differential reinforcement of other than vocalization as a control procedure in the conditioning of infant vocalization rate. *Journal of Experimental Child Psychology, 36*, 471-489.

Poulson, C. L. (1984). Operant theory and methodology in infant vocal conditioning. *Journal of Experimental Child Psychology, 38*, 103-113.

Poulson, C. L. (1988). Operant conditioning of vocalization rate in infants with Down Syndrome. *American Journal on Mental Retardation, 93*, 57-63.

Poulson, C. L., Andreatos, M., Parnes, M., & Kymissis, E. (1993). Generalized motor imitation in infants with developmental disabilities. Manuscript submitted for publication

Poulson, C. L., Gena, A. Kymissis, E., Andreatos, M., & Kyparissos, N. (1993). Generalized motor imitation in infants. Manuscript submitted for publication.

Poulson, C. L., & Kymissis, E. (1988). Generalized imitation in infants. *Journal of Experimental Child Psychology, 46*, 324-336.

Poulson, C. L., Kymissis, E., Reeve, K. F., Andreatos, M., & Reeve, L. (1991). Generalized vocal imitation in infants. *Journal of Experimental Child Psychology, 51*, 267-279.

Poulson, C. L., Kyparissos, N., Andreatos,M., Kymissis, E., & Parnes, M. (1993). Generalized imitation and response class formation in infants. Manuscript submitted for publication.

Poulson, C. L., & Nunes, L. R. P. (1988). The infant vocal-conditioning literature: A theoretical and methodological critique. *Journal of Experimental Child Psychology, 46*, 438-450.

Poulson, C. L., Parnes, M., Andreatos, M., & Kymissis, E. (1993). Generalized vocal imitation in infants with Down Syndrome. Manuscript submitted for publication.

Premack, D. (1976). *Intelligence in ape and man*. Hillsdale, NJ: Lawrence Erlbaum Associates.

Ramey, C. T., & Ourth, L. (1971). Delayed reinforcement and vocalization rates of infants. *Child Development 42*, 291-297.

Reeve, L., Reeve, K. F., Brown, A. K., Brown, J. L., & Poulson, C. L. (1992). Effects of delayed reinforcement on infant vocalization rate. *Journal of the Experimental Analysis of Behavior, 58*, 1-8.

Reeve, L., Reeve, K. F., and Poulson, C. L. (in press). Parameters of delayed reinforcement in young infants. *Journal of the Experimental Analysis of Behavior.*

Rheingold, H., Gewirtz, J. L., & Ross, H. W. (1959). Social conditioning of vocalizations in the infant. *Journal of Comparative and Physiological Psychology, 52*, 68-73.

Risley, T. R. (1968). The effects and side effects of punishing the autistic behavior of a deviant child. *Journal of Applied Behavior Analysis, 1*, 21-34.

Risley, T. R. (1977). The development and maintenance of language: An operant model. In B. C. Etzel, J. M. LeBlanc, & D. M. Baer (Eds.), *New developments in behavioral research*. Hillsdale, NJ: Lawrence Erlbaum Associates.

Risley, T. R., Hart, B., & Doke, L. (1972). Operant language development: The outcome of a therapeutic technology. In R. L. Schiefelbusch (Ed.), *Language of the mentally retarded*. Baltimore: University Park Press.

Routh, D. K. (1969). Conditioning of vocal response- differentiation in infants. *Developmental Psychology, 1*, 219-226.

Rumbaugh, D. (1977). *Language learning by a chimpanzee: The Lana Project*. New York: Academic Press.

Schroeder, G. L., & Baer, D.M. (1972). Effects of concurrent and serial training of generalized vocal imitation in retarded children. *Developmental Psychology,6*, 293-301.

Schumaker, J. B., & Sherman, J. A. (1978). Parent as intervention agent: From birth onward. In R. L. Schiefelbusch (Ed.), *Language intervention strategies, Vol. 2*. Baltimore: University Park Press.

Sheppard, W. C. (1969). Operant control of infant vocal and motor behavior. *Journal of Experimental Child Psychology, 7*, 36-51.

Sherman, J. A. (1965). Use of reinforcement and imitation to reinstate verbal behavior in mute psychotics. *Journal of Abnormal Psychology, 70*, 155-164.

Skinner, B. F. (1957). *Verbal Behavior*. New York: Appleton-Century-Crofts.

Terrace, H. (1979). *Nim*. New York: Alfred A. Knopf.

Wahler, R. G. (1969). Infant social development: Some experimental analyses of an infant-mother interaction during the first year of life. *Journal of Experimental Child Psychology, 7*, 101-113.

Weigerink, R., Harris, C., Simeonsson, R., & Pearson, M. W. (1974). Social stimulation of vocalizations in delayed infants. *Child Development, 45*, 866-872.

Weisberg, P. (1963). Social and nonsocial conditioning of infant vocalizations. *Child Development, 34*, 377-388.

Wetherby, B. (1978). Miniature languages and the functional analysis of verbal behavior. In R. L. Schiefelbusch (Ed.), *Bases of language intervention, Vol. 1.* Baltimore: University Park Press.

Young, J. M., Krantz, P. J., McClannahan, L. E., & Poulson, C. L. (1993). Generalized imitation and response class formation in children with autism. Manuscript submitted for publication.

Footnote

[1] Support for the preparation of this manuscript was made available by Grant HD 22070 from the National Institute of Child Health and Human Development.

Chapter 6

Arranging the Development of Conceptual Behavior: A Technology for Stimulus Control

Barbara C. Etzel
Susan R. Milla
M. Diane Nicholas[1]
University of Kansas

What we mean by knowledge, and how it is acquired, has always been a matter of debate among psychologists. Skinner (1938) proposed in *The Behavior of Organisms* that we could replace mentalistic notions of knowledge with the study of behavior. This was in response to the growing number of cognitive psychologists who approached the study of mental processes using structural descriptions.

Behavior-Analytic and Developmental Cognitivists' Approach to Conceptual Behavior

Behavior-analytic researchers work from within a natural-science framework in which functional relations between variables are the object of their study. Developmental cognitivists, correlate hypothesized cognitive structures residing within the organism with variables such as chronological age. Many of these structures, however, are circular with respect to their final explanations: They infer a structure, name it, study the relations it was invented to explain, and then conclude its existence (see Schlinger, 1992, for a detailed contrast of these two theoretical approaches). Hypothesizing cognitive structures may not be necessary. Skinner (1978, p. 97) stated, "The variables of which human behavior is a function, lie in the environment". As such behavior analysts do not infer internal processes. Rather, they make direct observations of stimuli in the environment and of the organism's responses; they systematically manipulate stimuli, and they specify functional relations between stimuli and responses. They generally ignore nonmanipulable variables (such as age and deficit) and instead study manageable environmental events. The fact that one manipulates conceptual behavior by environmental variables, rather than infer hypothetical internal processes, has ramifications far beyond substantiating the different theoretical positions mentioned earlier. From the applied perspective, it gives educators the opportunity to stop blaming the child's internal processes, over which they have no control, and to thus educate the child (Sidman & Stoddard, 1966).

The Behavior-Analytic Paradigm: The Three-Term Contingency

Behavior analysts illustrate their paradigm by a simple three-term contingency: SD-R-SR (see Figure 1). SD refers to a discriminative stimulus, R to the response, and SR to the reinforcing stimulus. The relationship between the R and SR describes how the presence of a consequent stimulus (the SR) maintains or increases the probability of the response (R). Another kind of relation involves the stimulus that precedes or accompanies the response. A stimulus can become discriminative (SD) when the organism begins to respond consistently in one way to one antecedent stimulus and not to other (and sometimes related) stimuli in the environment. Stimulus discrimination is the relationship between responses and controlling antecedent

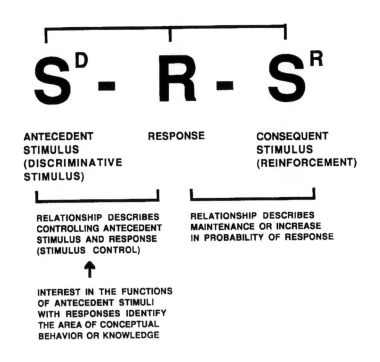

Figure 1. The behavior analytic three term contingency illustrating antecedent and consequent control.

stimuli. The term stimulus control is synonymous with stimulus discrimination, but carries with it no hypothesized internal process that might be connoted by the term "discrimination."

The Behavior-Analytic Locus of Control of Knowledge

Interest in the functions of the antecedent stimuli with responses identifies the area of conceptual behavior. Sidman (1978) made the distinction between behavior that is governed by reinforcement contingencies, "purpose", and behavior under stimulus control, "knowledge". This distinction is about the different relationships in the three-term contingency. Sidman (1978, p. 265) notes that research about the relationships between responses and reinforcers far exceeds research into the relationships between antecedent stimuli and responses.

The Behaviorist and Cognitive View of Concept

Bijou (1976), in discussing the development of conceptual behavior, contrasted the traditional child-development literature with a behavioral approach. For cognitivists, a concept is a mental entity formed by combining the characteristics of a class of objects. Differences in conceptual responses are due to differences in cognitive structures (such as age or intelligence). By contrast, the behaviorist views a concept as discriminated behavior in relation to stimuli. Differences in concept development are a function of a child's past interactions with stimuli (pp. 61-63). Bijou (1976) goes on to make a critical point: isolated properties of stimuli do not occur in an organized manner in nature. For a child to learn concepts, people must arrange relevant stimuli and reinforcement contingencies. When children are exposed to objects or events in their environments, others help the child learn to respond differentially as their culture prescribes (pp. 62-63). A concept, Bijou concludes (p. 64), is described by a relationship between a response that is controlled by a property of an antecedent stimulus, or combinations of properties in the physical world. These include letters, words, numbers, pictures, and social stimuli. The key to analyzing a child's concept is to observe the dimensions of an object that control the child's response. For example, give a child various objects of different colors, and ask that all the red objects be placed in a box; if the child picks only red items, the child's response is controlled by the property of redness. Parents often conclude, "My child knows red."

Simple Discriminations and Abstractions

Although much conceptual behavior starts with simple discriminations, it quickly extends to complex relations among stimuli (or events). The simplest level of relationships among stimuli are those that appear configurationally similar. They are probably taught by teachers and parents whose range of what, for example, is called a tree (culturally, not biologically determined), includes, a trunk, leaves, and branches and is rooted in the ground. Trees vary greatly; even so, the essential configurational similarities among trees that control our use of the word cause us to reinforce the child's word "tree" to some otherwise very different trees. In the same manner dogs are quite different from one another but similar configurations of "Dogness" can be identified.

However, in our culture, most relationships among stimuli are verbal or symbolic – that is, the relationships do not depend on shared stimulus features (Green, Mackay, Saunders & Soraci, 1990). For example, 2 and "two" share very few common characteristics, yet we know they correspond. These relationships are arbitrary, reflect the particular culture involved, and hence present a more difficult level of learning, often called Stimulus-Stimulus (s-s) relationships. While most normal children learn arbitrary s-s relationships easily, children with developmental delays do not. This is especially true when the s-s relationships involve cross-modal integration such as auditory-visual stimuli (Green, et al., 1990).

Error-Reduction Procedures for Teaching Individuals with Developmental Delays

Teaching by procedures that reduce errors during discrimination training has a long history. These procedures are in contrast to trial-and-error methods, in which the subject learns to respond less to the incorrect stimulus and more to the correct stimulus, but makes many incorrect responses in the process. Most of us have learned much that way.

Prior to the 1960s, research on error-reduction procedures used nonhuman organisms (e.g., Terrace, 1963). As interest in developmental delay increased, these procedures were extended to populations that did not readily acquire discriminations by trial-and-error. Sidman and Stoddard (1966) and Bijou (1968), began to develop procedures effective not only in reducing errors, but in teaching discriminations previously considered impossible.

Early research on error reduction in delayed populations, resulted in a variety of technological procedures that have the same goal: reducing errors. Such procedures have been termed "errorless stimulus-control procedures" (Etzel & LeBlanc, 1979); "errorless discrimination training" (Lancioni & Smeets, 1986); and "stimulus-control topographies" by McIlvane and Dube (1992).

The technology of error reduction includes a number of different procedures for manipulating the antecedent stimulus. As new procedures are developed, the issue of which procedure to apply, and when, will become more of a science than art. Lancioni and Smeets (1986) have noted a great deal of diversity in setting error criteria; number of responses per manipulation-step; number of steps in the program; manipulations on the S+ (SD) only, and the S- only, or both; and the type of task (e.g., number of choices available in a match-to-sample task). Their review of over 70 studies concludes that not all error-reduction procedures are successful, and that more research is required to make most of these procedures predictably successful. Even so, we know why some work better than others. Finally, if error reduction is desirable, we know procedures that will minimize them.

Descriptions of error-reduction procedures are presented in Table 1. Note that some reviewers do not consider some of these labels as procedurally different. For

TABLE 1

Error Reduction Procedures Identified in the Literature

Procedure	Description	Reference
Stimulus Fading (Criterion Related)	Uses an element of a stimulus along some physical dimension (intensity, size, color) that gradually changes across trials and is still present at the criterion (terminal) level.	Terrace, 1963 Schlosberg & Solomon, 1943
Stimulus Fading (Non-Criterion Related)	Uses an element of a stimulus along some physical dimension (intensity, size, color) that gradually changes on successive trials to transfer control of responding from one property to another at the criterion level.	Sidman & Stoddard, 1966 (circle-ellipse program) Reese, Howard & Rosenberger, 1977
Stimulus Shaping (Criterion Related)	Uses an element of a stimulus complex that is or quickly becomes the controlling element (becomes salient) of that stimulus. The stimulus and the element gradually change across successive trials and and the element is still present at the criterion level of the stimulus.	Sidman & Stoddard, 1966 (reversal program) Schilmoeller & Etzel, 1977 Schilmoeller, Schilmoeller, Etzel & LeBlanc, 1979
Superimposition and Fading	A stimulus is added to the criterion level stimulus (either both S+ and S- or to the S+ only). Gradually, across trials, the added stimulus is faded along some physical dimension (with the criterion level the same as entry level).	Rincover, 1978 Smeets, Lancioni, Striefel & Willemsen, 1984
Superimposition and Shaping	A stimulus is added to the criterion level stimulus (either both S+ and S- or to the S+ only). Across trials the added stimulus gradually changes in configuration and is incorporated into the criterion stimulus or removed by parts.	Etzel, LeBlanc, Schilmoeller & Stella, 1981 Smeets, Lancioni & Hoogeveen, 1984
Delayed Prompting (Delayed Cue)	A pretrained S+ stimulus is added to the criterion level of the to-be-trained S+. The first trials presented are: pretrained S+ on the to-be-trained S+ and the S- at criterion level. The pretrained S+ is then progressively delayed when presented with the to-be-trained S+. The S- remains at criterion. Transfer is observed when the subject responds to the to-be-trained S+ before the pretrained S+ is presented.	Touchette, 1971 Touchette & Howard, 1984
Within Stimulus Prompting (Intrinsic Fading) (Distinctive Feature Manipulations)	The stimulus element selected to serve as a prompt should be located within (as opposed to outside) the stimulus complex and is an element contained in the S+ and not in the S-.	Schreibman, 1975 Rincover, 1978
Equalization	Complex, multidimensional stimuli are initially presented exactly alike except for one element. When the S+ and S- elements have become discriminative for a particular response, the other stimulus features are rearranged or added slowly until the S+ and S- are at criterion.	Hoko & LeBlanc, 1988 Etzel, LeBlanc & McCartney, 1988

example, Deitz and Malone (1985) have proposed that there is no difference between stimulus fading and stimulus shaping, because "one common factor in errorless learning is that discriminations are established by transferring control from an effective stimulus to a different stimulus" (p. 260). However, Etzel and LeBlanc (1979) have suggested that transfer may not be necessary. If one incorporates from the beginning an element or part of a stimulus complex that, to use Dietz and Malone's words, is effective (salient), and continues to include that element through the shaping of the stimulus, and is present in the final criterion SD, transfer need not be involved.

Dietz and Malone also suggest that transfer is always involved in the stimulus-fading procedure. They use Rilling's definition (1977, p. 466) which emphasizes that "some property of a stimulus is gradually changed on successive trials to transfer control". However, the most successful early research using what could be called a fading procedure with a nonhuman subject (William James, 1890, pp.505-515; Pavlov, 1927, p.117; Schlosberg & Solomon, 1943; and Lawrence, 1952), uniformly began with large differences between the S+ and S-, and across presentations decreased to small differences between the S+ and S-. For example, if we wish to train a very close size discrimination between two circles (which trial-and-error training had shown to be a difficult discrimination), we start with a large circle and a small circle, ones the organism reliably discriminates. Then the sizes of the two circles can be faded until they are almost identical. No transfer is needed, because only size was manipulated. At criterion, the discrimination is still based on size. Using our terminology we would say that the fading was "criterion related", in that the same basis for making the original discrimination was still present at the criterion. What was transferred? A circle is still a circle and the size of one circle relative to the other is still the basis for responding. To see transfer here is to argue that all learning involves transfer, which makes the term meaningless. True, reproduction of a stimulus is never the same, nor is the learning environment. But these issues do not seem as important as whether or not transfer of some element of the controlling relation is or is not involved, and when it occurs (Stoddard, McIlvane & deRose, 1987; McIlvane & Dube, 1992).

Table 1 includes the procedures we propose. The references noted to the side give published examples. Often enough, probably similar or even identical procedures are reported with different names. The reason for listing similar (or same) procedures is to give the reader the descriptors needed to review the literature.

The procedures described in Table 1 were designed so that, from the beginning, the S+ has a higher probability of being responded to correctly than S-. Physiological measures taken during the acquisition phase of trial-and-error training, are different than those obtained during error reduction procedures (Berkler, Schilmoeller, Etzel, & LeBlanc, 1973; Berkler & LeBlanc, 1974; Reese, Howard & Rosenberg, 1977; and Reese 1981). Many teachers have reported anecdotally that children taught with error-reduction procedures are less emotional, happier, and more eager than those taught with trial-and-error procedures. Terrace (1966) first addressed "emotionality" when he suggested that wingflapping and pacing in pigeons during trial-and-error learning was due to the amount of S- responding the subject experienced under this procedure. However, Rilling (1977) suggested that emotional behavior is due to the withdrawal of the opportunity to receive reinforcers, not extinction per se. The S- is aversive but not because of the lack of reinforcement. In addition, Rilling noted that aggression was not due to extinction contingencies that prevailed during the S-condition, but rather to the contrast with the reinforcement contingencies operating during the S+ condition. Regardless, the applied studies reviewed later indicate less emotive responding when fewer errors occur for both normal and learning disabled-children.

A Theoretical Account for Unsuccessful Noncriterion-Related Fading

Referring again to Table 1, there is a distinction between "criterion-related" and "noncriterion-related" fading. Since some reference to the difference between criterion-related shaping and noncriterion-related fading will be made when we discuss exclusion, the following is offered as a possible explanation for unsuccessful noncriterion-related fading programs.

Errors during discrimination training are thought to occur as the result of "blocking". Blocking is said to occur when the subject has had some prior history with a stimulus that, when simultaneously presented with other stimulus elements, prevents stimulus control by those other elements. MacKintosh (1977), in reviewing blocking, suggested that it is similar to Pavlov's observation of overshadowing in which a more "salient" stimulus or more "valid" stimulus, prevents other stimuli from gaining control. "Salient" stimuli refer to stimuli closely associated with sensory processes of the subject and "valid" stimuli are more closely associated with reinforcement. Thus, another stimulus that is less salient will not develop stimulus control when a more salient stimulus is present.

Weidenman (1978) drew a parallel between blocking and the procedures involved in some fading programs. For example, an additional stimulus (cue) is added to the initial stimulus complex. Across trials, both the additional stimulus and the relevant stimulus (which should control responding at the criterion level) are equally available. The added stimulus is then faded until, at the criterion level it no longer exists, leaving only the relevant stimulus to control responding. When the added salient stimulus is irrelevant to the final discrimination, then procedurally, a fading program is similar to the experimental procedure used in the blocking paradigm.

In a review of the literature on errorless programs, Etzel and LeBlanc (1979) noted that some programs were successful and some were not. One distinction between these programs was the manner in which the stimuli were either changed across trials with regard to their total configuration (Sidman & Stoddard, 1966, their reversal program; Bijou, 1968), or, as outlined in the blocking discussion, by adding an extra physical dimension (e.g. color or size that was ultimately faded out by the criterion stage). Changes in total configuration were typically successful; the latter

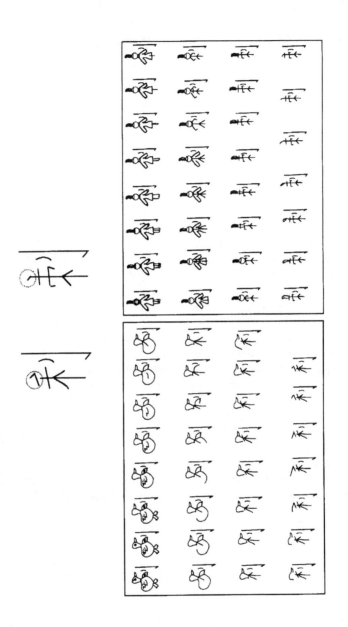

Figure 2. Two Kanji (Japanese symbol) stimuli at criterion level. Circled elements at the top of each figure are those selected for emphasis during the program. The left shaping sequence (The S-) illustrates the manipulation of the figure while the duck's bill was the last to be changed to criterion. After the S- is shaped to criterion, the S+ (which remained at entry level) is then manipulated with the Indian's feather, the last element to change to criterion.

had mixed results. This led Etzel and LeBlanc to describe one as stimulus shaping (the configurational change), and the other as stimulus fading of a noncriterion-related cue. The terms criterion-related and noncriterion-related were suggested by Bijou to replace "relevant" and "non relevant". The term "criterion" meant that the cue would be present at the criterion (final) level of training. This led us to develop a number of stimulus-shaping programs in which an element of the stimulus complex was made salient in the initial trials of the program. The cue undergoes some changes, but is always present, while the rest of the stimulus complex undergoes configurational changes. At the criterion level, the stimulus complex has been changed in terms of its TOTAL configuration, but the stimulus element (cue) selected still remains. The example Etzel and LeBlanc (1979) provided was the discrimination of two Kanji stimuli, as seen in Figure 2.

The circled elements at the top of each figure were those selected for criterion cues. The shaping of the S+ and S- stimuli are shown in Figure 2. The entry stimuli were drawn as a duck and an Indian woman. The duck's bill and the feather in the Indian's hair were the elements selected to be criterion-related cues. The shaping sequence was from a program developed by Stella and Etzel (1979).

There are two simple stimulus-shaping rules. First, the criterion cue that has been selected should be the last to undergo changes (Stella & Etzel, 1979). The rest of the stimulus complex is shaped to the criterion form first. In Figure 2 the duck's head and bill are the last to change, as is the Indian's feather. Although the duck's bill and the Indian's feather may not be the only controlling stimuli in the first few trials, they are the essential parts of the stimulus complexes that will make them different from other organisms (all ducks have bills and many Indian women wear feathers in their hair). The second rule is to shape the S- first. Keep the S+ at entry level, then shape the S+ (Stella & Etzel, 1978).

Stimulus shaping gives experimenters the opportunity to select controlling stimulus elements that will also be present at the criterion level. This avoids the problems encountered by fading a noncriterion-related cue. In the noncriterion fading procedure, the experimenter cannot be certain that the subject will transfer control from the added cue to the relevant cue. Arranging control is better than hoping for it.

There are, of course, programs that use noncriterion-related cues with fading procedures and succeed (e.g., Sidman & Stoddard, 1966, the circle/ellipse program; and Schreibman, 1975). An examination of these programs suggests that several procedures operate to insure transfer, despite the use of a noncriterion-related cue. For example, in both the Sidman and Stoddard (1966) and the Schreibman (1975) programs, initial control was established by using intensity as a cue. However, early in both programs, the noncriterion intensity cue was faded out and the only control was the relevant cue; no other basis for making the discrimination existed. Once control by the relevant dimension had occurred, the rest of the program was devoted to either adding redundant cues or fading in the S- stimulus.

Weidenman (1978) suggested another possible variable that may influence fading programs: the number of criterion trials present at the end of the program. For example, when using a trial-and-error comparison group, all trials are at the criterion level. However, if fading on a noncriterion cue continues up to the very last trials, the subject has little or no opportunity either to transfer or to practice. In both the Sidman and Stoddard (1966) and the Schriebman (1975) programs, many trials occurred after transfer that resulted in reinforcement, and hence control by the relevant cue.

Thus, several procedures can be applied to noncriterion-fading programs that increase the probability of successful transfer: Arrange for transfer early, and make sure that the discrimination can be made only on some aspect of the final relevant cue. The critical experiment to test this hypothesis has not been carried out. Sidman and Stoddard's (1966) earlier circle/ellipse programs were unsuccessful. They used an intensity cue (a noncriterion-related cue) from the beginning to achieve control of responding, and did not fade it out until the end of the program. Transfer to the circle-vs-ellipse problem (or at least circle vs. some S-) was never specifically arranged. In their last and successful program, intensity as a cue was eliminated early in the program, so the subject then had only the circle (S+) to discriminate the response. Once the circle controlled responding, the S-(ellipses) were faded in, completing the criterion discrimination.

Much of what has been covered so far has been a detailed analysis of stimulus-control analytic reasoning, designed for addressing problems in teaching academic skills. To understand stimulus control one needs to see what stimulus-control analysis looks like and what skills it requires.

A new area that has some promise for teaching applied academic skills is exclusion. We have detailed our procedures and our analyses so that one may go through the stimulus-control analysis and follow the necessary changes that the analysis requires. We were not always successful and we offer the reader explanations. But, by following our procedures during the development of the program and how we changed them, one will have a better model to follow than reading about a "polished" procedure. The field learned a great deal about error reduction by going through all of Sidman and Stoddard's (1966) unsuccessful programs.

Exclusion as an Example of Conceptual Behavior

We illustrate the development of conceptual behavior by environmental manipulation with the exclusion technique. This technique is not widely known, and it is currently being researched by a number of investigators (Dixon, 1977; Schusterman, Gisiner, Grimm, & Hanggi, 1993). A simple example is seen on multiple choice tests.

KANSAS IS A STATE IN THE UNITED STATES. THE CAPITAL OF KANSAS IS:
1) Los Angeles
2) Topeka
3) New York City

If you do not know the capital of Kansas, but choose #2 because you do know where Los Angeles and New York City are, you are correct through exclusion. Although correct now, if you are asked at the end of this chapter, "What is the capital of Kansas?" you may not be able to say "Topeka". The study of exclusion has addressed not only the initial correct response, through exclusion, but other procedures that are necessary to assure that correct responding will continue when the stimulus is not paired simultaneously with previously learned relationships (e.g., Los Angeles and New York City). Dixon (1977), using mildly retarded subjects, applied the term "exclusion" to correct responding, from the beginning, to an untrained s-s relationship, when other previously trained stimuli were simultaneously presented with the new untrained stimuli.

The format used in exclusion studies is usually match-to-sample. One common arrangement is for a sample stimulus to be located at the top and a row of possible choice stimuli below (Figure 3). The subject points to the sample stimulus first and then is instructed to find the stimulus below with which it goes. The match-to-sample format teaches s-s relationships. Sidman (1978, 1986) has noted that conceptual behavior is not the simple process of "hooking" responses to stimuli, but involves more complex conditional discriminations involving relations between stimuli. Such s-s relations are always involved in conditional discriminations, exclusion being one example. Figure 3 illustrates the first training and subsequent probe that suggests exclusion responding.

The subject is trained to respond to the choice, A2, when A1 is the sample. This initial training is carried out until the subject always points to A2 regardless of its position. The symmetrical relationship is also illustrated since it is sometimes trained (i.e., A2 sample with A1 as the match). Then probe trials are presented and B1 (which earlier in training was an incorrect choice stimulus) is presented as the sample and a new stimulus (B2) is included as one of the choices along with A2. If the subject on following probe trials then points to B2 (the new stimulus) when B1 is the sample, we note that a new relationship is observed, that has never been trained. Dixon (1977) found that as long as A2 was present as a choice, the subjects continued to respond to B2 when B1 was the sample. However, if B1 (sample) and B2 (choice) were presented without A2 as a choice (but with some other stimulus, (i.e., "C"), then correct responding was at chance levels. This suggests that correct relational responding for B1/B2 was dependent upon the presence of A2. Since Dixon's (1977) study, the term exclusion has been applied to cases where immediate correct responding occurred to an untrained s-s relationship when another previously trained stimulus was present and already under control in another relationship.

Controlling Relations in a Match-to-Sample Format

Different types of controlling relations can exist when using the match-to-sample format. For example the most straight-forward is the "SD rule" (Figure 4, top illustration). The subject learns that when A1 is the sample, A2 is the match.

Thus, the sample stimulus defines the correct (choice) comparison. The SD rule holds in match-to-sample formats across nonhuman subjects (Berryman, 1965; Cumming & Berryman, 1961; Urcuioli & Nevin, 1975), and humans as well.

Another type of controlling relation that can be systematically identified is the S-delta rule (or S- rule), as seen in the middle illustration in Figure 4. Here, the subject learns, in the presence of the sample stimulus, to not respond to the incorrect comparison stimulus. Berryman, et al. (1965) suggested this possibility, but could

**FIRST TRAIN THE A1-A2 RELATIONSHIP AND
THE SYMMETRICAL A2-A1 RELATIONSHIP**

PROBE FOR EXCLUSION

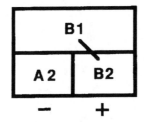

*Figure 3. Training and probe sequence to demonstrate exclusion responding in a
match-to-sample format.*

not verify it with nonhuman subjects. However, Dixon, Dixon, & Spradlin (1983),
confirmed that both normal preschool children and moderately retarded children
showed evidence of S-delta stimulus control.

Finally, there is a third type of relationship (bottom illustration, Figure 4), that
may be identified in match-to-sample formats and involved in exclusion responding.
The SX rule was suggested by Dixon et al. (1983). This rule expands the SD rule in
the following manner: The subject is trained in the presence of the sample A1 to
select choice A2. This is according to the SD rule. But, if some other sample stimulus
occurs besides A1, (such as B1), then it is not correct to select A2 since A2 is under
the control of A1. This is an expanded SD rule in that a qualification is added to

account for the instance when a particular sample stimulus is not present (such as A1) that would control the choice stimulus (A2). Thus, the subject selects the other available choice stimulus (B2). Dixon et al. (1983) showed evidence to suggest that SX stimulus control exists.

Control when Exclusion Is and Is Not Possible

Early research (e.g., Dixon, 1977) in exclusion training noted that although subjects were successful from the onset in exclusion probes of new stimulus-stimulus relations, such as B1/B2 (Figure 4, SX rule), they were not successful when one stimulus from the previously trained relationship, A2, was not present as a choice. Thus, they did not demonstrate direct control of the new (untrained) B1/B2 relationship. McIlvane and Stoddard (1981) have referred to this as an "exclusion-only outcome." That is, the new relationship is demonstrated only when a previously trained choice stimulus (A2) is present. However, as probes are continued when exclusion is possible (involving the new relationship), direct responding on the basis of the SD rule will apparently occur, and so the new relationship is formed (B1/B2).

Approximately 25 to 30 studies have shown exclusion in nonhumans, severely retarded children and adults, nonverbal, and normal subjects. The research has been primarily basic. Stimuli have included auditory-visual and visual-visual relations (McIlvane & Stoddard, 1985) and responses studied have been both receptive and expressive (McIlvane, Bass, O'Brien, Gerovac, & Stoddard, 1984). Since Dixon's first study in 1977, experimenters have gone on to ask what training procedures enhance exclusion performance and where control is located (e.g., McIlvane, et al. 1987).

Most exclusion studies have shown that direct training of a minimal number of relationships yields new relationships without direct training, given continued exposure to probes. The new relationships were formed and ultimately were maintained on nonexclusion trials. This suggests that exclusion could join the growing list of stimulus-control error-reduction procedures useful for persons with learning problems.

However, most exclusion studies have used only two or three choices in the match-to-sample format. Little has been studied applying exclusion to learning academic skills. Examples of skills that could be targeted are the training of arbitrary relationships found in reading, language, and mathematics. Workbooks and computer programs would be a natural mode of presentation.

To apply the exclusion methodology to applied problems, a number of other problems needed to be addressed. First, the number of choices needed to be expanded, if we are to teach a series of relationships, and not just one by exclusion. Also, more choices could review previously acquired relationships and allow more simultaneous comparisons of stimuli. Another problem is to use educational symbols that already control some responses, but not the one the teacher is trying to teach. An example of this will be given later.

DIFFERENT CONTROLLING RELATIONSHIPS POSSIBLE IN MATCH-TO-SAMPLE FORMATS

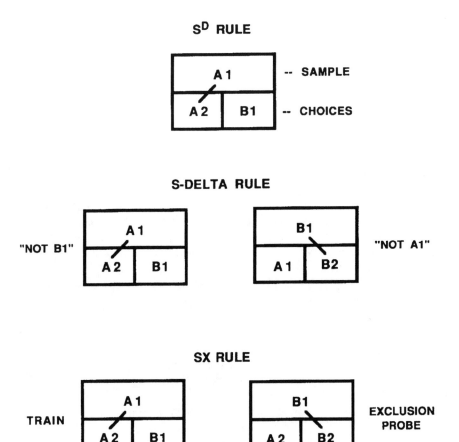

Figure 4. Different controlling relationships possible in match-to-sample formats: The SD rule; S-Delta rule; SX rule.

The Development of An Exclusion Program for Teaching Academic Skills: A "Case History"

Two experiments were carried out in this program. The first was considered basic, in that nonsense stimuli were used. The second experiment was considered applied because it used academic stimuli to which the child had been previously exposed. The purpose of the basic program was to develop procedures that would ultimately produce a near-errorless acquisition of the stimulus relationships.

The Basic Program: A Summary

The basic experiment consisted of three studies, to test three different exclusion programs. Only the third and final program will be summarized below along with the description of the procedures that were found to be the most successful from the first two programs. All children were normal three year olds. From the beginning,

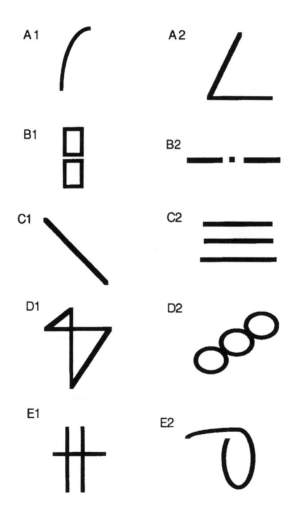

Figure 5. Five sets of stimuli utilized in Experiment 1: A1-A2, B1-B2, C1-C2, D1-D2, and E1-E2.

five pairs of two stimuli each were used, and by the end of the program the number choices in the match-to-sample format increased from three to five. The five pairs of stimuli used in the basic experiment are seen in Figure 5. All children were pretested to determine that no one pair (i.e., A1 and A2) was consistently responded to as being related. Figure 6 is an example of a trial at the end of the program when all five comparisons were present and C2 was the sample and C1 the correct choice. The instructions were: "Point to the picture on top", and then "point to the picture on the bottom that goes with it".

Step 1 of the program directly trained A1 to A2 and the symmetrical relationship A2 to A1 (as suggested by Stromer, 1986). The format was three-choice match-to-sample. The two distracter choices (S-choice stimuli) were two slightly different flowers. Table 2 summarizes this last program. As noted (Table 2), Step 2 was similar to Step 1, however B1-B2 and B2-B1 stimulus pairs were then trained, with flowers as distracters. Earlier versions of the program where the B stimulus pairs were introduced and were to be learned by exclusion (rather than directly trained as in this last program) indicated that many more trials would be required in the initial training of the A Set (using the B set as distracters) and many errors would result. The decision

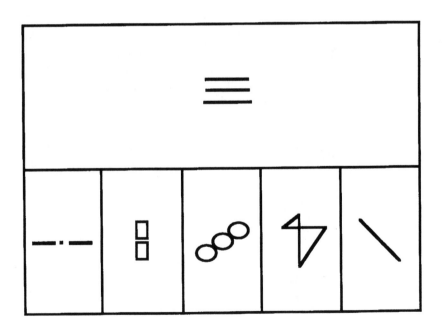

Figure 6. Example of trial toward the end of the basic program illustrating the five-comparison format with C2 as the sample and C1 (far right, position 5), as the correct choice.

TABLE 2
EXPERIMENT 1
BASIC PROGRAM

STEP	CONDITION	DISTRACTERS
1	Train A1-A2/A2-A1 (12 trials) Session 1	Flowers
2	Train B1-B2/B2-B1 (12 trials) Session 2	Flowers
3	A1-A2/A2-A1; B1-B2/B2-B1 intermix (14 trials) Session 3	Fade out first flower and fade in 2nd comparison (Criterion-related shaping suggested alternative)
4	A1-A2/A2-A1; B1-B2/B2-B1 intermix (14 trials) Sessions 4 and 5	Fade out second flower and fade in 3rd comparison
5	A1-A2/A2-A1; B1-B2/B2-B1 intermix (12 trials) [Exclusion] Sessions 6, 7, and 8	All distracters at full criteria either A or B stimuli
6	C1-C2/C2-C1 (12 trials) [Exclusion] Session 9	A or B stimuli
7	A1-A2/A2-A1; B1-B2/B2-B1; C1-C2/C2-C1 intermix (12 trials) Session 10	A, B, or C stimuli
8	5 comparison format with A, B, and C relationships (12 trials) Session 11	A, B, or C stimuli
9	D1-D2/D2-D1 (12 trials) [Exclusion] Session 12	A, B, or C stimuli
10	A1-A2/A2-A1; B1-B2/B2-B1; C1-C2/C2-C1; D1-D2/D2-D1 intermix (16 trials) Session 13	A,B; B,C; A,C; A,D; B,D; or C,D stimuli
11	E1-E2/E2-E1 (12 trials) [Exclusion] Session 14	A,B; B,C; A,C; A,D; B,D; or C,D stimuli
12	A1-A2/A2-A1; B1-B2/B2-B1; C1-C2/C2-C1; D1-D2/D2-D1; E1-E2/E2-E1 intermix (10 trials) Session 15	A,B; B,C; A,C; A,D; B,D; C,D; A,E; B,E; C,E; or D,E stimuli

to minimize errors dictated training both A and B Sets separately, with distracters (flowers) that could be easily discriminated as incorrect.

Step 3 (14 trials) then mixed (randomly) trials of "A" stimuli with flower distracters, and "B" stimuli with flower distracters. Step 3 also started a fading procedure applied to one distracter (see Table 2 column "Distracters"). In Step 4 (14 trials) of the program the trials continued to alternate randomly (A1-A2 and A2-A1 trials with the B1-B2 and B2-B1 trials). This Step in the program also completed the fading out of the last flower distracter and the fading in of A or B distracter stimuli (depending on whether the sample was B or A).

Step 5 of the program contained 12 trials of A1, A2, B1, and B2 serving as samples three times each, with the A and B stimuli serving as distracters. All stimuli were presented at criterion level. Since Step 5 ended direct training of the A and B stimulus relations it was then time to probe these two relationships before beginning C training by exclusion.

The first two studies in Experiment 1 indicated that nontraining test trials (probes) of the criterion relationships were necessary to determine if direct control of a relationship had been established. That is, when exclusion was not available for making a choice, would the child demonstrate control (directly) by the relationship between A1-A2, or A2-A1? The first two studies had shown that unless direct control was established, moving forward in the program would result in many errors.

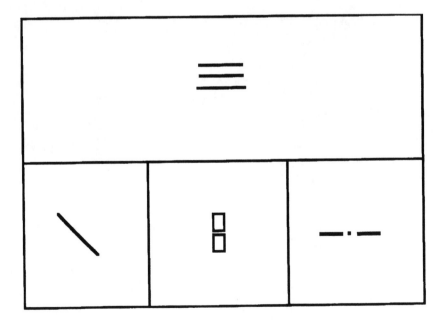

Figure 7. Example of C2 as sample and C1 (far left, position 1) as correct choice. B1 and B2 distracters (step 6).

Therefore, probes were developed to test direct control of s-s relationships after each Step in the program. If direct control of the relationships did not occur, the previous Step was repeated despite 100% correct responding - - such performance might reflect only exclusion responding, not direct control of an s-s relationship. The first probe followed Step 5, to determine if the A1-A2, A2-A1, B1-B2 and B2-B1 relationships were directly controlled. Illustrations and a discussion of these probes will occur after the final description of the program. Each Step from 5 on, was followed by probes.

Step 6 started the procedure of training by exclusion. Twelve trials (six with C1 as the sample and six with C2 as the sample) were presented. Six of the trials showed A1 and A2 as the distracter matches, and six showed B1 and B2 as the distracters. Figure 7 is an illustration of one of the trials where C2 is the sample, with B1 and B2 as the distracters. Following Step 6, the second probe tested the A, B, and C relationships. Step 7 involved the random intermixing of trials with "A", "B", or "C" as the samples and either the "A", "B", or "C" stimulus sets as distracters. This would be the first time that both "A" or "B" stimuli would be presented as the sample with the two "C" stimuli as distracters.

Step 8 (12 trials) started the five comparison, match-to-sample format. That is, there was one sample (either an "A", "B", or "C" stimulus) and five comparisons. The comparisons included two of the two s-s relationships as distracters, and the other the correct match. Figure 6 illustrates the five comparison format. No new relationships were trained in Step 8; the only addition was one earlier trained relationship added to the comparisons.

Step 9 (12 trials) then started "D" exclusion training. All of the sample stimuli contained "D" stimuli (6 trials of D1 and 6 trials of D2 as samples). The S-comparison stimuli were either pairs of "A" and "B" stimuli, "A" and "C", or "B" and "C". Step 10, as with Steps 5 and 7, involved 16 trials intermixing A, B, C, and D samples across trials. Now a pattern of procedures can be seen (see Table 2). When a new s-s relationship is first introduced, (for example Step 9) the samples in that Step contain only members of that relationship. Then the following Step (for example Step 10) intermixes the new and previously trained relations as samples across trials. Step 10 (as in step 7) contained all possible combinations of distracter (S-) s-s relationships. Following Step 10, another direct control probe was given for each member of the A, B, C, and D stimuli.

Step 11 (12 trials) introduced E1 and E2 as the sample (six with E1 randomly interspersed with six E2 stimuli). All combinations of "A", "B", "C", and "D" s-s relations appeared as matches for the E samples. Step 12 (like Steps 5, 7, and 10) intermixed all A, B, C, D, and E sample stimuli (randomly) across trials. Each member of a stimulus pair appeared only once, therefore there were only 10 trials in Step 12. There were also 10 combinations of two s-s relations possible, so each combination appeared only once. Finally, direct-control probes into the A, B, C, D, and E relationships were made.

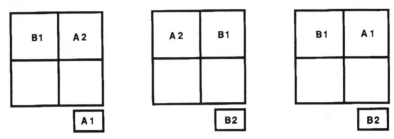

DIRECT CONTROL PROBE 1:

DIRECT CONTROL PROBE 2:

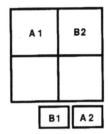

Figure 8. Examples of A and B direct probes 1 and 2. In direct probe 1, child was given a stimulus card and instructed to place it under its match. In direct probe 2 both cards were to be placed under appropriate matches.

Direct-Control Probes

There were two forms of direct-control probes. The first format was matching one of the s-s pairs (printed on a card) to the other stimulus (of that pair), while other members of other trained pairs were also present. Figure 8 illustrates this in the probe format in the top three squares. The child took the card (represented by the small box below the squares) and placed the card beneath the other member of that s-s pair. Correct responses were not reinforced or errors corrected. The other format appears in the lower right box of Figure 8. Selected samples of all possible combinations of s-s pairs that had been trained to date were tested. The child was instructed to place each card (located below the squares) "beneath the shape it goes with". It should be noted that this second probe is not as "rigorous" as the first type of probe. For example, in the first type of probe, the child may have acquired the A1-A2 and A2-A1 relationships but not the B relationships. The child could be correct on the top left box (placing A2 under A1) but may not be correct in placing one or both of the B cards beneath the B stimuli in the other two squares. However, in the second type of probe the child may respond correctly with both cards, knowing only the A relationship. The B card would be placed correctly only because one space was left. The chances of correct responding on the first type of probe were 50% for the A and B relations. As more s-s pairs were added as the program progressed, the chances were reduced to 33%, 25% and 20%. Even though the second type of probe could be responded to by exclusion (i.e., first place the cards on the stimuli where the relationship has been acquired and then place the last card in the space that is left) it was considered to be fairly difficult since the child had to attend to all stimuli simultaneously. Figure 9 illustrates the two types of direct probes after the E relationship was presented.

The results of the one normal subject (age 3 1/2) that was given this version of Experiment 1, are presented in Figure 10. For purposes here, 90% or better correct responding was the criteria for moving to the probes, otherwise the step was repeated. The solid circle represents correct responses on the program materials (probe results will be presented later). During "A" training (Step 1) and "B" training (Step 2) the child responded 100% correctly to all trials. Correct responding decreased to 93% when Step 3 was presented. The procedure then in effect was the fading out of the first flower (distracter) and the fading in of one stimulus of the "B" s-s pair (this condition is noted as the second comparison fade). Step 4 was then presented with the third and last comparison fading in (i.e., the other flower was faded out and the other "B" stimulus of the "B" s-s pair faded in). Correct responding fell to 71%. Step

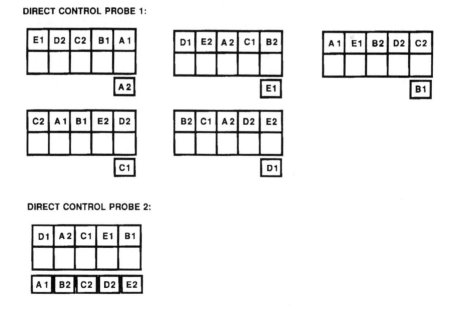

Figure 9. Example of direct control probes 1 and 2 after E exclusion training (after step 11).

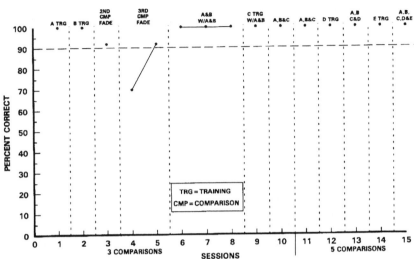

Figure 10. Results of Experiment 1, study 3. Three comparison format from sessions 1 through 10, and five comparison format from sessions 11 through 15.

4 was repeated in the next session (5) since responding was below 90%. Comments on the fading procedure used in this program will be given later. The repeat of Step 4 resulted in 93% correct responding. Step 5 which intermixed the "A" and "B" trials across the session (with all distracters at criterion) resulted in 100% correct responding. Inadvertently the usual first direct probe did not follow immediately after Step 5 (session 6), so Step 5 was repeated again on session 7 with the child again reaching 100% correct responding. However, when the probe followed this repetition of Step 5, direct probe 1 was at chance (50%) and direct probe 2 was 100%. If both types of probes were not at 100% correct responding, the training session was repeated the next day. Step 5 was therefore presented for the third time (session 8) and 100% correct responding occurred. The probe after session 8 also produced 100% correct responding. As Figure 10 illustrates all further introductions of new relationships through exclusion (C, D, and E) and all intermixing of the various s-s pairs resulted in 100% correct responding.

Figure 11 illustrates the results of direct probes 1 (solid bar) and 2 (criss-cross bars). No probes were given until Step 5 (after fading was completed). For this child, session 7 was the first probe of Step 5. As mentioned above, the direct probe 1 had 50% correct responses and direct probe 2 had 100% correct responses. That resulted in repeating Step 5. On session 8, the probes were both at 100%. The probes for all further relationships remained at that level.

This program had a total of 150 trials from beginning to end. Approximately 5 minutes per Step (per day) was usual which would add up to one hour of instruction time across days if the child did not repeat any Step. Acquisition was accomplished by directly training two s-s relationships and three s-s relationships by exclusion. The use of direct probes allows immediate assessment before progressing.

If there were any changes to be made in program 3, it would appear to be in the method of introducing the criterion-level distracter after the "A" s-s relationship and the "B" s-s relationship (with flowers as the entry distracters) had been taught (Steps 3 and 4). Research on fading in or out stimuli has not been as successful as a procedure known as shaping (e.g., Schilmoeller, Schilmoeller, Etzel, & LeBlanc, 1979). Our best recommendation at this time would be to avoid fading and instead change the configuration of the flower (for the "B" distracters) slowly across trials, by shaping it into each of the criterion stimuli. An illustration of the shaping process that could be used (many are possible) is seen in Figures 12 & 13. Each shaping of the new distracter would occur one at a time as in the fading program. Step 3 would still have one flower present and the other flower would shape into one of the criterion level distracters (of the B s-s pair). Then Step 4 would contain one correct match, one S-distracter that had been shaped to criterion the previous Step, and the other flower shaping into the criterion form of the other B stimulus of the "B" s-s pair. We have

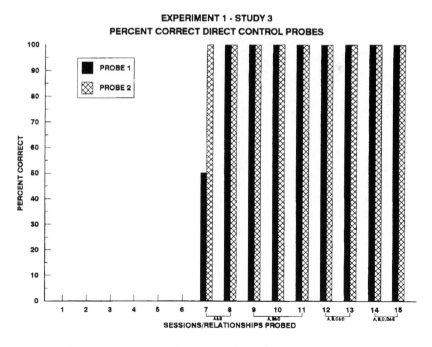

Figure 11. Results of direct control probes 1 (shaded bars) and direct control probes 2 (crossed bars) starting with session 7 when A and B stimuli were at full criterion.

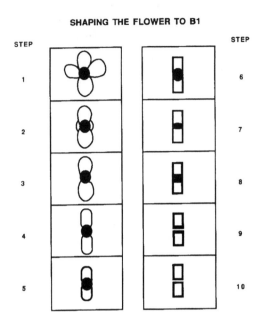

SHAPING THE FLOWER TO B1

Figure 12. Suggested shaping of flower to B1 criterion stimulus.

no empirical evidence that this would be successful, but it may avoid the problem of the child attending to the intensity (not the form) of the stimulus when fading is used. Intensity is not a cue that is present at the final criterion level. Therefore, when it is no longer present the child may not be under control of the form of the stimulus, only its intensity. By shaping the actual configuration from one form to another, we know that the child will observe the changing form (see Stella & Etzel, 1986). For the shaping of the A1 and A2 s-s stimuli when they serve as distracters during "B" training, we considered two simple line drawings of different sailboats that would undergo a similar configurational change into the criterion A1 stimulus and the criterion A2 stimulus. These are not illustrated.

Conclusions From Experiment 1

The three studies in Experiment 1 suggested several procedures that were then applied to Experiment 2.

1) The first s-s relationship ("A") that is directly trained, can be introduced in a three-choice format if the distracter stimuli are discriminably different from the pair being trained (such as familiar objects like flowers). However, the two distracter objects should not be identical since they ultimately will become different stimuli (the next to be trained s-s relations) through shaping or fading.

2) The second s-s relationship ("B") that is directly trained should follow the same procedure as in the first directly trained relationship.

3) Errors occurred when the distracter flowers were faded out and the B stimuli were faded in. A different procedure (shaping) was suggested for introducing the second to-be trained stimuli as distracters when the first trained stimuli serve as sample and match.

4) When introducing stimulus pairs, the symmetrical relationship should be trained at the onset by having both members of the pair serve as samples.

5) Intermixing trials (within a session) of all previously trained (either directly or by exclusion) relationships should occur before moving on to training a new relationship.

6) Introducing the five comparison format (from a three comparison format) should be carried out when the three s-s pairs are 100% on probes.

7) Probe after every training step. Errors on probes will indicate which training should be repeated. Move forward only when probes are 100% correct.

8) Feedback on correct responding should be provided on all training sessions (directly trained or exclusion sessions). Probes should not have reinforcement for correct responding. "Working hard"; "looking carefully"; or a similar acknowledgement is appropriate for preschool children to assure continued responding on probes.

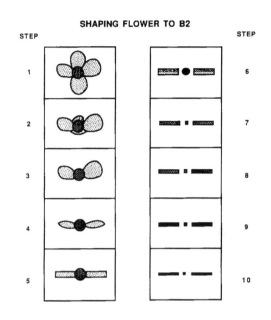

Figure 13. Suggested shaping of other flower to B2 criterion stimulus.

Experiment 2

An Applied Exclusion Program Teaching Quantity to Numeral

An applied program was used to determine if stimuli that were familiar to children would present any problems compared to "nonsense" stimuli. Another goal of this series of experiments was to examine the feasibility of using exclusion as an errorless procedure when error reduction is indicated for some children.

The Program

The stimuli used consisted of five pairs where A1, B1, C1, D1, and E1, were numerals (1, 2, 3, 4 and 5) and the A2, B2, C2, D2, and E2, were the matching quantity.

Figure 14 illustrates the pairs of numerals and quantities, and the configuration of the quantities used in training. The stars, spiders and faces, however, appeared with every numeral so it was not the type of object but rather how many of the objects were present that determined the relationship between numeral and objects. The configurations of the quantities that were trained were always in the "domino" style[2], as illustrated in Figure 14, A2 control for this configuration was built in the probes, where the child responded both to the trained configurations and untrained (different) configurations. One example of the untrained configurations is seen in Figure 15 with the spider stimuli. There were three different untrained configurations used in probes.

Following a pretest, during which each stimulus was presented as a sample at least once (in both a three-comparison and a five-comparison format), A1/A2 and A2/A1 training began. Table 3 summarizes the applied program, indicating the steps, condition and distracters used. The A1 and A2 stimuli were the numeral 1 and one object respectively. A three comparison format was used. For six trials A1 was the sample with A2 randomly interspersed as the sample in the remain-

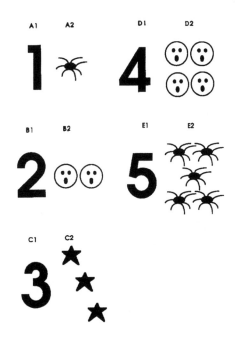

Figure 14. Stimuli used in experiment 2. A1 through E1 were numerals 1-5. Objects were combinations of spiders, faces, and stars, but were never consistently associated with any specific numeral.

ing six trials. There were no other S- (distracter) stimuli in the two remaining empty (comparison) windows. The instructions to the child were the same as in Experiment 1, "point to the picture on top", and then "point to the picture on the bottom that goes with it".

Step 2 took 2 sessions and continued with A1-A2/A2-A1 training for ten trials each session. B1 (the numeral 2) faded in during the first ten trials. Figure 16 illustrates the intensity levels. The third distracter window was still blank in this first session of Step 2. The second session of Step 2 completed the fading-in of the third window with B2 (the quantity). The stars, spiders and faces that represented the quantities were intermixed randomly across trials. These objects were faded in a similar manner as illustrated in Figure 16, by increasing the intensity levels. A1-A2/ A2-A1 served as samples and comparisons during the second session of Step 2.

While Step 1 resulted in 100% correct responding during the training of A1-A2/ A2-A1 (without distracters), Step 2 (sessions 2 and 3), that programmed for the fading in of B1 and then B2, resulted in the first problem that confronted us when using stimuli that evidently had a history for the child. An analysis of the errors during

Figure 15. One example, of three different untrained configurations of objects used only in probes.

sessions 2 and 3 indicated that a numeral class had been acquired by the child so that when a numeral "1" was the sample the child would respond to numeral "2" (not one object). That is, A1-B1 was the s-s controlling relation for our subject. The child's performance in the applied program is graphed in Figure 17. Sessions 2 and 3 resulted in 65% and 75% correct responding, indicating the errors on the numeral to numeral "bias".

A revision was then made in the program (T3) to avoid the opportunity for the child to have further experience with the numeral-to-numeral relationship during training in the following relationships in session 4. This session (4) started with three trials of A1 (numeral 1) as the sample, intermixed with three trials of A2 (quantity of one) as the sample, with no distracters. These six trials were then followed by ten trials of A1 and A2 as the sample (intermixed) with the B2 (quantity of two objects) fading in. This avoided a response to B1 when A1 (numeral "1") was the sample. This fourth session brought responding back to 100%.

The second program (session 5) revision was to train B1-B2/B2-B1 for six trials, randomly using B1 and B2 as samples with no distracters. This was followed by fading in A2 (the object) in the second window, with no distracter in the third window. This too prevented the child from responding numeral to numeral, and introduced the B1-B2/B2-B1 relationships for the first time. This second program (Step 4, session 5) revision also resulted in 100% correct responding (see Figure 17).

Step 5 then picked up where Step 3 had ended. A1-A2/A2-A1 training was resumed with the B2 distracter (the two objects) at full intensity, and B1 (the numeral "2") fading in across the ten trials. Toward the end of the fading procedure (session 6), the child resumed the numeral-numeral ("1"-"2")error, and correct responding was at 70%. Step 5 was then repeated two more times (sessions 7 and 8), and correct responding increased to 80% and then 90%. We were only partially successful in eliminating the numeral-numeral bias. We decided to use extended training (with feedback) to finish training the A1-A2/A2-A1 and the B1-B2/B2-B1 relationships; however, as discussed earlier, this is not good programming.

TABLE 3
EXPERIMENT 2
NUMERAL TO QUANTITY--QUANTITY TO NUMERAL PROGRAM

STEP	CONDITION	DISTRACTERS
1	Train A1-A2/A2-A1 (12 trials) Session 1	None (blank windows)
2A	Train A1-A2/A2-A1 (10 trials) Session 2	Fade in B1 (numeral)
2B	Train A1-A2/A2-A1 (10 trials) Session 3	Fade in B2 (two objects); B1, the numeral, at criterion intensity
	- REVISION -	
3	Train A1-A2/A2-A1 (16 trials) Session 4	First six trials no distracter; next 10 trials B2 faded in as distracter
4	Train B1-B2/B2-B1 (12 trials) Session 5	First six trials no distracter; next six trials A2 faded in as distracter
5	Train A1-A2/A2-A1 (10 trials) Sessions 6, 7, and 8	B2 at full intensity (as at the end of Step 3); B1 faded in across 10 trials
6	Train B1-B2/B2-B1 (10 trials) Sessions 9 and 10	A2 at full intensity (as at the end of Step 4); A1 faded in across 10 trials
7	Train B1-B2/B2-B1 (10 trials) Session 11	All distracters (A1 and A2) at full intensity
8A	Exclusion training C1-C2/C2-C1 (12 trials) Session 12	Distracters are "B" stimuli at full intensity
8B	Train C1-C2/C2-C1 (12 trials) Session 13	Distracters are "A" stimuli at full intensity
9	Five comparison format with A, B, and C relationships (18 trials) Sessions 14 and 15	A, B, or C stimuli
10	Exclusion training D1-D2/D2-D1 (18 trials) Sessions 16, 17, and 18	A, B, or C stimuli
11A	Exclusion training E1-E2/E2-E1 (12 trials) D1-D2/D2-D1 (6 trials) Session 19	A and B stimuli - 4 trials B and C stimuli - 4 trials D and A stimuli - 4 trials A, B, and C stimuli
11B	E1-E2/E2-E1 (12 trials) Session 20	A and C stimuli - 4 trials B and D stimuli - 4 trials C and D stimuli - 4 trials
11C	E1-E2/E2-E1 (12 trials) Sessions 21 and 22	A, B, C, or D stimuli

Figure 16. Fading steps involved in fading numeral 2.

Step 6 (sessions 9 and 10) was designed to complete B1-B2/B2-B1 training where Step 4 ended. A2 (one object) was at full intensity as one distracter, and across ten trials A1 (numeral 1) was faded in. Step 6 was presented in session 9 and repeated in session 10, with correct responding at 80% and then 90%.

The final training program revision (session 11) for B (numeral 2 and two objects) was the last Step in the direct training of the "A" and "B" relationships. The first two s-s relationships were directly trained, not acquired by exclusion. Figure 17 (session 11) indicates that the subject was 100% correct on B1-B2/B2-B1 training with the A distracters at full intensity. The numeral-to-numeral (error) relationship had been changed to a numeral-to-quantity relationship.

Step 8 started exclusion training for the C1-C2/C2-C1 (numeral "3" to three objects). Unlike the basic program (Step 6) the "C" relationship in the applied program was introduced first with B distracters only (session 12), followed by A distracters only (session 13). The child's history of numeral-to-numeral errors suggested this slower introduction of distracters. Both sessions (12 and 13) of C training (continuing with a three-comparison format) were at 100% correct responding.

The five-comparison format was then introduced with A, B, and C relationships. The first four trials had A1 and A2 as samples (two each). The next four trials used B1 and B2 as samples, and the following four trials used C1 and C2 as samples. The last six trials (of 18 total) intermixed A, B, and C trials, with A1, B1, C1, A2, B2, and C2 serving as samples. The subject was 88% correct in session 14, and 100% correct in session 15.

"D" exclusion training was started with Step 10 (session 16). The D1-D2 (numeral "4" to four objects) and D2-D1 (four objects to "4") sample-matches were intermixed throughout the 18 trials. All of the distracters were composed of all combinations of A-B, A-C, and B-C. Although the subject was 100% correct in session 16, the direct probes (same type as Experiment 1) did not indicate complete control. "D" exclusion training was then repeated for two more sessions (17 and 18). Session 17 training was at 94% correct, but direct-control probes still indicated more training was necessary. Session 18 training was again at 100% correct responding as were the probes.

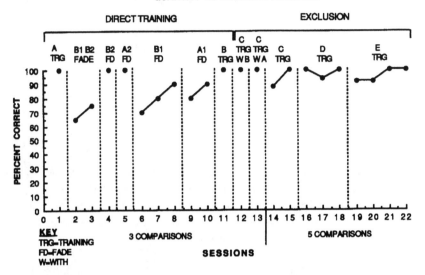

Figure 17. Results of Experiment 2. Sessions 1 through 13 had a three-comparison format, and sessions 14 through 22 a five-comparison format.

The final exclusion training of numeral "5" to five objects (E1-E2) and five objects to numeral "5" (E2-E1) was started in session 19. Three "D" training sessions (training between 94% and 100% correct) brought the probes to between 50% to 100%, indicating that the "D" relationship had been slowly acquired. Therefore, the "E" relationship was introduced in stages. The first (session 19) E1-E2/E2-E1 exclusion session started with 12 trials of E1 and E2 intermixed as samples, and the first four of these trials had the "A" and "B" stimuli as distracters. The next four trials had "B" and "C" stimuli as distracters, followed by 4 trials of "D" and "A" distracters. The last 6 trials (18 total trials) again presented D1-D2/D2-D1 as samples and comparisons with "A", "B", "C", and "D" pairs of relations as distracters. The subject was 92% correct in the exclusion training but probes were only in the 90s, indicating more exclusion training should occur.

Session 20 included only "E" exclusion training for 12 trials. The first four trials had "C" and "A" stimulus pairs as distracters, followed by "B" and "D" pairs, and finally "C" and "D" pairs. The subject was again at 92% correct responding on the training. Probes ranged from 82% to 100%.

The last two sessions (21 and 22) had the same "E" program (12 trials) with "A", "B", "C", and "D" pairs of stimuli as distracters. Correct responding in both training sessions and on all probes was 100%.

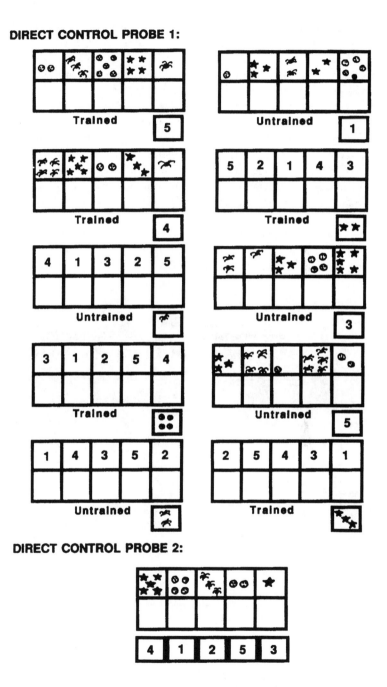

Figure 18. Direct control probes 1 and 2 used in experiment 2, including illustrations of trained and untrained configurations in probe 1.

The rules used in Experiment 1 for moving to the next training Step were used in the applied study. Probes for the applied program started in session 11 for the "A" and "B" relations. Both types of probes, as illustrated in Figure 18, were used. As mentioned earlier, this experiment always trained the object stimuli arranged in a "domino-type" configuration. On direct-control probes both trained and untrained configurations were presented. This probe procedure would indicate if the configurations of the stimuli per se or the number of stimuli in any configuration were controlling the relationship. There were three different arrangements of untrained configurations. Figure 18 gives an example of direct probe 1 and 2 for the final criterion behavior. Figure 18 further identifies which trials during direct-control probe 1 contained either trained or untrained configurations. In this example there were 5 trained and 5 untrained object configurations. The probe procedure was the same as in Experiment 1.

The subject's performance in trained and untrained (Direct Probe 1) configurations appears in Figure 19. With one exception, trained configurations were either equal to or had higher percentages correct than untrained configurations. Consis-

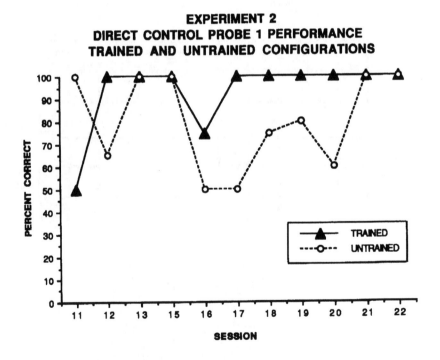

Figure 19. Results of direct control probe 1 for trained and untrained object configurations across sessions.

tent 100%-correct responding to the trained configurations occurred four sessions prior to 100%-correct responding to the untrained configurations. Since the last two probes (sessions 21 and 22) were 100% for both types of configurations, it would seem that at least for the three types of untrained configurations probed, the subject was not controlled by the "domino-type" of configuration at the end of the study. We do not know if the subject was counting the objects or just learned a variety of different configurations. If learning a variety of configurations did occur, it had to occur during probe trials as the untrained configurations occurred only in probes.

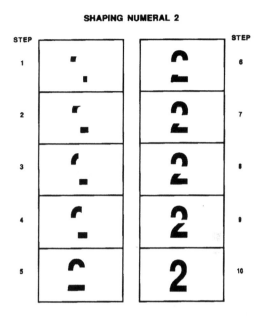

Figure 20. Suggested shaping of numeral two across ten trials.

Experiment 2 (the applied program) introduced S- choice stimuli more gradually than in Experiment 1, but the fading in of the S- choice stimuli was still used. Earlier research in our laboratory had frequently introduced S- stimuli by the fading procedure, and then trained the criterion discrimination through stimulus shaping (e.g. Schilmoeller and Etzel, 1977; Stella and Etzel, 1986). We suspect that fading in the S- in the present two programs did not succeed because in exclusion training the S- on some occasions also becomes the S+, as is typical in conditional discriminations. The stimulus that is the sample determines which stimulus is the correct match. Therefore, all stimuli serve as S+ and as S- on different occasions. The fading procedure presented problems in both Experiments, but in Experiment 2 these may have been due to the subject's history of numeral-to-numeral relationships. We suggest a shaping procedure to introduce the distracters, as illustrated in Figure 20. This might have avoided errors of immediately matching "1" to "2" or "2" to "1". The actual shaping of the "2" is not completed until many trials of "1" to one object have occurred. It is important to note that the shaping of the numeral "2" has to occur with more than one element present in the choice window; otherwise one element would be as appropriate a choice as the one object stimulus to the numeral "1" relationship. These suggestions mean further empirical study. This program needs other revisions, but, it serves as a model of how a technology can be developed, and, when problems arise, how a further analysis can produce other procedures to train conceptual skills quickly and effectively.

This program used 192 trials to reach criterion performance, but many trials were due primarily to the revision that was necessary as the result of the child's history of numeral-to-numeral correspondence. Those 22 sessions were never longer than five minutes. A program such as this could be adapted to workbooks or computers for children learning letters from upper case to lower case (and visa versa), picture to word and word to picture correspondences, as well as numeral to quanity and quanity to numeral. As the technology of error reduction continues, refinements will continue. Bridges are built better, operations are less invasive, and children can learn more efficiently, especially those with learning problems.

Conclusions

Packer and Weisberg (1982) noted that of all the studies in the *Journal of Applied Behavior Analysis* related to academic or classroom settings, 76% dealt with reinforcement to modify student behaviors. They also note that many of the studies also describe academic problems as being correlated with other behavioral deficiencies. If academic skill deficiencies had been modified, would the other deportment (social) problems have disappeared? Parker and Weisberg suggested that research on antecedent events, specifically instructional variables including error reduction, should be the future direction of behavior analytic academic research.

A year prior to the Parker and Weisberg paper, Weeks and Gaylord-Ross (1981) noted the correlated incidence of difficult academic tasks and aberrant behavior, in contrast to errorless tasks and the lack of such behaviors. They too discussed the need for more research in the area of reducing maladaptive behaviors through curricular modifications, rather than through consequence-manipulation procedures.

These comments, and others (e.g., Vargas, 1983), are now a decade old. Have behavior analysts identified the basic problem in school failures? In the '70s we reduced aberrant behavior by differential reinforcement or time out. Classrooms today still teach little; the reasons usually given are greater social problems, lack of an intact family, race relations, and poverty, to name a few. But if classrooms became discriminative for successful learning and progress, perhaps academic skills would supplant disruptive social behaviors.

Baer (1987) has argued that one difference between basic and applied behavior analysis is one behavior: identifying a practical problem. Another problem for the applied science of behavior, Baer suggests, is one other behavior (usually a chain of behavior). The chain (Baer, 1987) starts with our cultural custom of evaluatively labeling behavior by complaining. When someone complains, others act on those complaints. But that may not be the end of the chain, since others may complain about those actions, and then engage in other behavior because of their own complaints.

Consider a hypothetical account (but a common scenario) often encountered in family-school interactions. Billy was sent to summer camp; when he wrote letters to his parents, they could not read his handwriting, and many words they could read were misspelled. The parents complained to the school. The school replied that Billy was out of his seat too often, and creating such disturbance that he never finished his work. A conference between school authorities and the parents resulted in a program for modifying Billy's out-of-seat behavior. This included time-out, recess denied, notes back and forth between school and family on daily progress, and positive consequences when he remained in his seat for most of the time that was scheduled. What happened to Billy's penmanship and spelling? Billy sat in his seat more frequently but he still got Ds in writing and spelling.

As Baer suggests, unless applied researchers use design and measurements to demonstrate that changing a target behavior will also modify the complained-about behavior and all of the subsequent chain of complaining, we have not engaged in applied research. Thus, "...the first hallmark of applied research [is] the demonstration that changing the target behavior was an analysis of the complaint and its subsequent chain" (Baer, 1987, p. 104). In addition to this first requirement, Baer adds three other criteria for specifying when applied research is distinct from basic research. These are: (1) Was changing the complaint worth the effort? (2) Was there some other way to change the complaint? (3) What problem did changing the complaint solve?

Applying these four criteria to the example of Billy, we could conclude that the incorrect target behavior was identified. Billy still cannot write or spell very well. Was adopting the school's complaint rather than parents' worth the effort? From the school's point of view, Yes: Billy is not disrupting the group. From the parents', No: He still does not write or spell well. Is there a more direct way to change their complaint? We could tutor Billy in writing and spelling, starting with an analysis of his current skills so as to program success in acquiring the indicated new skills. Finally, what problem was solved? Children staying in their seat, but not learning? But is that the purpose of education today?

It is possible that where educational studies are concerned, behavior analysts have not researched the basic target behavior. Research on the development of conceptual behavior – that is, research on antecedent stimuli and the relationship between those stimuli and academic skills – has long been ignored. This area is the behavior analysts' domain. Cognitive psychologists have extensively written about the development of cognitive behavior by suggesting hypothetical structures that are involved in mental processing and they have proposed models for developing materials to exemplify those structures in students' minds. As Johnson and Layng (1992) point out, this approach has been and is the accepted model for U.S. educators. Yet United States education continues to make little progress. There are at least two questions we are asking:

1.   Is there anything in the cognitive literature that suggests better or effective procedures for designing educational material or is it simply symbolism over substance?

2. Is our time better spent analyzing the antecedent stimulus - response relations and manipulating those stimuli directly – those stimuli that are responsible for the development of conceptual behavior?

References

Baer, D. M. (1987). The difference between basic and applied behavioranalysis is one behavior. *Behavior Analysis, 22,* 101-106.

Baer, D. M. (1991). Tacting "to a fault". *Journal of Applied Behavior Analysis, 24,* 429-431.

Berkler, M. S., Schilmoeller, K. J., Etzel, B. C., & LeBlanc, J. M. (1974, August). *Response latencies as a function of discriminations acquired during trial-and-error and errorless procedures.* Paper presented at the meeting of the Kansas Psychological Association, Topeka, Kansas.

Berkler, M. S., & LeBlanc, J. M. (1974, August). *Heart rate as a physiological correlate of schedules of reinforcement in third- and fourth-grade children.* Paper presented at the meeting of the American Psychological Association, New Orleans, Louisiana.

Berryman, R., Cumming, W. W., Cohen, L. R., & Johnson, D. F. (1965).Acquisition and transfer of simultaneous oddity. *Psychological Reports, 17,* 767-775.

Bijou, S. W. (1976). *Child development: The basic stage of early childhood.* Englewood Cliffs, NJ: Prentice-Hall, Inc.

Bijou, S. W. (1968). Studies in the experimental development of left-right concepts in retarded children using fading techniques. In N. R. Ellis (Ed.), *International review of research in mental retardation.* (pp 65-96) New York: Academic Press.

Cumming, W. W., & Berryman, R. (1961). Some data on matching behavior in the pigeon. *Journal of the Experimental Analysis of Behavior, 4,* 281-284.

Dietz, S. M., & Malone, L. W. (1985). On terms: Stimulus control terminology. *The Behavior Analyst, 8,* 259-264.

Dixon, L. S. (1977). The nature of control by spoken words over visual stimulus selection. *Journal of the Experimental Analysis of Behavior, 27,* 433-442.

Dixon, M. H., Dixon, L. S., & Spradlin, J. E. (1983). Analysis of individual differences of stimulus control among developmentally disabled children. *Advances in Learning and Behavioral Disabilities, 2,* 85-110.

Etzel, B. C., & LeBlanc, J. M. (1979). The simplest treatment alternative: The law of parsimony applied to choosing appropriate instructional control and errorless-learning procedures for the difficult-to-teach-child. *Journal of Autism and Developmental Disorders, 9,* 361-382.

Etzel, B. C., LeBlanc, J. M., Schilmoeller, K. J., & Stella, M. E. (1981). Stimulus control procedures in the education of young children. In S. W. Bijou and R. Ruiz (Eds.). *Contributions of behavior modification to education.* Hillsdale, NJ: Lawrence Erlbaum Associates.

Etzel, B. C., McCartney, L. L. A., & LeBlanc, J. M. (1986, May). *An update on errorless stimulus control technology.* Paper presented at the 12th Annual Convention of the Association for Behavior Analysis. Milwaukee, Wisconsin.

Green, G., Mackay, H. A., McIlvane, W. J., Saunders, R. R., & Soraci, S. A. (1990). Perspectives on relational learning in mental retardation. *American Journal of Mental Retardation, 95,* 249-259.

Hoko, J. A., & LeBlanc, J. M. (1988). Stimulus equalization: Temporary reduction of stimulus complexity to facilitate discrimination learning. *Research in Developmental Disabilities, 9,* 255-275.

James, W. (1890). *Principles of psychology.* New York: Holt.

Johnson, K. R., & Layng, T. V. J. (1992). Breaking the structuralist barrier: Literacy and numeracy with fluency. In K. A. Lattal (Ed.), Special issue: Reflections on B. F. Skinner and psychology. Washington, D. C.: *American Psychologist, 47,* 1475-1490.

Lancioni, G. E., & Smeets, P. M. (1986). Procedures and parameters of errorless discrimination training with developmentally impaired individuals. *International Review of Research in Mental Retardation, 14,* 136-145.

Lawrence, D. H. (1952). The transfer of a discrimination along a continuum. *Journal of Comparative Physiological Psychology, 45,* 511-516.

MacKintosh, N. J. (1977). Stimulus control: Attentional factors. In W. K. Honig and J. E. R. Staddon (Eds.), *Handbook of Operant Behavior.* Englewood Cliffs, NJ: Prentice-Hall, Inc.

McIlvane, W. J., Bass, R. W., O'Brien, J. M., Gerovac, B. J., & Stoddard, L. T. (1984). Spoken and signed naming of foods after receptive exclusion training in severe retardation. *Applied Research in Mental Retardation, 5,* 1-27.

McIlvane, W. J., & Dube, W. V. (1992). Stimulus control shaping and stimulus control topographies. *The Behavior Analyst, 15,* 89-94.

McIlvane, W. J., Kledaras, J. B., Munson, L. C., King, K. A., deRose, J. C., & Stoddard, L. T. (1987). Controlling relations in conditional discrimination and matching by exclusion. *Journal of the Experimental Analysis of Behavior, 48,* 187-208.

McIlvane, W. J., & Stoddard, L. T. (1981). Acquisition of matching-to-sample performances in severe retardation: Learning by exclusion. *Journal of Mental Deficiency Research, 25,* 33-48.

McIlvane, W. J., & Stoddard, L. T. (1985). Complex stimulus relations and exclusion in severe mental retardation. *Analysis and Intervention in Developmental Disabilities, 5,* 307-321.

Packer, R. A., & Weisberg, P. (1982). What is the behavior analyst doing in the classroom? The incidence of reinforcement versus instructional-based solutions to classroom problems. *Alabama Studies in Psychology, 1,* 57-62.

Pavlov, I. P. (1927). *Conditioned reflexes.* London: Oxford.

Reese, E. P. (1981). *Physiological and behavioral coorelates of errors during discrimination training.* Paper presented at the 89th Annual Meeting of the American Psychological Association, Los Angeles, California.

Reese, E. P., Howard, J. S., & Rosenberger, P. B. (1977). Behavioral procedures for assessing visual capacities in nonverbal subjects. In B. C. Etzel, J. M. LeBlanc, &

D.M. Baer (Eds.), *New developments in behavioral research: Theory, method and application.* Hillsdale, NJ: Lawrence Erlbaum Associates.

Rilling, M. (1977). Stimulus control and inhibitory processes. In W. K. Honig and J. E. R. Staddon (Eds.), *Handbook of operant behavior.* Englewood Cliffs, NJ: Prentice-Hall, Inc.

Rincover, A. (1978). Variables affecting stimulus fading and discriminative responding in psychotic children. *Journal of Abnormal Psychology, 87,* 541-553.

Schilmoeller, K. J., & Etzel, B. C. (1977). An experimental analysis of criterion-related and noncriterion-related cues in "errorless" stimulus control procedures. In B. C. Etzel, J. M. LeBlanc, and D. M. Baer (Eds.), *New developments in behavioral research: Theory, method and application.* Hillsdale, NJ: Lawrence Erlbaum Associates.

Schilmoeller, G. L., Schilmoeller, K. J., Etzel, B. C., & LeBlanc, J. M. (1979). Conditional discrimination responding after errorless and trial-and-error training. *Journal of the Experimental Analysis of Behavior, 31,* 405-420.

Schlinger, H. D. (1992). Theory in behavior analysis: An application to child development. *American Psychologist, 47,* 1396-1410.

Schlosberg, H., & Solomon, R. L. (1943). Latency of response in a choice discrimination. *Journal of Experimental Psychology, 33,* 22-39.

Schreibman, L. (1975). Effects of within-stimulus and extra-stimulus prompting on discrimination learning in autistic children. *Journal of Applied Behavior Analysis, 8,* 91-112.

Schusterman, R. J., Gisiner, R., Grimm, B. K., Hanggi, E. (1993). Behavior control by exclusion and attempts at establishing semanticity in marine mammals using match-to-sample paradigms. In H. Roitblat, L. Herman & P. Nachtigall (Eds.), *Language and communications: A Comparative perspective.* Hillsdale, NJ: Lawrence Erlbaum Associates.

Sidman, M. (1978). Remarks. *Behaviorism, 6,* 265-268.

Sidman, M. (1986). Functional analysis of emergent verbal classes. In T. Thompson and M. Zeiler (Eds.), *Analysis and integration of behavioral units.* (pp 213-245). Hillsdale, NJ: Lawrence Erlbaum Associates.

Sidman, M. & Stoddard, L. T. (1966). Programming perception and learning for retarded children. In N. R. Ellis (Ed.), *International review of research in mental retardation.* (pp 151-208). New York: Academic Press.

Skinner, B. F. (1938). *The behavior of organisms: An experimental analysis.* New York: Appleton-Century-Crofts.

Skinner, B. F. (1978). *Reflections on behaviorism and society.* Englewood Cliffs, NJ: Prentice-Hall, Inc.

Smeets, P. M., Lancioni, G. E., & Hoogeveen, F. R. (1984). Using stimulus shaping and fading to establish stimulus control in normal and retarded children. *Journal of Mental Deficiency Research, 28,* 207-218.

Smeets, P. M., Lancioni, G. E., Striefel, S., & Willensen, R. J. (1984). Training EMR children to solve missing minuend problems errorlessly: Acquisition, generalization and maintenance. *Analysis and Intervention in Developmental Disabilities,* *4,* 379-402.

Stella, M. E., & Etzel, B. C. (1978). *Procedural variables in errorless discrimination learning: Order of S+ and S- manipulation.* Paper presented at the 86th Annual Meeting of the American Psychological Association, Toronto, Canada.

Stella, M. E., & Etzel, B. C. (1979). *Manipulation of visual orientation on correct (S+) stimuli during acquisition.* Paper presented at the Biannual Meeting of the Society for Research in Child Development, San Francisco, California.

Stella, M. E. & Etzel, B. C. (1986). Stimulus control of eye orientations: Shaping S+ only versus shaping S- only. *Analysis and Intervention in Developmental Disabilities, 6,* 137-153.

Stoddard, L. T. McIlvane, W. J., & deRose, J. C. (1987). Transferencia de controle de estimulo com estudantes mentais: Modelagem de estimulo, superposicao e aprendizagem em uma tentativa. [Transfer of stimulus control with mentally retarded students: Stimulus shaping, superimposition, and one trial learning.] *Psicologia, 13,* 13-27.

Stromer, R. (1986). Control by exclusion in arbitrary matching-to-sample. *Analysis and Intervention in Developmental Disabilities, 6,* 59-72.

Terrace, H. S. (1963). Discrimination learning with and without "errors". *Journal of the Experimental Analysis of Behavior, 6,* 1-27.

Touchette, P. E. (1971). Transfer of stimulus control: Measuring the moment of transfer. *Journal of the Experimental Analysis of Behavior, 15,* 347-354.

Touchette, P. E. & Howard, J. S. (1984). Errorless learning: Reinforcement contingencies and stimulus control transfer in delayed prompting. *Journal of Applied Behavior Analysis, 17,* 175-188.

Urcuioli, P. J., & Nevin, J. A. (1975). Transfer of hue matching in pigeons. *Journal of the Experimental Analysis of Behavior, 24,* 149-155.

Vargas, J. S. (1983). What are your exercises teaching? An analysis of stimulus control in instructional materials. In W. L. Heward, T. E. Heron, D. S. Hill, & J. Trap-Porter (Eds.), *Focus on behavior analysis in education.* Columbus, OH: Charles E. Merrill.

Weeks, M., & Gaylord-Ross, R. (1981). Task difficulty and aberrant behavior in severely handicapped students. *Journal of Applied Behavior Analysis, 14,* 449-463.

Weidenman, L. E. (1978). *A comparison of fading, non-fading and a combination of procedures in training word recognition with moderately retarded adults.* Unpublished Masters Thesis. University of Massachusetts, Amherst, MA.

Footnotes

[1] The authors extend their appreciation and thanks to Donald M. Baer for his helpful comments during the writing of this chapter. We also thank Ellen P. Reese and George B. Semb for their expert editing skills.

2 The domino configuration was used when presenting the quanity because many preschool materials initially use this method of displaying amounts of objects. However, by kindergarten most arrangements of quantity are random. Training on domino configurations and probing on both domino and random configurations enabled us to evaluate the effect of this arbitruary change in configuration.

Chapter 7

Development and Causality

Josep Roca i Balasch
Institut Nacional d'Educació Física de Catalunya
Universitat de Barcelona

It has been said that curiosity is the basic characteristic of philosophers and scientists but, because of the enormous amount of information and data and theories that can be found in contemporary science and in psychology, it is necessary to add that more than being imquisitive, we must have an orientation. It seems to me that this is the main goal of our work as psychologists: to become oriented in respect to human behavior in general. And when I say "orientation" I mean to say: put some order in our discipline and try to give a good and structured knowledge to society.

This is the reason why I have decided to present a topic as general as development and causality. I have tried to set up some principles and general ideas that could be helpful in my work dealing with the extraordinary world of human development, hoping that my reflections can also be used by others in their own work.

Methods in Science

There are different ways of working in science. This is an idea that appears to be useful to understand the different perspectives of study in human development. Logic and mathematics can be seen as social conventions and agreements previous to the subsequent scientific activities of description, analysis and intervention. Each individual has to manage these conventions in order to coordinate his particular work with others.

Technologies are a kind of scientific activity focused on intervention. They are disciplines that integrate different kinds of knowledge in order to apply them to specific situations; knowledge that come from logic and mathematics, from descriptive and explanatory sciences and, also, from experiential knowledge. Engineering, medicine and education are echnologies.

Morphological sciences are descriptive and pre-explanatory. The kind of knowledge these produce does not inform us about the functional aspects of nature but of its appearence in terms of spatial forms, topographys, etc. When we talk about development we have to take into account, from the start, this kind of science.

Functional sciences are analytic and explanatory. They try to build up knowledge about the organization of nature and try to show its functioning through experimentation and theorization. Physics, biology, psychology and sociology are functional sciences dealing with a specific level of organization of nature.

These four ways of working in science have to be known. But when we try to explain development we have to manage directly the last two: the descriptive and the functional. This is what I am going to talk about.

Morphological or Descriptive Sciences

First of all we look for a **descriptive** studying phenomena scientifically. This is the first step carrying outscientific work. The classification of animals or minerals are two clear and primary examples. But anatomy and linguistics are also descriptive sciences. Anatomy describes the organs and systems in their morphologies and situations. Linguistics also describe verbal morphologies and their "situations" or uses in social behavior.

The fact that they do not give an explanation is comon to all these sciences. In other words, they do not provide a functional analysis of natural events. Anatomy, for example, does not explain the physical or physiological functioning of the organism. Biomechanics and physiologist are those who do this functional analysis, being the anatomic descriptions useful for both. The same happens with linguistics:their descriptions can be used by sociologists and psychologists in their functional analysis of language and speech. But linguistics is not, in itself, an explanatory science.

Then we can say that scientific activity that consists in describing, classifying and comparing is not an explanatory science and, moreover, does not have an univocal relationship with one functional or explanatory science. In accordance with this, differential psychology is also a descriptive science. It describes how people react according to their sex, social position or job; but this is nothing more than the first and pre-explanatory step in the construction of global knowledege. On the other hand, differential psychology just as the other descriptive sciences can be used by the explanatory sciences as, in this case, sociology and psychology.

In a second step we can say that descriptive work in science has undergone some changes, mainly because of the historical perspective which has been necessary to adopt in some cases. Geography, the classification of minerals and some other descriptions do not have to be, primarily, historical but the classification of species and animals does. This is what Darwin (1859/1982) claimed in *The Origin of the Species*. He said that instead of synchronic classification, geneaológic or diachronic classification had to be used.

It is relevant to the descriptive activity of differential psychology to note how the genealogical description became necessary in such a way that developmental psychology appeared, basically presented as a scale of things to be done or usually done in each age, period or stage. Gesell's and Piagetian theories had been undertaken with this general idea of showing the genealogical classification of human development closely related to biological growth.

Genealogic perspective in biology has been developed, on the other hand, with the idea of a unique animal phylum and the "scala naturae". It is interesting to note how a very simplistic idea of organising genealogical classification has been promoted. Hodos and Campbell (1969) used this to offer an alternative view in which the idea of different phylums took the place of that single and unique "scala naturae". Developmental psychology appeared with the same simplistic idea of a unique phylum of evolution instead of accepting the diversity of phylums. I mean to say: when we consider the descriptive activity of presenting the different levels of performance through the ages, we still think in a unique pattern of evolution underlying each individual, instead of thinking in different patterns and ways of development.

Apart from this, the important thing for Darwin was to settle the ways of explanation of genealogical classifications, and this is also the important point for us. Descriptive activities, even when they are synchronic or geneaologic, are not explicative activities even when they are usually accompanied by some beliefs about plans or pre-determinations that cause the evolution described and that can be used against the true activity of explanation. The idea of the existence of different species independently of the physical and specific biological conditions of animals and "maturity" theories are a clear example of explanation in terms of predetermination.

I do not want to conceal the fact that Darwin himself promoted the idea of biological predetermination of mind when he suggested an understanding of higher intellectual functions as a result of animal evolution. But this is something that has to be allied with his general method of explaining evolution; and not to be taken separately.

The claim for a historical description by Darwin had a double consequence. The first was to promote a genealogical classification of animals, having an influence in the adoption of the genealogical classification of human development, but the second was the explanation itself of the functional changes underlying and explaining that genealogical description. We are going to continue talking about this last subject and also referring to Darwin to help us in our reasoning.

Science: the Study of Causes

Behaviorists have been reluctant to use the word "cause" because of the close relationship to a spiritistic understanding of it; mainly as a creative cause. I do not want to analyse this, but merely use it as a starting point supposing a certain coincidence within us about that statement.

The important thing to establish here is the Aristotelian principle which tells us that the **true science is the one treating the causes**.

When we are talking about explanatory or functional sciences we are talking about sciences directly involved in causality. And, I think, we have to get rid of our fears and apprehensions about it. I believe that psycholgy needs to be clear on this general subject in order to face the conceptual problems contained therein and which are deeply rooted in the cultural way of understanding human beings and our role in explaining their behavior.

I have mentioned Aristotle which I want to justify and also the continous use of some terms directly related to him that I am going to use from now until the end of this paper. First of all: I do not think, as some people claim, that Aristotle has said almost every thing there is to be said or that after him nothing else can be said... Rather, I think that Aristotle was a philosopher who is especially suggestive to psychology in order to solve its conceptual problems. This was the idea of Kantor (1963-1969) when he emphasized the top naturalistic level of his scientific thinking. But, we do not have to repeat him verbatim, rather we have to take and adapt his naturalistic way of thinking and apply it to the actual questions of psychology and the organization of scientific knowledge.

The Criterion of Change or Movement

Before talking about causality it is necessary to talk about the criterion that exist in the understanding and interpretation of the natural world. This criterion has to be the first, most general and preeminent principle in that understanding and interpretation of nature. Historically, the criterion of movement has been presented as an alternative to that of extensión (Roca, 1988, 1990), assuming that nature is better understood when we represent it as something primarily and essentially dynamic. Movement is the concept used for announcing this general principle of representing nature.

All those who talk about behavior for defining what the mind is, with a radical interpretation of a kind of action or organization of nature, have taken up that Aristotelian criterion of movement as the main principle in philosophy and science. There are a lot of things in behaviorism that could be a cause for desagreement in relation to this criterion but I do not want to go into it here. What has to be settled here is the coincidence between Aristotelian thinking and behaviorism in that criterion of taking movement or behavior as the first and more general concept to define the science of psychology. But this coincidence is not enough. It seems to me that it is necessary to go beyond the limited concept of behavior to understand the magnitude of the concept of movement and its relevance in order to improve the understanding of the same concept of behavior and the general contents of our science.

Aristotle, in an amplification, used to talk about different kinds of movement, or also change. As Averroes (1987) has pointed out in his review of Aristotle's Physics, there are four kinds of movement: translation, alteration, increase and decrease, and generation and destruction.

I do not want to talk about these old terms but rather those that, in my opinion, actually mean the same thing in the organization of science. It can be agreed that there are three kinds of movement. The first is the *qualitative movement* describing the change related to different types of behavior that can be found. It can be said that this "qualitative movement" is coincident with alteration movement and includes local movement, a specific organization of nature magnified by Aristotle for reasons that I do not want to go into now. The second is the *"quantitative movement"* describing the change in increase and decrease. And the third is the *developing movement* which refers to the change of generation, evolution and destruction.

What we call "basic sciences" are focused on these three types of change. They try to explain first, the different types of behavior; second, the quantitative changes inside each behavior and third, the behavior that means generation and evolution, integrating both qualitative and quantitative movements.

Science, as we know it, develops a systematic analysis of these three types of change, coincidentally with that old Aristotelian concept.

The Concept of Cause

The concept of "Cause" has no clear and univocal meaning in aristotelian literature. A clear difference is not evident between "cause", "principle" and other terms, and in any case, "cause" means different things or can be said in different ways as was normal in aristotelian reasoning (Prevosti, 1984).

In a very abstract formulation, "Cause" can be defined as the principle –or the essence– of a movement, and the interaction between movements. Perhaps in a more simple way, "cause" means the interdependencies in the functioning of nature, being interdependencies describing a movement or interdependencies between movements.

This is the idea that I employ in order to see how the global functioning of natural events, especially psychological events, can be represented in their singularities and in their interdependencies.

The formal cause, the material cause and the final cause. These three types of cause are directly related to the description of the functioning of the qualitative movement.

"Formal Cause" means the kind of organization or functioning itself of each qualitative movement that can be observed in nature, each one of these differentiated movements are called **behavior** . This is why we usually talk about physics, biology, psychology or sociology as sciences studying a *form* of organization of nature and we say that they study different behaviors. When we are centered on the study of a form of movement we try to establish what its primary and essential feature is, showing the difference in respect to another behavior. This primary feature is its formal cause.

"Material Cause" shows the dependence of a form of behavior upon another form which is the basic condition for its occurrence. Biological behavior is the material cause of psychological behavior as physical behavior is the material cause of biological behavior; while psychological behavior is the material cause of social behavior. Here the concept of cause means dependence and is clearly shown by the concept of a behavior being a **condition** for the existence of another behavior.

"Final Cause" means the form of behavior that acts as a specific exigence of adjustment to another form of behavior. "Cause" in this case means the dependence of one behavior upon another behavior that acts as an exigence of adapatation.

Biological behavior has to be adapted to physico-chemical environment while psychological behavior has a broader universe which appears as a cause, in the sense of being in **need** of adaptation; the psychological adjustment is carried out in relation to biological, physico-chemical and social behaviors as universes which cause specific adjustments in the sense of being behaviors in order to whom the psychological behavior is formed.

When psychologists like Ribes and Lopez (1985) define psychology as "the adjustment of the organism, as a whole, to the physico-chemical, biological and social conditions of the environment" we are joining these three types of causality: the first is "adjustment" as a kind or a form of behavior; the organism "as a whole" means biological behavior acting as a material basement and, the third –"physico-chemical, biological and social conditions"– means the finalities to which adjustment is made.

The factors or variables in an explanatory field as causes. Each science, after selecting a *form* of movement and presenting it as a behavior and showing its functional relation to other behaviors, acts in a complementary way, carrying out the analysis of the quantitative movement. They observe and manipulate a set of factors which are causes for the quantitative variations of a specific behavior. Here, the concept of cause means the changes in the formal organization of a behavior which produces increase and decrease. "Intensity" is a factor in **reactive** or biological behavior and "Probability" is a factor in **associative** or psychological behavior, to put two clear examples.

Each scientist has to deal with these factors that explain variations, which means to say: increase and decrease movement in a specific behavior. The "laws" of a science are the formulation of this quantitative movement.

For psychology this is a relevant goal so as to put some order in the knowledge that actually exists, apart from being a necessity in demonstrating the existence of this kind of movement in our object of study.

An essay, representing psychological events with these concepts describing both qualitative and quantitative Movements, has been done starting from interbehavioral positions and the field model (Roca, 1993). What I am trying to do now is to continue with the functional analysis but opening it to development and differentiation. When planning to do this, the concept of efficient cause becomesuggestive.

The Efficient Cause. The aristotelian metaphor of the statue is usually evoked when talking about "efficient cause". I have to say, nevertheless, that this is a dangerous metaphor, as are all metaphors when they are not being used only as a form of interpretation.

This metaphor is of use for showing the relation between material and formal cause. It is easy to understand that the stone is the material and the statute itself is the form; but a lot of confusion is produced when one talks about the "final cause" . This causality has no clear representation in the metaphor or induces an inadequate idea, such as that of supposing the ideal image in the sculptor's mind. It is inadequate because it can be suggested that the ideas and the human mind, in general, is the final cause and the upper level in the organization of nature which acts as a the central point of reference for all things.

But the metaphor is especially dangerous when we try to understand the concept of "efficient cause" from a naturalistic point of view because it induces the interpretation that the sculptor's mind produces from nothing the concrete form of the statue. This interpretation has, in my opinion, the defect of offering an spiritization of mind and an organocentric understanding of events in nature.

If we take the criterion of movement as the main and general criterion for the representation of nature, then the "efficient cause" can be understood not as a production of something by someone but the **effectation of one movement by another**.

I am going to spend the rest of this paper developing this concept of "efficient cause" of a movement, or a behavior, affecting another, and show its relevance to the naturalistic understanding of development.

Qualitative forms of behavior affecting psychological development. The metaphor of the statue is valuable in introducing the idea of how a person can affect another person by influencing and teaching him in such a way that he reaches a new level of skill or learning.

When a teacher manages things in such a manner that a boy can learn the skill of throwing a ball properly into the basket, he is acting as an efficient cause of this learning. This behavior of teaching is not the material cause of the psychological behavior, which are visual, auditive and propioceptive reactions as elements; it is neither the formal cause which is the interdependencies of elements which constitute the psychological act of perceiving and nor is it the final cause which is the physical behavior to which the act of perceiving means adaptation.

So, this behavior of showing and instructing about how to throw a ball in the proper manner is a behavior that affects the specific way of throwing of an individual and which we call "efficient cause".

From this example we can make a generalisation: the teaching behavior of man is one of the most important and efficient cause in the humanisation of individuals. It seems to me that it is easy to concur with this idea of education as a behavior being efficient cause. And we can go a step further and suggest that the social education system is also a behavior which through different ways affects the psychological acts of adjustment to the physical, biological and social behavior itself. Culture means, among other things, a system of teaching and instructing individuals in their psychological adaptation. Teachers, specifically and professionally, promote this adaptation. But social organisation has ways of influencing human development that are much broader and less intentional than the formal institution of teaching, in order to get specific human adjustments. And, it is broader in a very important aspect: it instructs in the very relevant aspect of the habits and customs related to economic and social structure beyond the values that can be taught in school.

It is necessary to note that the social education system is not a thing but the behavior of "arbitrary" conventions held by a group and linked to other social "conventions" like that of economic relationship between cultures, nations, groups or individuals, and between other kinds of conventions. Similarly, the act of teaching; is not a production or effect of a thing called the mind but the behavior of referring through the vocal or gestural morphologies; and it can be another person referring or the same individual when it is himself referring rules or knowledge culturally established. I mean to say: it is the behavior of referring which matters and not the identification of a body doing it.

There is one aspect especially important when talking about the efficient cause in general and which it is opportune to note here: it is always a specific psychological behavior that is taught. I mean to say: teachers do not teach perception in general but specific acts of perceiving directly related to situations and manners. When we talk about "formal cause" we talk about perception but when we talk about "efficient cause" we talk about a concrete perception. I mean to say, efficient cause describes a **concrete** form of behavior and completes the determination of a specific psychological event. This is the complementary role of efficient cause in the explanation of psychological adjustment; a role that means a natural explanatory approach to differential and developmental psychology.

Development means not only changes in specific behavior but also in quantitative variations. The development scales show, for example, quantitative variations in reaction time, in time of realization of a coordination or in precision.

The effects of a behavior upon development can also occur directly affecting these quantitative changes.

Let me give, as an example, some data of a work done some years ago (Roca, De Gracia, & Martinez, 1988) on differential and developmental reaction time. We studied the difference between men and women and boys and girls from five to twenty years old.

Regarding the sexual differences in reaction time, a better performance in men than in women has been observed. And a biological explanation has been offered: maybe the smaller and less heavier brain of women is the cause (Sic!) (Welford, 1980). A naturalistic approach can be made to the sexual differences in reaction time when instead of general population, we look at students of physical education and sports of both sexes; there is no difference between sexes and this is probably due to the fact that this group shares the same interest, motivations and skills related to velocity and attention in performances involving speed reaction. But what I want to show is how specific teaching caused a better reaction time performance in very slow women of the normal population.

They were taught to observe the salient aspects of a specific situation of measurement such as the apparatus noises which act as a warning signal and also, instructed about the convenience of thinking only in the needle of the chronometer and trying to avoid a big displacement, etc. The result of these simple instructions and teachings caused a dramatic change in reaction time reaching values better than the normal male population, even sportsmen (Figure 1).

It also ocurred in regard to developmental reaction time that children of 5 and 7 years old changed their reaction time, with statistical significance. This can be seen in Figure 2 where two registers are presented. The left shows the different ages before training; the right is the performance of the 5, 7 and 13 year old boys after training.

This study is an example of the effects of referencial behavior on quantitative perceptual behavior and it is representative of the important role of referencial speech when explaining both differential and developmental differences, including differences in specific behaviors and in variations in some quantitative dimension.

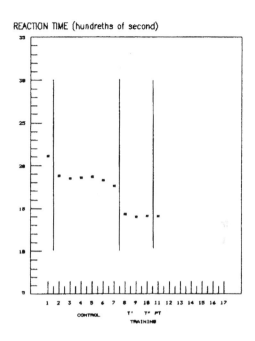

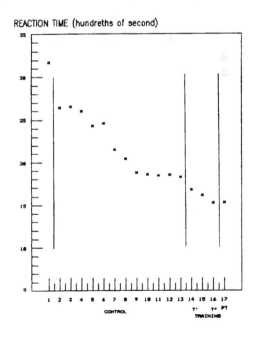

Figure 1. Measures of reaction time in two women with a standard measure -pre test-, only practice -control-, training -treatment-, and a post test measure.

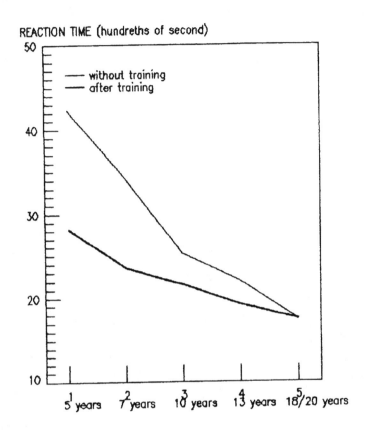

Figure 2. Registers of evolutive reaction time before and after treatment.

In general when we think about education and training as systems of intervening in human adaptation –biological or health adaptation, perceptual and motor adaptation and social adaptation– we are describing that type of causality that can be called "efficient". And we insist: this efficient cause makes it possible to reach the level of explanation of the complete and specific psychological events, especially in human beings where a teaching and instructing system is continuously present; a level that is impossible to reach with only categories of formal, material and final causes on one hand, and factors or variables of a field on the other.

Quantitative variations affecting psychological development. The general idea here is to show how quantitative movement is also efficient cause of differentiation and development.

When reading *The Origin of the Species* of Darwin (1859/1982) the concept of "variation" plays a big role in the explanatory system of evolution. Here "variation" means the changes in the functioning of the organisms that can signify or can act as a cause of life –reproduction and continuity, in general– of an organism or of a species. This movement is clearly underlined in the face of other causes of evolution such as t physical changes –structure and movements in the earth or climatic conditions– that could signify presence or absence of life.

Obviously, variation is related to the quantitative movement of biological behavior as a form of behavior but showing the important fact of continuity in quantitative change that life, as a qualitative form of behavior, can undergo. This enormous variation is taken by Darwin as the main cause when we try to understand differentiation and evolution of animals as organism or life systems.

It seems to me that it has to be easy to transfer this idea to the explanation of psychological differentiation and evolution. We have only to consider the enormous variations in conditioning, perceiving and understanding –this last one as representative of social adjustment– to see how differentiation and development are built upon this quantitative movement.

These variations are due to the field factors that have to be established by psychology but that can be already listed now when talking about practice and kind of practice, regularity, probability, contiguity, generalisation and inhibition , all referring to the quantitative relations between the elements participating in a field (Roca, 1993).

Regarding probability it is easy to see how variations occur and their consequences in the developing process of an individual. Let me mention an example from sporting life. It sometimes happen that a sportsman –tennis player or skier– usually wins during a period while he is playing in a particular category but when, because of age is forced to change this category, loses a lot of matches or races. What usually happens then is that the sportsman loses motivation in playing or competition, displaying different sorts of expressions and producing arguments to justify his decrease in performance and motivation. This is a clear example of the concept of "extinction" by forcing the ratio of reinforcement. This is the risk of winning continously.

The point is that depending on the program of reinforcement that each individual has, variations in the effects of forcing the ratio of reinforcement are observed. And these variations mean the continuity or not in that sport and when continuing, the doubts about his own sporting capacities, self esteem, etc.

This variation that we have limited to an ideal situation of an only dependence due to the factorprobability, is what can act as an efficient cause of an interest for the sport in general, or the motivation for winning in a specific match; both things being important in a given moment in the history of an individual, in order to explain his continuity in that sport and kind of life.

As used to happen in the concept of variation between organisms in the fight for survival in the theory of animal selection, the variation in psychological aspects in the struggle to win are also critical. The small differences in that variation of motivation or interest are very important in determining the survival and continuity of an individual in that sport and kind of life.

But probability is only one factor. We have to think about all the factors and the different adjustments that have to be made and their interrelation to have a first hand idea of what "variation" can mean in developmental and differential psychology.

Other evolutionary movements affecting psychological development. I have mentioned that Darwin did not give much importance to climatic and geographical changes in his explanation of evolution. Probably they are not so important as "variation" and this was due to the fact that the **physical** evolution of the earth is something relatively less important in respect to biological evolution than the quantitative variation in biological behavior itself. But when we think on the psychological differentiation and development of the individuals things change: **A human being grows, changes his proportions, learns constinously and, also, social behavior evolves and changes his conventions.** I mean to say: although "variation" is an important, efficient, cause when considering psychological differentiation and evolution; the historical changes in the other behaviors are not less important.

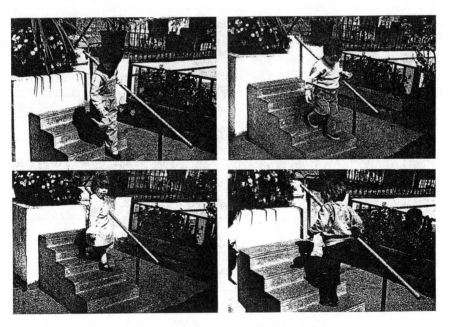

Figure 3. Photographs of children between 1 and 2 years old showing alternancy in ascending and descending.

As an example of this we can consider how swimming skill was not taken into account in educational programs some years ago; Gesell's scale can be consulted, for example. While nowdays these skills are progressivelly included in educational programs in our western schools.

And the same occurs with some other activities like managing computers: they call "mutant children" those who act in a very specialised and autistic way with a computer, but it is the social evolution that creates these machines and the exigences of manipulating it; and the children change because society evolves; and this evolution is not material cause, neiher formal, nor final, it is an efficient cause.

On the other hand, growth that means both biological evolutionary change and physical evolutionary change has also to be taken into account.

Let me continue with an experimental observation (Roca, 1986) in which we studied the development of alternancy in ascending and descending stairs. The observation of Gesell, Ilg and Ames (1940-1958/ 1973) on the evolution of this skill established that children used to ascend without alternation at the age of eighteen months, ascend alternating at the age of 36 months, start to descend without alternation at the same age and start to descend by alternating at the age of forty eight months. Nevertheless, when a special staircase was used with reduced steps, children of eighteen months easily showed alternation both ascending and descending (Figure 3); with the oldest children the presence of alternating was still easiest.

I would like to point out that physical evolution is the cause of alternating and the development of this skill. I mean to say: growth means a lengthening of the leg and acts as a mechanical facilitation to alternation. And it can be said that it is the a physical evolution that causes development.

Along the same lines we can consider biological changes as natural determinants of development. The increase of the force directly related to muscular growth can be seen as an example of how biological changes cause the presence or the absence of a skill and the development of the different postural positions and some other abilities related to force.

In all these cases, we have evolutionary changes affecting the existence of a specific psychological adjustment. I mean to say, these movements do not explain the psychological behavior of walking or balancing the body; but they are causes in the sense that this presence as a movement co-determine the existence of these psychological behaviors.

Development and Differentiation: the Integration of Causes.

The main idea that I have tried to demonstrate is that of psychological evolution and differentiation being a movement caused by qualitative movement, the quantitative movement and the other evolutive movements; integrating and closing the arc of the mutual effectations of any kind of movement and behaviors upon others.

I have not shown all the specific ways in which efficient causality can be demonstrated but I hope that what has been said can help to clarify the perspective that I think has to be taken for a naturalistic reinterpretation of the data that we have and promote new and systematic research.

I think when we reach to knowledge of the enormous complexity that the explanation of individual evolution signifies that we can have a more adequate idea of the work that has to be done,and also the ideas that have to be abandoned.

Psychology needs to confront not only the definition of its form of movement; presenting a clear definition of psychological behavior and presenting laws referring to the quantitative movement but has also to deal with development which integrates these synchronic movements in the diachronic or evolutive movement, which is the most comprehensive movement in nature.

From this point of view it is easy, first of all, to abandon the idea of the scales denoting a biological plan, as a trascendent plan fixed beyond the natural interdependencies of movements and behaviors.

Secondly, when describing differentiation and development it is not adequate to maintain the discussion between nature and nurture conceptions. First of all because it is a dilemma based on the stimulus-response scheme which corresponds to the biological form of behavior and not to psychological form. And secondly because the question is to have a broad conception of causality and , especially, go through another dimensión of causality: The dimension of efficient causality that makes it possible to understand, in a naturalistic approach, differentiation and development but also the relation between the formal cause that describes a general and abstract process with the efficient cause that allows us to describe concrete actions of ontogenetic adjustment.

On the other hand it makes no sense to think of evolutionary psychology as something separated and autonomous in respect to general psychology. There are no different psychologies but different movements and causalities and it makes no sense to explain development through an autistic language separated from that general, naturalistic and most comprehensive interpretation made by the use of the criterion of movement and the concept of causality. Psychology has to deal with all the movements and causes that are related to its behavioral events, its quantitative changes and its evolution and concretion in particular beings.

It seems to me that it will be through this broadening explanatory perspective that we could be a complete science and offer an usefull information to technologies such as education or medicine.

References

Aristóteles (1988). *Metafísica*. Madrid: Espasa Calpe.

Averroes (1987). *Epítome de Física*. Madrid: Consejo Superior de Investigaciones Científicas.

Darwin C. (1982). *L'origen de les espècies*. Barcelona: Edicions 62/ Diputació. (Original work published 1859)

Gesell A., Ilg F.L., & Ames L.B. (1973). *Psicologia Evolutiva de 1 a 16 años*. Buenos Aires: Paidos (Original was published 1943-1958).

Hodos W., & Campbell C.B.G. (1969). Scala Naturae: Why there is no theory in comparative psychology. *Psychological Review. 76*, 337-350.

Kantor J.R. (1963-1969). *The scientific evolution of psychology.* (Vols. 1-2) Chicago: The Principia Press.

Prevosti A. (1984). *La Física d'Aristòtil.* Barcelona: P.P.U.

Ribes E., & Lopez F. (1985). *Teoria de la Conducta.* México: Trillas.

Roca J. (1986). Registros Evolutivos Motores. Una observación crítica. *Apunts. Educació Física.* No. 6, 61-64.

Roca J., de Gracia M., & Martinez M. (1988). Evolución del Tiempo de Reacción: ¿Què evoluciona, el sujeto o la relación? *Apunts. Educació Física i Esports.* No. 13, 67-71.

Roca J. (1988). On the organism and the environment. *Behavior Analysis. 23*, 101-105.

Roca J. (1990). El papel de las Instituciones Cognoscitivas en la ciencia Psicològica. *Actas del encuentro "Psicologia: Ciencia, Enseñanza y Profesión".* Caracas.

Roca J. (1993). *Psicologia: Un enfoque naturalista.* Guadalajara: E.D.U.G.

Welford A.T., (1980). *Reaction Times.* London: Academic Press.

Chapter 8

Setting Factors in the Behavior Analysis of Human Development

Sidney W. Bijou[1]
University of Nevada

Twenty years ago, Gerwitz (1972), in an anthology on social learning theory, surveyed the determinants of stimulus potency and concluded that more research on contextual conditions would advance our understanding of social development. But during the ensuing two decades relatively few studies on the subject have appeared in the developmental literature.

Over ten years ago, Wahler and Fox (1981), whose research emphasizes the application of behavior principles to children with problems and their parents, proposed that the field of applied behavior analysis pay more attention to the concept of "setting events." A review of the titles in the *Journal of Applied Behavior Analysis* since the publication of that paper suggests that their message was not received.

This paper is, in a sense, still another appeal. Specifically, it aims to describe and illustrate the term "setting factors," which is conceptually similar to "contextual determinants" and "setting events." Our hope is that this paper will sensitize developmental psychologists to the need to identify and study the variables in the immediate locus of the stimulating situation and responding individual (Pronko, 1988).

The first part of the paper deals with the meaning of setting factors; the second part with categories of setting factors.

Meaning of Setting Factors

Early on, some of the conditions that influenced an interaction were referred to as drive or motivation. The difficulty with these terms is that they imply unobservable, subjective, physiological states such as arousal, and the impossibility of control.

Skinner (1931) referred to drive and motivation as terms included in the "third variables" and later (1957) he used "motivational operations" to refer to conditions that affect contingent stimuli and therefore whole interactions. Although he included several categories of physiological-state variables such as fatigue and drugs, he emphasized the role of deprivation of reinforcing stimuli and aversive stimulation.

Brady (1968) also avoided the terms drive and motivation, and suggested "potentiating operations" which he defined as conditions that "...determine the potency of the consequences that functionally defines the behavioral process" (p. 19). And,he added, "Such consequence-potentiating operations can obviously occur in any temporal relationship to the behavioral response process, i.e., either before or after the response" (p. 19). Categories of potentiating operations include the deprivation-satiation continuum, the functional physical equivalence of satiation and deprivation, and acquired potentiation developed by conditioning and generalization.

Goldiamond and Dyrud (1968) used the term "potentiating variables" and defined it as "...those procedures which potentiate the consequence, or make the reinforcing event effective" (p. 69). They elaborated by saying: "In the behavioral language employed, they [potentiating variables] serve many of the same functions as terms like motivation, but differ in that they refer to procedure rather than unobservable or inferred states" (p. 69).

Michaels (1982) argued that the concept of motivational or potentiating operations should be replaced with the term "establishing operations" which is defined as "...any change in the environment which alters the effectiveness of some object or event as reinforcement and simultaneously alters the momentary frequency of the behavior that has been followed by that reinforcement" (p. 150-151). He held, further, that establishing operations increases the reinforcing strength of unconditioned reinforcement whereas establishing stimuli increases the strength of conditioned reinforcement. In a later publication (Michael, 1993) Michael offered a more refined definition of establishing operations: "...an environmental event, operation, or stimulus condition that affects an organism by momentarily altering (a) the reinforcing effectiveness of other events, and (b) the frequency of occurrence of that part of the organism's repertoire relevant to consequences by events" (p. 38). He thought of establishing operations as consisting of two classes–unconditioned (UEOs) and conditioned (CEOs)–each with its own set of subclasses.

Morris (1988) treats motivational factors as contextual conditions, some historical and some current. "The function of the historical context–both phylogenic and ontogenic–is to establish what stimulus and response functions may occur in behavior, whereas the current context–its structure and its function–establishes what particular behaviors *can* and *will* occur, respectively" (p.309). He goes on to say that the historical context establishes the form and function of behavior and that the current context functions to actualize stimuli and responses for behavior

Others have offered still different terms and definitions of conditions that influence the occurrence or strength of an interaction. Sidman (1986) referred to "conditional stimulus control" as a general influencing condition in stimulus equivalence; Schlinger and Blakely (Blakely & Schlinger, 1987; Schlinger & Blakely, 1987) used "functional altering contingent-specifying stimuli" as a prevailing influencing condition for rule-governed behavior; Bijou and Baer (1961, 1978) and Wahler and Fox (1981) employed the term "setting events" as the "selective mechanism" for a response in normal and deviant child development; and Gerwitz (1972) offered "contextual conditions" to account for the potencies of stimuli.

As Morris (1988) has pointed out, some of these terms pertain to general but limited relationships and others to specific categories of stimulus funtions. An exception is Michael's concept of establishing operations (Michael, 1992,1993), Morris' historical and current context, and Kantor's setting factors (Kantor, 1959), the formulation which we will discuss in this paper.

Setting factors are defined as the general surrounding circumstances that operate as inhibiting or facilitating conditions in a behavioral unit. "Such setting factors as the hungry or satiated condition of the organism, its age, hygienic or toxic condition, as well as the presence or absence of certain environing objects clearly influence the occurrence or non-occurrence of interbehavior or facilitate the occurrence of the activities in question in varying degrees" (Kantor, 1959, p. 95).

According to this perspective, as a consequence of a person's history, objects and events acquire many stimulus functions . For example, a typical person learns, on the basis of past interactions, that a chair as a stimulus has many functions: It is something to sit on to eat a meal; it is something to stand on to reach an object on a high shelf; it is something to slouch in to watch T.V., and so on. Which particular stimulus function a chair has for a certain person in a given situation will depend on the setting factors in that situation. Another example, one involving verbal behavior: A person may have learned several ways of greeting another person. So on seeing a friend, he or she may ignore him, simply nod, say "Hi," shake hands and say, "It's great to see you again," and so on. The particular greeting that occurs for that person in a given situation depends on the prevailing setting factors.

Categories of Setting Factors

Conditions that influence the strength or selection of a response have been grouped in different ways. Gerwitz classified contextual determiners into concurrent, preceding, and maintaining conditions, and Bijou and Baer (1978) grouped setting events into organismic or biological, physical and chemical, and social and cultural. We suggest here a variation of the Bijou and Baer scheme, namely: (a) operations or events that affect the physiological state of the behaving person, (b) physical circumstances, and (c) sociocultural conditions.

Operations or Events Affecting Physiological States

High on the list of operations or events that affect the physiological state of a behaving person are the deprivation and satiation of organic needs, such as food, water, air,sunlight, and sexual contact. It is a commonplace observation that even mild deprivation of food initiates in a baby many aspects of the responses associated with obtaining and ingesting food; extreme deprivation of food brings about other behaviors usually described as "emotional."

While physical illness, injuries, chronic pain, and diseases are of course biomedical conditions they function at the same time as physiological state setting factors. Under such aversive conditions, there is a strong tendency to engage in escape and avoidance behavior, like taking analgesic medication.

In that they have stimulating or depressing properties, some drugs function as setting factors since they change behavior in complex ways. Included here are the so-called psychoactive drugs. Most of the field of psychopharmocology may be thought of as studies in physiological state setting factors.

The high and low points of physiological cycles, such as the sleep cycle, menstrual cycle, and circadian rhythms all have pervasive effects on behavior and therefore function as setting factors. Some are manipulable; some are not.

An individual's age, as an index of his or her biological growth or decline over time, is a non-manipulable physiological state setting factor. Age is a particularly important setting factor in developmental psychology where there is a special interest in a person's ability to perform a certain act, for example, an infant's ability to balance the head in an upright position.

Physiological state setting factors may also be generated by extreme fatigue from strenuous activity, as after running a race. The immediate reactions are well known and include sitting or lying down, drinking liquids, gasping for breath, and a slowing down of thinking and talking.

The final item in this category consists of strong feeling states, particularly fear, anger, and joy, resulting from a prior interaction. Such states are usually treated as moods or emotions with overlapping motivational characteristics. Since strong feeling states are not ordinarily viewed as setting factors, an illustration is in order. Each morning, Billy, a lively 4-year-old, dashes into the nursery school room with a cheerful "good morning" to his teacher as he runs to his locker, throws in his coat, and races across the room to ride a tricycle. One morning he comes in with a sad face, ignores the teacher, and sits on the floor near the locker without removing his coat. Recognizing the difference in Billy's behavior, the teacher immediately comes over, sits next to him, holds his hand, and asks, "What's the matter, Billy?" After some hesitancy, followed by tears and sobs, Billy confides that he was unfairly spanked by his father for having spilled milk on the rug, when in fact his younger sister was responsible for the mishap. The teacher encourages him to talk more about what happened, and before long Billy's face brightens. He tosses his coat into the locker, and runs over to ride his favorite tricycle.

Billy's unusual behavior on entering the nursery school room (deviation from his baseline performance) can be considered a function of a "feeling" setting factor brought about by a prior interaction. Getting him to talk revealed that he was angry because he felt he had been unfairly punished. Talking about the precipitating event with a supportive person dissipated the angry feeling and allowed Billy to engage in his usual morning activities.

Feeling state setting factors influence not only momentary interactions, as in the above example, but also correlated ways of interacting, referred to as "predispositional" behavior (Skinner, 1957). A man in love not only behaves amorously toward his beloved but he also "sees the world through rose-colored glasses": everyone is beautiful, kind, and generous; the sky is the bluest ever, the sunset is breath-taking, and so on. So, too, the dyspeptic. He is not only grouchy with people but he also tends to be a pessimist.

Physical Circumstances

Physical circumstances may serve as background to antecedent stimuli or as conditions pervading an interaction. Setting factors that influence antecedent stimuli are traditionally treated in psychology as perceptual problems. It is a well-recognized phenomenon that the way a person perceives an object and reacts to it is influenced by the setting or background—the well known figure-ground relationship. A person's reaction to a showy red design on a white T-shirt might be quite different from his or her reaction to the same design on a black T-shirt. So, too, one's reaction to a piece of music played as a violin solo would very likely be quite different from the response to the same music by the same soloist backed-up by a full symphony orchestra. The influence of background on a figure not only pertains to visual and auditory modalities, but also to interactions involving smell, taste, and touch.

Physical conditions affecting an entire interaction include temperature, humidity, and air and sound pollution. An example of temperature as a setting condition affecting behavior change was offered by Skinner (1961) in describing the rearing of his second daughter, Deborah, in a baby box/air crib. He noted that by slightly raising the night time temperature in the crib, she slept later in the morning, thereby delaying the time for the first feeding of the day.

Sociocultural Conditions

Sociocultural conditions include (a) cultural institutions, (b) the presence and actions of a person or group, and (c) verbal stimuli in the form of spoken or written rules.

The first category, cultural institutions, includes settings such as the home, school, church, playground, theatre, and court of law. Each requires prescribed forms of behavior taught on the basis of contingencies by parents, teachers, and others, as the child develops. For instance, a young adult engaging in jovial conversation with a friend while walking to church may lower his voice to a whisper, may even change the topic of conversation, or stop talking altogether as he and his friend approach and enter the house of worship. Skinner attributed the influence of such cultural institutions to the conditional reinforcers that develop during verbal interactions (Skinner, 1957).

The second category consists of the presence and actions of a person or persons having either strong reinforcing or aversive characteristics for the responding person. The presence of a mother in her child's preschool is an example of the former; the presence in the classroom of the serious-looking school principal accompanied by members of the school board exemplifies the latter.

The third sociocultural category—verbal stimuli in the form of spoken or written rules—is of two types. One consists of prescriptive rules imposed by parents, teachers, governmental agencies, religious leaders, and others. Blakely and Schlinger (1987), referring to this type of setting factor as contingency-specifying stimuli, CSSs), define the term as follows:

> Specifically, CSSs must describe at least two components of a contingency, that is, either a relation between behavior and consequences, behavior and antecedent stimuli, two or more stimuli, or antecedent stimuli, behavior, and consequences. By definition, then, CSSs are verbal stimuli; nonverbal stimuli cannot be contingency-specifying (p.183).

Rules imposed by others play a significant role in child-rearing practices. A mother says to her young son as she leaves him with a neighbor, "Now be a good boy while mommy goes shopping." Such a rule or instruction may control the child's "good" behavior for some time while in the neighbor's house in the sense that some of his "good" behaviors are facilitated and some "bad" behaviors are inhibited.

In addition to prescriptive rules, there is another type of rule which refers to agreements by the participants in an activity (Bijou, Umbreit, Ghezzi, & Chao, 1986). When rules are agreed upon they serve to control the behavior of the participants for a prescribed time or in a particular situation. As an example, two children may be engaged in spontaneous conversation and suddenly one suggests that they play the "knock-knock game." The other agrees and they take turns saying "Knock-knock, who's there?", giving answers, and laughing at them. Their agreement to play a game changes the course and nature of their verbal interactions. Another example: A group of adults gathered in a room are making "small talk." One person stands up and says in a loud voice, "It's time to begin the meeting." All conversation stops, those standing take their seats, and talk and comments are now sequential following Robert's rules of order.

Combinations of Setting Factors

Although we have analyzed setting factors as single sets of conditions, they (the setting factors) usually occur in everyday living in all sorts of combinations (Parrott, 1987). For instance, Johnny's behavior in the classroom at a given time may be influenced by (a) the presence of the school principal who recently reprimanded him for a minor infraction, (b) the teacher's recent dictum, "Behave like responsible citizens, or you will all stay after school," and (c) the children and the classroom. The chances are that Johnny will comply with the teacher's order.

In other instances, multiple setting factors can strengthen incompatible behaviors and generate conflict, and in some cases compromise response patterns. A four-year old boy may resolve the problem of a strong urge to go to sleep and a strong desire to stay up to watch a TV cartoon with his older siblings by standing near the doorway leading to his bedroom, watching the TV screen, sucking his thumb, and clutching his favorite blanket.

Summary and Conclusion

This paper has reviewed the concept of setting factors in a unit of psychological behavior. The meaning of setting factors as conditions influencing an interaction has been elaborated and a three-fold classification system put forth.

The role of setting factors in general developmental psychology is not yet fully appreciated, having either been ignored, or treated as stimuli, or as innate characteristics. When setting factors are (a) recognized as conditions such as operations and events affecting physiological state conditions, usually subsumed under drive or motivational operations; (b) physical circumstances including figure-ground relations in perception, and (c) sociocultural conditions including prescriptive rules, further advances in knowledge about individual human development and decline can be expected.

References

Bijou, S.W., & Baer, D.M. (1961). *Child development: A systematic and empirical theory* (Vol.1). Englewood Cliffs, NJ: Prentice-Hall.

Bijou, S.W., & Baer, D.M. (1978). *Behavior analysis of child development.* Englewood Cliffs, NJ: Prentice-Hall.

Bijou, S.W., Umbreit, J., & Ghezzi, P.M., & Chao, C.-C. (1986). Manual of instructions for identifying and analyzing referential interactions. *The Psychological Record, 36,* 491-518.

Blakely, E., & Schlinger, H. (1987). Rules: Function-altering contingency-specifying stimuli. *The Behavior Analyst, 10,* 183-187.

Brady, J.V. (1968). Potentiating operations. *Neuroscience Research Program Bulletin, 6*(1), 19-21.

Gerwitz, J.L. (1972). Some contextual determinants of stimulus potency. In R.D. Parke (Ed.), *Recent trends in social learning theory* (pp. 7-33). New York: Academic Press.

Goldiamond, I., & Dyrud, J.E. (1968). Some applications and implications of behavioral analysis for psychotherapy. *Research in Psychotherapy, 3,* 54-89.

Kantor, J.R. (1959). *Interbehavioral psychology.* (2nd rev. ed.) Bloomington, IN: Principia Press.

Michael, J.L. (1982). Distinguishing between discriminative and motivational functions of stimuli. *Journal of the Experimental Analysis of Behavior, 37,* 149-155.

Michael, J.L. (1993). *Concepts and principles of behavior analysis.* Kalamazoo, MI: Society for the Advancement of Behavior.

Morris, E.K. (1988). Contextualism: The world view of behavior analysis. *Journal of Experimental Child Psychology, 46,* 289-323.

Parrott, L.J. (1987). On the distinction between setting events and stimuli. *Experimental Analysis of Human Behavior Bulletin, 5,* 6-11.

Pronko, N.H. (1988). *From AI to Zeitgeist.* New York: Greenwood Press.

Schlinger, H., & Blakely, E. (1987). Function-altering effects of contingency-specifying stimuli. *The Behavior Analyst, 10,* 41-45.

Sidman, M. (1986). Functional analysis of emergent verbal classes. In T. Thompson & M.D. Zeiler (Eds.), *Analysis and integration of behavioral functional units* (pp. 213-245). Hillsdale, NJ: Lawrence Erlbaum Associates.

Skinner, B.F. (1931). The concept of the reflex in the description of behavior. *Journal of General Psychology*, *5*, 427-458.

Skinner, B.F. (1953). *Science and human behavior*. New York: MacMillan.

Skinner, B.F. (1957). *Verbal behavior*. New York: Appleton-Century-Crofts.

Skinner, B.F. (1961). Baby in a box. In B.F. Skinner (Ed.), *Cumulative Record* (enlarged ed.) pp. 419-426. New York: Appleton-Century-Crofts.

Wahler, R.G., & Fox, J.J. (1981). Setting events in applied behavior analysis: Toward a conceptual and methodological expansion. *Journal of Applied Behavior Analysis*, *14*, 327-338.

Footnote

[1] The author is grateful to Patrick M. Ghezzi for his most helpful comments on an earlier draft of the paper.

Chapter 9

A Behavior-Analytic View of Development

Jesus Rosales-Ruiz
University of North Texas
Donald M. Baer[1]
University of Kansas

From Behavior Change to Development

As infants turn into children, children into adolescents, adolescents into adults, and adults into aged adults, we see changes not only in their anatomical and biochemical functions, but in their behavioral functioning as well. From birth to death the organism acquires a behavioral history. Organisms are always doing something, and are always doing new things; there are no holes in the stream of behavior (Bijou & Baer, 1961; Schoenfeld & Farmer, 1970; Skinner, 1953; Watson, 1926). But there are behavior changes, from moment to moment and phase to phase, across the life span; on the face of it, they demand analysis, and some of them will repay analysis. Thus, psychology, like embryology, genetics, and evolution, posits continual change; more significantly, it posits a continuous process of change, and hence a term to index it: "development." The fact of change is undoubted; the problem is to explain its process—or processes.

What we mean by "process," however, is probably what we mean by "explain." We want a description of all the facts of behavioral change; much more, we want those facts organized by some principles, so that they are easy to understand, teach, and apply, despite their immense diversity of detail. We want the facts of change stated so that they are seen to be predictable, and perhaps manageable. Thus, we need them restated in terms of other processes that we already understand. A reinforcement theorist will assume that at least one developmental process is the sequence of powerful differential-reinforcement contingencies that an organism's repertoire encounters as life goes on. A cognitive theorist will assume that at least one developmental process is the succession of important conceptual schemata the organism acquires, constructs, reconstructs, or is endowed with as life goes on. And, indeed, the distinctions between "acquires, constructs, reconstructs, or is endowed with" can control which already understood process we ensconce as explanatory, just as the choice of what we consider explanatory can control whether we explain acquisition, construction, reconstruction, or endowment.

It follows that explanations of psychological development, and the proper ways to study it, are thoroughly controversial, even when we agree that "ways" is plural.

The classic problems of development (e.g., process-processes, nature-nurture, continuity-discontinuity, etc.) generate enduring debate and diverse positions, across and within disciplines. Harris (1957), like many observers across the decades, has noted that psychologists use a concept of "development" like the god Proteus, by giving it many shapes: They characterize it variously as a product, process, achievement, principle, mechanism, research strategy, explanatory strategy, professional strategy, world view, and more. That diversity, and the corresponding diversity of research, teaching, and professional strategies it engenders, is symptomatic of longstanding, underlying, unresolved philosophical debates. Developmental psychology in particular often moves from diversity to disagreement. The durability of the resultant debates suggests that perhaps they are not meant for resolution so much as for exploration of their consequences.

At least, development describes behavior change in time: sometimes simply as sequences of change, sometimes according to a calendar of when to expect those sequential changes. Interestingly, very many of the facts of development prove relatively easy to organize in those ways. However, modern developmental psychologists do not often find this kind of organization sufficient to define their discipline. They argue as if the timing and sequence of change is not sufficiently explanatory to qualify as development. As the etymology of the word suggests, the key to behavior change is that it not only changes, but also advances. That term helps to specify a more precise meaning for development, in that it requires a statement of the goal toward which the advance is made. It also helps to maintain the controversy, in that *advance* allows a very wide, and not necessarily precise, specification of those goals. Sometimes the goal is stated no more specifically than as higher levels of "complexity" or as some end state of "organization." Thus, behavior change over an organism's life-span cannot alone be the phenomenon of interest; it requires a theoretical construct to define either a product or a process of change, or both: "an *ideal* ordering of organizations, systems of transaction, principles of mental functioning" (Kaplan, 1967, p. 84). That kind of development will be used not to describe behavior change so much as to interpret it—to decide if the change is merely a change, or is a developmental change (Collins, 1982; Kaplan, 1967; Harris, 1957; Lerner, 1986; Miller, 1983; Reese & Overton, 1970; Wertheimer, 1982).

Even so, in the most general sense, psychological development must at least begin with and must always refer to behavior change. However, no developmentalist will find this characterization completely satisfactory until it distinguishes developmental psychology from psychology in general.

Developmental Psychologies

So what is the essence of a developmental psychology? Perhaps the answer should begin by examining the significance that researchers give to time, structure, and progression.

Time and Development

Ausubel and Sullivan (1970) distinguish between contemporaneous and developmental phenomena; for them, although both these phenomena take place in time, the developmental approach sees that time as essential, whereas the other approaches see it as incidental or nominal—as representing no more than the fact that changing behavior usually takes at least a little time, and can be seen to have happened at a certain time. Then it is not merely change that concerns the developmentalist; "change as a function of time is itself the phenomenon under investigation" (p. 2).

This statement has been central to the definition of developmental phenomena for some psychologists. For them, time is not simply a dimension along which behavior change is studied; it has been made into the "age variable." Thus age is to be found either as an independent variable, or as part of the dependent variable. Age as an independent variable has been one of the most popular variables organizing developmental research. This can be easily seen in the titles of developmental journals and in the discussion of the results of that research. Hence the phrase, "a function of age." However, some psychologists have objected to this notion as representing a false functional relation (e.g., Baer, 1970; Bijou & Baer, 1961; Baltes & Goulet 1970; Gewirtz, 1969; and Wohlwill, 1970). That is, although behavior change usually occurs with increasing age, age does not determine behavior change. This has lead to a reformulation of age as part of the dependent variable, which recognizes that other variables may affect development, and restricts development to those changes that are age-related, uniform, and consistent across a wide range of individuals and environmental conditions (e.g. Baltes & Goulet, 1971; Wohlwill, 1970). For example, an organized, systematic increase in a child's speed in solving arithmetic problems need not be considered developmental, because it may be optional: That kind of change is available to those who wish to program it, is unlikely to occur otherwise, and probably can be programmed with equal success almost any time after mastery of the skill in question has been achieved. Similarly, behaviors such as writing, swimming, reading, or "other responses acquired through directed teaching, differential reinforcement, or exercise would not qualify as developmental" (Wohlwill, 1970, p. 52). Apparently development must be less optional and more successive than that; it should be not only age-correlated (as is any behavior change that requires some time, such that students are a little older after the change than they were before), but to some degree age-dependent as well.

Other developmentalists argue that the business of dating behavior changes does not convey their concern with developmental *processes*. For them, development means something more, something explanatory of why those behaviors change at those times. *Why* is not ordinarily answered by normative approaches: Only when we see that a certain change *never* occurs before a certain age can we at least guess that the conditions characterizing the prior ages must be insufficient, which offers us a small part of *why*. Ordinarily, normative strategies merely differentiate behavior according to some chronology (see Ausubel & Sullivan, 1970; Daehler & Bukatko,

1985; Kessen, 1960, 1962). Thus, change over time is essential but incomplete in defining developmental psychology. This is an interesting point, especially when made by developmental psychologists who see development as invariant across individuals: If development is indeed predetermined, the normative method will surely document its unfolding, even if it cannot explain that unfolding. Indeed, if we assume a predetermined unfolding, the normative methods become methods of choice, and their lack of explanatory power is minor, in that we have already decided on at least the form of the explanation. But whereas predetermination implies an invariant unfolding sequence, the observation of an invariant unfolding sequence need not imply predetermination—it may as easily represent cultural practice or the logical necessities of task analysis, for examples. Thus, those developmentalists interested in more than cataloging predictable, orderly behavior changes over time sometimes ask an additional question about necessary structure.

Structure and Development

For Werner (1940), the concern is not if a given behavior "is early or late in the historical scale, but whether it represents a low or a high level of mentality." (p. 17). Hence, development is not restricted to processes unfolding over time; rather it refers to processes of organization: "an orthogenetic principle which states that wherever development occurs it proceeds from a state of relative globality and lack of differentiation to a state of increasing differentiation, articulation, and hierarchic integration" (Werner, 1957, p. 126). Those three endpoints, vague as they are, nevertheless must be dealt with simultaneously: This kind of development, said to proceed simultaneously from undifferentiated to differentiated, from unintegrated to integrated, from rigid to flexible, from unstable to stable, etc., thereby requires the theorist (and observer) to define a differentiation that is not the opposite of integration, flexibility, stability, etc., even though the everyday connotations of those terms may cast them as polarities rather than concomitants.

Although Werner's approach is not typical of contemporary structural or organismic approaches to development (see Glick, 1992), his orthogenetic principle seems prototypical for them, even paradigmatic. In some form or another, structural approaches postulate progression from state to state through some sort of structural reorganization, be it one of differentiation and integration, or one that simply points to "qualitative" changes in some sort of capacity, ability, or cognitive functioning. Thus, development is often characterized as an invariant sequence of stages of psychological functioning, whose timing could be accelerated or retarded by external forces, but only to a limited extent, and whose organizational structure is largely immune to such forces.

Our emerging argument—that development can be characterized by structure and age—is not meant to be categorical. Developmental change is better conceptualized as some mixture of these characterizations, and we should postulate mechanisms that control that mixture, and that can be confirmed by research. Perhaps a minimal definition of development should cite a lawful succession of seemingly universal states, stages, age-correlated abilities, etc., to mark what seem to be qualitatively different behavioral organizations, each dependent on the preceding or on age. But that kind of definition is indeed minimal; it merely notes a regularity in the behavioral content of stages, and supposes a lawfulness in their sequence, or in their dependence on age. Developmentalists usually supplement that minimalism with additional notions of gradualness, purposiveness, progressiveness, or directionality.

Progression and Development

Lamarck provides an instructive case in point. He saw evolution as moving progressively toward an idealized form. He could not specify the ideal *a priori*; he could only hope eventually to induce it from the changes that had been and would be seen to occur. Thus he would be forced to interpret those changes as progressive, would require a principle of progressivity to do so, and would either induce it or invent it (which sometimes are the same process). Developmentalists place themselves in a similar situation, when they make development refer to an overall continuity in attaining higher, more complex, more rational, more adaptive, or more *something* forms of being. Small wonder that its end points are sometimes described as intellectual and aesthetic pinnacles (Baldwin, 1902), equilibrations finally at the highest levels of cognitive functioning (Piaget, 1971), a more mature sexuality (Freud, 1905), an integrated self (Erikson, 1950), a rational moral philosophy (Kohlberg, Levine, & Hewer, 1983), awareness of one's role in culture and ecology (Bronfenbrenner, 1979), and still others (see, Gollin, 1981; Kagan, 1983; Morss, 1990), either singly or in various combinations.

Clearly, these uniquely developmental supplements are meant to be more than romantic metaphors; they are used as central concepts in describing how development proceeds. They may often be intended to also explain why development proceeds as it does, and so become regulatory principles; an interesting question is to what extent they succeed in that. The answers to that question in turn will hinge on what we mean by explanation; within the community of developmentalists and quasi-developmentalists, we probably mean some quite different things. And even when we have opted for a linear concept of development driven either by its end state or by the need to maintain some equilibrium, we at least sometimes are fascinated by counter-examples. Some we find in dynamical systems theory, wherein we discern processes that create order from an initial disorder (or chaos), yet have no necessary or specifiable end state, goal, or equilibrium to maintain (Gleick, 1987). Others we find in the genetic algorithms (Holland, 1992), wherein we choose a goal, end state, or solution, and then search for the total diversity of methods that could accomplish it. In the genetic algorithms, organized complexity evolves not from a supreme organizing principle governing the parts of a system, but from simple rules, each of which governs the interactions between some of those parts.

Both of those formulae might be a fair characterization of the reinforcement, discrimination, and other behavior-shaping and behavior-organizing contingencies that behavior analysts see as the "analytic" processes of development. These contingencies are in theory, and to a considerable degree in fact, capable of taking any initially disordered or partially ordered state of behavior and making it into any of a wide diversity of better, more thoroughly, or at least differently ordered end states, none of which need be an end state; alternatively, given an arbitrarily chosen end state, we can see a considerable number of programmed sequences of those contingencies capable of achieving that end state.

However explanatory they may prove to be, these metaphors for progress and directionality are so central to mainstream developmental psychology that even contextualist approaches like Lerner's (1986) add organismic models to give direction and order. Otherwise, the approach would seem dispersive and nondirectional, as contextualist world views must (Pepper, 1942). Perhaps what we mean by contextualist world views are any views burdened by too many well established facts to allow a small, simple set of principles to explain them all.

Several authors have pointed to the biological origin of the concepts of gradualness, purposiveness, progressiveness, and directionality, and the impact they have had on mainstream developmental psychology—notably Costall (1986), Ghiselin (1986), and Morss (1990). Of these, Morss (1990) is most interesting for our present discussion, because he argues that the biological and philosophical concepts of change that have shaped the whole of developmental psychology are outdated: They represent a preDarwinian concept of evolution and an eighteenth-century concept of associationism.

Interestingly, Morss (1990) did not review a behavior-analytic view of development. Of the central contributors to behavior-analytic science, he briefly mentioned J. B. Watson as a "minor figure." But even so, Morss recognized that it was Watson's behavioral formulations rather than Thorndike's Darwinistic arguments "that seemed to provide the major alternative to recapitulationary viewpoints in the early decades of the present century" (p. 53). However, that alternative was often transformed by its audience into a naive environmentalism (i.e., ignoring biological factors) and a naive reductionism (i.e., reducing the individual's complex behavior to movements of glands and muscles). This outlook is still used to describe Watson's position—or what some theorists would like Watson's position to be, so that it will prove easy to controvert—and it is also extended increasingly to modern behavior analysis.

Behavior-Analytic Views of Development

Modern behavior analysis does indeed constitute a challenge to any teleological components of developmental theories, and to any theorists who assume that because orderliness can be driven by its end state, it always is. In addition, behavior-analytic views are not committed in principle to a purely environmental account of behavior. Interestingly, Watson did not seem to subscribe to that pure an account, either, although it is often claimed that he did. Notice that in his now infamous quote, "give me a dozen healthy infants, well formed, and my own specified world to bring them up..." (1926, p. 10), he did not ask for just any babies, but for "healthy," "well formed" ones. His writings do not deny the role of biology in the account of behavior; they do oppose the unempirical "biologizing" of behavior, and any corollary idea that must see only biological determinism in all psychological events. Thus, Watson was largely silent on the biological mechanisms of development, because he needed first direct empirical evidence of their existence. (Yet he did question the "evidence of inferiority in the negro race"–p. 10). Modern behavior analysis has further clarified the reality of organismic-environmental interactions. It recognizes that "every psychological occurrence is in itself a biological occurrence" (Bijou & Baer, 1961, p. 10), and that both biological descriptions and psychological descriptions are legitimate and desirable. However, although behavior analysis recognizes the necessary role of biological factors, its account of behavior is complementary to biology rather than reduced to it. (We shall return to this issue.). Furthermore, its concept of environment has become broad enough to encompass biological events as part of the environment, and at the same time keep the social and cultural factors of development that Morss could see any biological analysis of development would require.

Similar to modern evolutionary theory, behavior analysis is free of purpose, intention, and predetermined design as explanations of behavior change. It offers a logical analysis for abandoning those explanations, and when it analyzes the causal roles of environment, it does so, ultimately, in terms of selection by environmental consequences. That may seem to invite two classes of teleological restatement: (1) Development is driven by its end state, which is to maximize some of those consequences and minimize others of them. But that is a logical error; it creates a goal of change by equating it to the processes of change. The processes are only processes. (2) Development is driven by its end state, which is to maximize a generalized "control" over all those consequences. But the concept of generalized control is nothing but a concept, a behavior of the theorist; it is not an event that could be programmed as a consequence of a behavior that might "develop" that behavior. Instead, we should recognize that we can use some real events to establish behaviors that control *those* real events, that we can use the same real events to establish behaviors that an observer will interpret as "helplessness," that both outcomes represent the results of what are fundamentally the same processes, and that neither outcome is inevitable.

The idea that behavior change processes can accomplish any topography of behavior change, and yet remain the same processes no matter what topographies they accomplish, is one of the central tenets of the behavior analysis espoused by Skinner (1981). For behavior analysis, development is a process of individualization. The individual's behavior ultimately is accounted for by the interplay of phylogenic contingencies of survival and ontogenic contingencies of reinforcement and punishment, of which cultural practices are a special case. In Skinner's (1969) words: "Phylogenic contingencies are responsible for the fact that men respond to stimuli, act upon the environment, and change their behavior under contingencies of reinforcement....Ontogenic contingencies are responsible for the fact that a man reacts to only some of the stimuli to which he is sensitive, makes only some of the responses of which he is capable, and does so with given probabilities upon given occasions" (p. 296). Is it not interesting that the actual position is consistently ignored, and is instead equated to the naive environmentalism imputed to Watson, thereby to become easy to dismiss? This misattribution still haunts behavior analysis. (Is it not interesting that almost every modern scholarly view of behavior analysis is identical to some journalist's 1971 account of it in Time magazine, when its cover story cited Skinner as the most influential American psychologist? If Time was correct in so labelling Skinner, it thereby became his successor: It apparently is, or might as well have been, the most influential source for subsequent textbook authors attempting to characterize something called behaviorism. It must be remembered, of course, that the cost of an accurate account is to read several thousand pages. Start with Zuriff, 1985. By the same token, it must be remembered that we may not have read all the relevant pages in constructing this comparison and contrast of a behavior-analytic view of development with other views. Be warned.)

Progressive Changes

A little more than 30 years ago Bijou and Baer (1961) defined psychological development as "progressive changes in the way an organism's behavior interacts with the environment" (p. 1). However, in their approach, "progressive" was not an essential qualification, as it has been and is in so many other approaches. That kind of "progressive" did not require developmental changes to be unidirectional movements toward some externally defined ideal of improvement, betterment, or finality. Thus it did not mean to limit the scope of inquiry to such cases. This was not always understood, and so its updated definition added the word "regressions" (Bijou & Baer, 1978; Bijou, 1989). Nonetheless, the significance of progression-regression seemed relevant to a behavior analysis of development in at least two contexts.

1. One context was to describe successive qualitative differences in organism-environment interactions. The heuristic exemplar offered by Bijou and Baer compared the eating interactions of an infant and a toddler. In both cases, the effects of eating are essentially the same. In both cases, deprivation is an important setting factor, but with some difference in how quickly and severely it operates since the last meal. However, some stimulus and response factors change significantly: Aspects of the breast and its milk are operative stimuli for an infant's sucking-swallowing chains; aspects of quite different objects, such as cereal, juice, spoons, and cups are operative stimuli for the toddler's manipulation-chewing-swallowing chains. In this example, the changes may be called "progressive," but doing so does not alter the nature of the behavior changes in any essential way. The only role intended for "progressive" is to acknowledge that each successive behavior change is made on the basis of the environment-behavior interactions that precede it—that any behavior change is

always built on the interactions already existent in the organism's interactions with its own characteristics and its environment.

Giving "progressive" any other meaning complicates analysis, perhaps unnecessarily and fruitlessly, just as do the concepts of pathology, abnormality, delay, and retardation when they are imposed on behavioral processes. They impose external criteria where nature does not demand it (cf. Baer, 1985).

2. A second context was to single out developmental disciplines as specially concerned not merely with the interactions immediately preceding any behavior change, but with as much of the entire span of historical variables that would prove relevant: "with the effect of past interactions on present interactions" (Bijou & Baer, 1961, p. 14).

Neither of these purposes differentiates developmental behavior analysis from behavior analysis in general. Behavior analysis remains an unencumbered description of developmental phenomena: orderly changes in the ways an organism's behavior interacts with the organism's characteristics and its environment, and with changes in the organism's characteristics and environment. We call these changes orderly because they may prove predictable, especially at certain points in certain sequences. And we can call these changes orderly for a better reason: that they prove to be experimentally controllable. If we can arrange the conditions for their occurrence, we can be useful as well as understanding.

We note that several developmental theories could have predicted at least some of those changes, and that several others could postdict them. Thus, it is only a personal value to prefer looking for order where we are curious about order, and to explain it by the processes that allow us to gain experimental control of it, rather than to begin looking for order where a theory predicts it will be found, and to remain interested in the theory even when experimental control over its explanatory causes typically proves impossible. Clearly, both strategies characterize the behavior of scientists.

Developmental Stages and Behavior-Analytic Cusps

The stage concept is another important part of mainstream developmental psychology that needs consideration within the behavior-analytic approach. We can all see that development progresses in a stage-like manner, yet the meaning of stage remains ambiguous. Perhaps that is why we can all see that development proceeds that way. Piaget had to complain about its imprecise use in other psychologies:

Psychologists have relied too much on the notion of stage. Some speak as though it were nothing but a series of actions, not always, though 'generally,' in a constant order, and supposedly sharing a dominant characteristic, nothing more—which opens the door to arbitrary thinking. This is what Freud means by stages... (1971, p. 17).

Piaget's stage concept requires three criteria:

First, where the series of actions is constant [independent of chronological age]; second, where each stage is determined not merely by a dominant property but by a whole structure which characterizes all further actions that belong to this stage; third, where these structures offer a process of integration such that each one is prepared by the preceding one and integrated into the one that follows. (p. 17)

The second criterion is interestingly agreeable to behavior analysts: Piaget was not satisfied with mere action; he required interaction. (Behavior analysis might well require a more operational specification of just what interacts with just what, but it is an agreeable and very basic principle.) This insistence on interaction can be seen most clearly in Piaget's description of the early behavior of the sensori-motor stage, the essence of which is the reflex and the conditioned reflex. The major problem a behavior-analytic approach will find in this conceptualization is its unnecessary reliance on unobservable, internalized, and therefore inferred, schemata.

For Piaget, conditioning works because it interacts with a sensory schema designed to note stimulus-stimulus (and, we might as well add, response-stimulus and stimulus-response-stimulus) correlations in the environment (Piaget & Inhelder, 1969). We do not know that such a schema exists, of course; the argument is inferential. If such a schema existed, it would constitute a higher-level explanation of the observable facts of conditioned reflexes. The underlying strategic question is whether we value apparently higher-level explanations more than we value verifiable explanations.

In modern psychology, the stage concept remains ambiguous and diverse. As discussed by Flavell (1982), Lerner (1986), and Wohlwill (1973), it refers vaguely to a structure that guides action, a structure said to be universal, qualitative, mental, cognitive, and moral—whatever needs explanation. Interestingly, cognitive psychologists agree that a person's developmental stage or level should "ideally be based on that person's modal response pattern" (Lerner, 1986, p. 223). Many other stage principles have emerged in developmental psychology. In their multiplicity, they seem to suggest that the important unresolved questions are the criteria that will determine how to define or identify a stage, how many stages are needed for reasonable explanation, and, interactive with that, how to define transitions from one stage to the next. (See Brainerd, 1978, for comment and an illustrative example of these unresolved questions.)

Some developmental psychologists (e.g., Flavell, 1982; Fisher, 1980) are pessimistic about achieving an overall picture of cognitive development based on the stage concept. They have begun to look instead for invariant sequences within much more restricted domains: e.g., skill acquisition (Fisher, 1980), social skills (Damon, 1977), word acquisition (Clark, 1973) and the sophistication of rules used in certain abstracted forms of problem-solving (Siegler, 1981). For the most part, these relatively new ventures are descriptions of particular developmental sequences, pursued as if such facts can eventually lead to explanatory principles. Even so, from a behavior-analytic point of view, they can represent an admirable development within the discipline. Smaller arenas of analysis allow a much more intimate interaction between research and data, and they allow more of the data to be experimental, very much in accord with behavior-analytic values and strategies. More important, restricting analysis to much smaller domains indirectly parallels another strategy of behavior analysis: If (1) behaviors are studied as the fundamental topic of analysis, and if (2) most of the analysis in hand so far is based on the extreme power of certain environmental contingencies (such as reinforcement and discrimination contingencies) to determine how the response that contacts those contingencies will operate in the future, then (3) it is likely that every response of an organism that could meet different environmental contingencies than another response meets is to that extent likely to come under different control than that other response, and if that is an impressive extent, then (4) an overarching stage-like organization of a great deal of the organism's behavior is improbable, and our research *ought* to look first for regularity in much smaller domains, and then ask about experimental control of some of that regularity within those domains. True, behavior analysis sketches some mechanisms for bringing a great deal of an organism's behavior under homogeneous control, as if something that could be called a stage were operative—but those mechanisms are difficult to make happen and maintain on a large scale, which adds even more to a disciplinary scepticism about the likelihood of overarching stages.

For behavior analysis, the stage concept seems neither essential nor explanatory; but it is clearly heuristic. It is a convenient way to organize the immense and complex scope of what we know and would like to know about life-span behavior changes. We reach for the convenience of stage segmentation to help describe those transitions when interactions change in qualitatively different ways and remain stable for enough time to justify a shift in conceptualizing what is happening. That criterion has suggested, for a start, a sequence of foundational, basic, and societal stages, much as J. R. Kantor proposed in 1959. When the changes described by a stage concept show great generality across behaviors, settings, and contexts, the concept of stage becomes correspondingly serious; when we know, or think we know, how to diminish or disassemble some of that generality by fairly straightforward environmental interventions (as behavior analysts at least think they know for at least some cases), the concept of stage becomes correspondingly more arbitrary.

However, the moment when a child achieves generalized imitation may be seen as a developmental stage by the same criteria, and if not as a developmental stage, then as a developmental *cusp*: It marks a time when the expansion of the child's repertoire is likely to become explosive, and when the deliberate management of the child's behavior becomes pragmatically different than it was before. The moment when a child learns to read skillfully marks another such stage, and if not a stage, then again a cusp. A cusp is an interaction, or complex of interactions, that enables access to new reinforcers, new contingencies, and new communities of reinforcement and contingencies—and thus to new behaviors. And to new cusps, not all of which need be seen by all of us as positive or desirable. Introducing a child to an addiction is an obvious example of a cusp that most of us will deplore; teaching a child to always seek help rather than ever master the task at hand is a more subtle example.

In less systematic terms, a developmental cusp is a special instance of change; whether it is seen as a change in behavior, skill, ability, discrimination, perception, affect, or motivation, nevertheless it is crucial to what should or can come next in development. A cusp is a change that (1) is often difficult, tedious, subtle, or otherwise problematic to accomplish, yet (2) if not made, means that little or no further development is possible in its realm (and perhaps in several realms); but (3) once it is made, a significant set of subsequent developments suddenly becomes easy or otherwise highly probable, which (4) bring the developing organism into contact with other cusps crucial to further, more complex, or more refined development in a thereby steadily expanding, steadily more interactive realm.

Cusps can range from quite large to quite small changes. An obvious example of the former is generalized imitation: For children who acquire this skill, quite casual instruction and demonstration will accomplish a wealth of social, communicative, self-help, and motor-skill advances that would prove very difficult to convey to children who do not acquire it. An example of the latter is seen in an anecdote from a parent rearing a profoundly retarded child at home: Teaching this child to manipulate the door and screen-door latches separating her from the outside fenced yard transformed her from a child who tried, often unsuccessfully, to request that doors be opened for her frequently throughout the day, to one who could manage them herself, which transformed her opportunities for learning and activity from mainly indoor ones, obviously enhanced her control over some of her daily life, and transformed her family's perception of her from eternal frequent problem to a learner whose skill acquisitions could improve everyone's life—from someone to be managed into someone to be taught more and more independence.

For children we call normal, many cusps are achieved and surmounted through the ordinary events of life. The children we call deviant are often enough called that because they have not acquired some cusps crucial to what we will call normalcy through their everyday experience. Yet all the literature of applied behavior analysis argues that these cusps are learnable by even severely deviant children, given careful task analysis and powerful, systematic teaching technique.

Thus, normal children get through cusps to what follows, usually by extensive if casual teaching (e.g., imitation and spoken language), and aided by various skills acquired through prior cusps that makes them better and better at self-teaching (e.g., self-regulation); less fortunate, less endowed, less skilled, and less well taught children do not, and become problems in diagnostic labelling and the pragmatics of careful teaching. The pragmatic is not the theoretical; the principles of behavior change do not change at the point of a cusp, but results and techniques can.

Stages have always lent themselves to finer divisions and revised boundaries; those refinements are often based on the cusps of development (cf. Bijou, 1989). In many ways, some of the cusps may prove more interesting in a behavior-analytic approach than the stages within which they occur.

Clearly, developmental cusps can be organized on at least two continua: (1) the difficulty of accomplishing the cusp, and (2) the scope, magnitude, and value of the behavior changes and new opportunities that getting by the cusp enables. Both have obvious significance for development: Easy cusps are more likely to be achieved than difficult ones, and thus the changes they enable are more likely to occur; and cusps that enable many wide-ranging subsequent behavior changes of great use in the organism's environment will be seen as more developmentally significant than cusps that enable few, highly similar changes of little use.

All of these parameters are subject to contextual evaluation. For example, in the authors' experience, getting to enter a university was a cusp: It made a great difference in the character of much of our subsequent lives. Some of that difference lay in the nature of what happened during those years, and some of it lay in the credential that those years produced. Others testify differently: What happened during those years made little difference in their current or subsequent lives—it was "just four more years of high school, but harder" and they "don't remember anything they learned for those tests"—but the credential achieved made a considerable difference in what happened next. Still others say virtually the reverse—that what the university taught them enduringly enriched their subsequent lives, but the credential was never used.

For the second author, soon after entry to the university, one minute finally devoted to learning the several meanings of a term—"criterion," plural "criteria"—proved to be a significant cusp within the larger cusp of what the university would accomplish: Prior to that knowledge, lecturers' explanations of how decisions were justified in intellectual discourse often seemed incomprehensible; subsequently, they were clear, which opened the door to intelligent counter-argument, which in turn opened the door to further shaping.

Thus, the time and difficulty of getting by a cusp has little relation to the scope and value of what it enables; quick, easy cusps can have large consequences, and long, difficult cusps can have small ones. All these parameters depend on context, and much of what we mean by context consists of what other cusps the organism has passed. Sequence, both necessary and merely societal, can be essential to this concept of development; but it is the cusps that need to be analyzed first. As we understand them, we will then be in better position to learn when their sequences are crucial.

Behavior-Environment Interaction

So far the issue has been the concepts of progression, which may be seen as a sequence of stages, or as a sequence of cusps. It is time to integrate the issue of interaction. Once again, the behavior-analytic position is usually misunderstood or fractionated by developmental theorists, who see behavior analysis as adhering to only the simplest forms of interaction—sometimes as nothing more than reinforcement, sometimes as those considered "mechanistic" (Lerner, 1986; Overton & Reese, 1973; Reese & Overton, 1970). Although Skinner did not, some developmentalists characterize his concept of reflex as a response automatically, inevitably, and hence "mechanically" elicited by the relevant stimulus; thus they recall, label, and maintain a now largely extinct, largely fictitious event known as S-R psychology. This restricted characterization has made the behavior-analytic view an easy target for criticism, and it certainly contributes by default to the strength of an alternative formulation, such as any of the several organismic models. It also leaves behavior analysts looking in puzzlement for a colleague who does that kind of S-R work, or explains it that way.

Similarly, the behavior-analytic view has been and still is characterized from outside as nothing but environmentalist, such that it must see the organism as either passive, reactive, or empty, like a machine prior to its switch closure or a puppet prior to its string jerk. Behavior analysis has thus been seen as elementarist, reducing human function to the elements of those stimulus-response connections, as if they could be combined by the organism's teachers but never by the organism into a new, emergent behavior. In these ways, behavior analysis was reduced to knowing nothing more than how to increase the number of stimulus-response connections in an organism's repertoire. Skinner (1953) denied that view; he argued that the organism is not a machine. We may understand its ways through the same analytic methods we would apply to understanding a machine, but we will find that, unlike a machine, its behaviors are determined by their consequences much more than by its structure.

Where did these views of behavior analysis develop? One is tempted to invoke the Freudian mechanism of fixation to explain their insistence and durability—but in what frustrations of what stage of psychosexual development? Neither Skinner nor Bijou and Baer offered this view of interaction between the organism and its environment. Perhaps the impetus for seeing nothing but robot-like interactions in the behavior-analytic view arose from propositions like the following: "An interaction between behavior and environment means simply that a given response may be expected to occur or not, depending on the stimulation the environment provides" (Bijou & Baer, 1961, p. 2). But here Bijou and Baer were only defining the necessary structure of an organism-environment interaction, not characterizing them all, and not establishing a single direction of causality. Changes in a response should be related to the responsible prior changes in the environment, and to the systematic consequent changes in the environment, which in turn should be related to any further changes in the response, and so on. Anything to be termed an interaction between behavior and environment should include all these components. Thus their heuristic exemplar noted that sudden exposure to bright sunlight can cause a person to squint, which reduces the visual field, thereby negatively reinforcing squinting as a response to sunlight, but also producing some strain, which in turn leads to a search for sunglasses, which, found and worn, reduces both the sunlight and the strain, etc. We should note, as Bijou and Baer did, that this exemplary interaction was not meant to characterize development, only the continuity of most interactions between the organism and its environment—"how behavior affects environment and environment affects behavior" (Bijou & Baer, 1978, p. 2). These were successive interactions, and in a trivial sense they were progressive. However, much of this progression (sunlight-squint-relief-strain) could have occurred at almost any time in the organism's post-infancy life; there is little systematic or important dependence of these interactions on the preceding ones. However, the final step of strain-sunglasses reminds us that almost any instance of behavior can reflect a prior history: It is only children who have learned about sunglasses and have access to them who will respond to eye-strain in that way; younger or less advantaged children will respond with perhaps a turn of the head away from the light, a shielding hand, or a search for shade. And each of those skills is in turn a product of some small prior history of behavior-environment interaction. Even so, they all represent interactions that could occur at a very wide range of moments in a child's development.

Reading beyond page 2 of Bijou and Baer (1961, 1978) will reveal a full exposition of what is meant by behavior-analytic interactions relative to a concept of development. Indeed, the very next paragraph noted that a toddler's eating represents a qualitatively different interaction from an infant's eating, by virtue of the elements changed in the interaction (as noted earlier here). We may remind ourselves that when an infant acquires the skills of self-controlled eating with utensils and containers, another of those developmental cusps has been attained: the domain of eating will be pragmatically different thereafter, even though the laws of behavior have not changed.

We should also ask for the quantitative changes in the toddler's eating that make it qualitatively different from the infant's, so that we can see more clearly what we mean. For one thing, the infant's nipple-sucking has gone to zero rate; for another, hand motions that grasp and manipulate forks, spoons, and cups have gone from zero rate to high rates; for another, the stimuli that previously had zero control over those manipulations now have near-100% probability of evoking them; for yet another, the responsiveness of the feeding interactions to the toddler's state of food deprivation has become less intense than it was in the infant, in terms of hours of deprivation necessary to produce the same reliability of these interactions; etc. What we will call a qualitative change can often be described with this kind of quantitative specification, but usually need not be for ordinary communication (and perhaps had better not be for ordinary communication). However, when communication is not ordinary, but instead is about the philosophical assumptions underlying an approach, the convenience of shorthand expressions such as "qualitative changes" should at least momentarily give way to quantitative specification. There is a question to be asked: Can every qualitative change be reduced to the quantitative presence or absence of certain elements? Tchaikovsky and Shostakovich might well be seen as qualitatively different composers, yet each is essentially a producer of sound patterns. The question is the extent to which their differences can be reduced to the relative frequencies of certain sound patterns, kinds of sound patterns, and patterns of sound patterns in each one's composing.

Is asking that kind of question the analytic habit that is seen as mechanistic? The result need not look like a mechanism; it will be a statement of the controlling variables and the contextual factors that determine their effectiveness. What is at issue is lawfulness, not mechanism. The lawfulness is there to be seen; it is not a matter of choice. If a mechanism is there as well, it should be discovered and proven, not presumed.

Perhaps we should also remember Watson's (1919) words:

A marine gas engine is made up of a number of parts, such for example as the carburetor, the pump, the magneto, the valve system, the cylinders with their pistons and rings, connecting rods, etc. Separate tests of each part may show that it functions perfectly when working alone....Unless all the parts are properly interconnected and timed the engine as a whole will not perform its function, that is, *turn the propeller*. When we speak of the action of the individual as a whole, we mean something of this nature....No mechanical contrivance yet hit upon approaches the human organism in its multiplicity of possible functions and in the rapidity with which co-ordinations of separate functions can be so rapidly shifted for each new duty of the machine as a whole. (p. 392)

Watson also knew that only when we know "enough about the parts of any mechanical contrivance, the nature of the interlocking systems and the various interdependent functions, we can make safe predictions about how it will work under new conditions or specify the changes which will have to be made if the contrivance must perform some new function" (p. 393). That is mechanism, no doubt. The interesting question for here is whether human development can be understood well enough to make safe predictions about how it will go in new conditions, or how it can be made to go better when it has gone badly. Perhaps it is Mechanism that insists on that as the goal; perhaps it is behavior analytic to instead ask how closely we can approximate any of that.

Verifiability and the Concept of Development

So far, this discussion of behavior analysis and its interaction with the conventional notion of development and its own concept of development has been theoretical. An alternative approach would ask first not what we insist is the proper way to think about these problems, but rather what we can prove about them. That might lead us to the following interesting null hypothesis: Consider the possibility that, upon analysis, development will prove to be a negatively defined concept. That is, development will be the label applied only to processes that cannot be seen in terms of simpler or more familiar concepts. (Whether those processes that cannot be seen in terms of simpler or more familiar concepts can eventually be seen (seen, not postulated) in terms of larger or more complex concepts remains to be seen, not taken for granted.)

Suppose that, much as did Bijou and Baer (1961), we characterize development as progressive, orderly changes in the way an organism's behavior interacts with its environment. We call these changes progressive if they seem to accomplish a greater capability of the organism. We call them orderly if they seem predictable; they may prove predictable because they emerge dependably at certain ages, or because they emerge dependably in certain sequences, or because they emerge just as some theory predicts.

Progressive, orderly changes in the way an organism's behavior interacts with its environment are nonetheless behavior changes. We know a fair amount about changing behavior by managing the way it interacts with its environment; and that knowledge has been organized as a discipline. The name of that discipline is not developmental psychology but behavior analysis. Our question here might be stated as whether what we know about behavior analysis is sufficient to explain what we need to know about progressive, orderly behavior changes; but a better question would be whether the strategies that behavior analysis uses to learn more about behavior changes will be sufficient to learn what we need to know about progressive, orderly behavior changes. If so, then the discipline of behavior analysis may replace the discipline of developmental psychology (depending, of course, on how each of us in that "we" decides how much we need to know). If not, then the interesting question is what else we must know to explain progressive, orderly changes in the way an organism's behavior interacts with its environment, and whether that something else can be understood by and integrated into behavior analysis, and if so, whether the result is what should be called developmental psychology.

The simplest possibility is that by development, we mean no more than the description of the progressions and order that typify the behavior of the organism under study—a listing of the orders in which they change and the ages at which that usually happens. Description does not require explanation, and often proceeds without it. Indeed, occasionally the content of developmental psychology has been nothing more than a description of the typical orders in which children's behavior change, and the ages at which that usually happens.

But psychology, like most sciences, usually demands a reason for what it can describe. Among the natural sciences, psychology is perhaps distinctively likely to invent reasons rather than discover them, and perhaps is distinctively likely to fall into tautology when doing so. Thus a few descriptions of behavior changes as usually occurring at certain ages have also made age seem the explanation for those changes, as if to say that if they usually occur at those ages, those ages must have caused them to occur. Similarly, a few descriptions of behavior changes as usually occurring in certain sequences have also made sequence seem the explanation for those changes, as if to say that if one usually occurs after another has occurred, the occurrence of the first must have caused the occurrence of the second.

However, tautology is usually seen for what it is—eventually. When that happens, then either the tautology must be abandoned as nonexplanatory, or an explanatory mechanism must be found that encompasses it, or, if finding one seems too tedious, then one may be invented, the positive word for which is "inferred." Thus age, when seen as a tautological explanation of age-related behavior changes, has sometimes been transformed into an inferred age-correlated biological mechanism: We are told that it is of course not age that causes age-related behavior changes, but maturational changes in the organism's structures, musculature, neural operations, and biochemical processes that occur at those ages and thereby enable or produce those behavior changes.

If these maturational causes could be specified and experimentally proven as biological processes, that would of course be superb science. It would also create an occasion for even more superb science: If the reason that behavior changes so reliably at certain ages is that biology changes so reliably at those ages, then we need to explain why biology changes so reliably at those ages. The same drama may be played out again: We may tautologically see age as the cause, not of behavior change this time, but of biological change. As soon as we recognize that as tautology, we shall then have to find biological mechanisms that explain why those biological changes occur at those times; as ever, we shall have the opportunity to find their real causes, or to invent some. Invention is always easier and quicker. Occasionally, it provokes the analysis of real causes; often, it does not, and remains a work of art. Science inventions invite evaluation by science criteria; when they fail to provoke verifiable analyses, perhaps they then invite evaluation by art criteria.

Indeed, mere inference is often called science; but, as sciences go, it is surely one of the cheaper forms. Perhaps that is why the insistence that age regularities must be based in biology is sometimes used by theorists who have never held a scalpel in hand, never inserted an electrode in a nervous system, never altered an endocrine balance, never blocked an enzyme receptor, and never studied the relevant biology beyond the introductory level.

We do not deny the involvement of biology in much of what we call development; it seems undoubtable. For us, the point is to discover the biology, not merely invent it. Discovery, whether prompted by verifiable invention or not, requires training in biology, which usually is quite different from training in psychology. Consequently, we do not do it ourselves; we watch respectfully as those who know how discover it—but we ignore those who only invent it.

Similarly, sequence, when seen as a tautological explanation of typically sequential behavior changes, has sometimes been transformed into a sequence-correlated mechanism, such as prerequisite necessity. We are then told that it is of course not sequence that explains sequential behavior changes, but the fact that each is prerequisite for the following one. Quite often, we are told that each behavior is a member of a schematic class or stage of thinking or perception, and that it is less the sequence of the behaviors than the sequence of those stages that we should understand—their sequence is the true cause of the sequence of their members.

Whether we are discussing a sequence of behaviors or a sequence of hypothetical stages that organize them, we still need to understand that sequential dependency. A stage concept may well seem to explain the behaviors that belong to it, but a sequence of stages needs explaining just as much as a sequence of behaviors. Whether we are discussing a stage or a behavioral member of a stage, if the nature of each one's dependency on the preceding one could be specified and experimentally proven as such, that would of course be superb science. However, there is again a cheaper alternative; it is to infer that some kind of dependency must be operative.

Again, it is remarkable how often this cheaper alternative is used by theorists who have never task-analyzed a problem or, having hypothesized a task analysis for their problem, have never tested its reality, its efficiency, its necessity, or its alternatives (but cf. Siegler, 1981, for an interesting counter-example).

Perhaps this is the moment in evaluating any concept of development to inquire into the meaning of prerequisite. We shall begin with the problem of proving that when one behavior almost always emerges before another, the one that emerges first is prerequisite to the one that emerges subsequently. But first note that the strategy of beginning with proof is both arbitrary and crucial to what follows; it is a strategy quite different from its more popular alternative, which is to start with theory.

How can we prove that First Behavior is a prerequisite for Second Behavior? We might show that we have never found Second Behavior in the absence of an older First Behavior. But that is no proof of anything; it is merely a description of the generality of the sequence that provoked our inquiry. Our question is about necessity, not generality; if necessity could be proven, generality would follow automatically; but if generality is proven, that does not establish necessity. Believing that it does is a standard logical error exposed as such in all introductory logic courses, where it is labelled as affirming the consequent. (Often it is accompanied by a homely case in point: Since dogs are hairy, live with humans, and have four legs, a tail, and sharp teeth, then the organism meowing at the door, which also is hairy, lives with humans, and has four legs, a tail, and sharp teeth, must be a dog.)

Consider a reduction to absurdity: You will never see piano-playing in any child who had not previously exhibited the Moro reflex; but most of you do not see the Moro reflex as a prerequisite for piano-playing. Of course, one might claim that the Moro is evidence of the integrity of the nervous system, and claim that integrity of the nervous system is a prerequisite for piano-playing. But first, note that it is not the Moro that is established as prerequisite by that argument; it is something called the integrity of the nervous system. Second, and more important, note that terms like "the integrity of the nervous system" have no useful meaning, although they are good show business. What we need to understand is how the nervous system underlies and enables behaviors like piano-playing; very likely we shall eventually understand that, but only through many decades of extensive, painstaking, difficult-to-predict research. When we do understand it, we may also see what connection the Moro reflex has to the way in which the nervous system mediates piano-playing, and then we may be in a position to evaluate its importance as a prerequisite for piano-playing, or, perhaps, as a nonprerequisite but useful tracer variable. Right now, it is difficult to be optimistic about its usefulness in either role. Yet we never see piano-playing not preceded by the Moro.

How else could we prove the necessity of First Behavior for Second Behavior? We might find that we could experimentally control First Behavior; if so, we could ask if when we cause it to emerge, Second Behavior invariably follows it on some predictable timetable. If we showed that, it would be superb science, but it would have proven the sufficiency of First Behavior for Second Behavior, not its necessity.

We would need to show as well that as long as we prevent the emergence of First Behavior, we never see the emergence of Second Behavior. Events other than First Behavior might also be sufficient to provoke the emergence of Second Behavior, yet we have not looked for any such events.

Then perhaps we should look for some. We need to show more than that when we cause First Behavior, we get Second Behavior thereafter. We also need to show that as long as we prevent First Behavior, we never see Second Behavior emerge, even though we allow all other possible causes of Second Behavior to occur. The logic of that tactic is excellent, but there are three impossibilities in it: One is that "never" is too long a time for definitive research; another is that we do not know what range of possible other causes of Second Behavior to promote while we are preventing First Behavior; and the third is that merely allowing "all" other possible causes to occur while we are preventing First Behavior is intrinsically inconclusive, because for all we know, the membership of that "all" may be very improbable events, for which waiting may take too long for definitive research.

It begins to look as if there is no practical way to prove that First Behavior is a prerequisite for Second Behavior. But it also appears that we might readily prove that First Behavior is not a prerequisite for Second Behavior: In the process of preventing First Behavior while we await or promote the occurrence of any other events that might cause Second Behavior, we might find one. The discovery of just one cause of Second Behavior other than First Behavior is enough to show that First Behavior is not prerequisite to Second Behavior; it is merely sufficient for Second Behavior.

Then perhaps we cannot build a verifiable developmental psychology on the concept of prerequisites. To this there are of course two replies: (1) The very common reply is to deny that a verifiable developmental psychology was ever wanted all that much, and to assert that inferential theory not only can fill the gaps where proof is missing, but can indeed be more comprehensive, cohesive, logical, satisfying, postdictive, and, in short, more beautiful than mere proofs, which invariably prove to be incomplete. To this very frequent assertion, we nod respectfully—it is the majority view—but we also report that, perverse as it may be, we find beauty elsewhere, especially in proof. (2) The other reply is that those few of us committed to a verifiable discipline may still build a developmental psychology on our increasing knowledge of the specific First Behaviors that are sufficient, even if not prerequisite, for certain Second Behaviors. However, implicit in a commitment to proof is a commitment to provable explanation; the next question must be to ask for an empirically verifiable or falsifiable hypothesis about why First Behavior is sufficient to evoke Second Behavior.

Behavior Analysis and the Explanation of Development

It is time to return to our underlying question: whether what we know about behavior analysis is sufficient to explain what we need to know about progressive, orderly behavior changes, and whether the strategies behavior analysis uses to learn more about behavior changes will be sufficient to learn what more we need to know about progressive, orderly behavior changes. Because if so, then we may propose replacing the discipline of developmental psychology with the discipline of behavior analysis.

Behavior analysis can cite and often apply a small number of behavior-change processes that need not be considered developmental, in that they can be applied to a given response at almost any time in an organism's life with equal effect. To be declared developmental as well as behavior-analytic, a behavior-change process must not be one of those. A much greater number of behavior-change processes can be applied at almost any time but not with equal effect; the degree of effect depends on the preceding history, the elements of which may be labelled biological or environmental without altering the subsequent argument. Such behavior changes might be called developmental because of that dependence on the preceding history.

But then the same question must be asked about the preceding history: Could that history have been supplied at almost any time in the organism's life and equally well have affected the subsequent behavior-change process that depends on its prior occurrence? To find out requires that we be able to supply that history, experimentally, at any time in an organism's life. If we know enough to do that, we can begin answering these questions. If we do not know enough to do that, we have several alternatives:

We can wait until we do.

We can deduce the answers from our favorite theory.

We can invent the theory from which we see that we can deduce the particular answers we want. (But if we want certain answers prior to their proof, we must be in the grip of something other than curiosity about the truth— something like school loyalty, politics, lifestyle, or an axe to grind).

What is called behavioral science is full of all those approaches; our argument here is only to evaluate the development concept from the first of them: in terms of what can be verified or falsified. That implies waiting without an answer until experimental techniques are developed to allow a verifiable answer.

Remember that the point of being able to create interesting histories experimentally is to discover whether the dependency of a given behavior-change process on a particular history is uniform across almost all of an organism's life. If so, why call that developmental? Why not just call it the chain of conditions sufficient for the outcome under study? Or is that all that "developmental" will mean in the eventual shape of behavioral science? And if not, then we shall have to ask why that history does not affect that behavior-change process uniformly across the organism's life, and a high-priority question will be to ask if the history itself requires a certain earlier history to have the effects on the behavior-change process that it does. That kind of question, in addition to being pleasingly contextual, as modernity requires, also allows hypotheses that can prove verifiable or falsifiable, to the extent that we develop two classes of technique: (1) the experimental techniques suitable for supplying histories at many points in an organism's life, and (2) the observational techniques that can show us whether significant experimental histories have real-life parallels.

Indeed, a behavior-analytic developmental psychology very likely will be a collection of behavior-change processes, some of which will depend on certain prior histories for their effectiveness. The function of those prior histories sometimes in turn will depend on certain even more prior histories, which in turn will sometimes depend on yet more prior histories, etc., etc., as far back as the truth requires, or as interest in producing a usable truth requires, or as curiosity justifies.

If progressive, orderly changes in behavior are to be analyzed as exercises in behavior analysis, i.e., as collections of behavior-change processes whose effectivenesses sometimes depend on prior histories which in turn depend for their effectivenesses on even earlier histories, etc., we still may ask why there is so much order and so much progression in children's behavior changes. One eventually verifiable or falsifiable type of answer is that the behavior-change processes that can accomplish those progressive, orderly changes simply get applied in a correspondingly progressive and orderly manner—that the source of the progression and order is less in the organism and the organism's history, and more in the social environment that determines when those processes and their sometime-crucial histories are applied. The most obvious, and thus most conservative answer to why behavior change is progressive and orderly has always been that the child's environment, especially the social environment, does a great deal of teaching in a progressive, orderly way. If so, we then get to ask what taught the teachers to teach in that way. Will that prove developmental, or merely behavior-analytic, sociological, and the like?

The hypothesis is that much of what looks like development depends simply on teachings arranged in that order, and that we need to investigate the extent to which that is true, and when it is true, its causes, which in turn may be much like it. That hypothesis need not always be correct; indeed, it may often be incorrect. Even so, it is an obvious possibility and a very parsimonious one. On those grounds, it deserves investigation and falsification before going on to any more complicated propositions about either within-the-skin and outside-the-skin histories. But to investigate this simple, conservative possibility requires that we analyze teaching, deliberate and accidental, societal and natural, in all its varieties, and after that analyze the causes of those kinds of teachings. Behavior analysis is exactly such a discipline; it knows a great deal about what gets called teaching, and steadily produces even more knowledge about it. Thus, one conservative answer nominates behavior analysis as a well developed line of inquiry into progressive, orderly behavior changes; and because that discipline is large and complex, we see that this will be a very long line of at least occasionally fruitful inquiry. In sum, then, if our first criterion is to produce science propositions about progressive, orderly development that are verifiable and falsifiable, but only when that is our first criterion, is there any case for seeing developmental psychology as more than behavior analysis? We argue that there is not.

Finally, consider the usual case in point: When a quite young child fails in some training program, we usually question the training program rather than the developmental state of the child's biology or cognitive schema. After all, we can sometimes improve the training program, produce prompt success in accomplishing the behavior change in question, and thus dissolve the question about the current teachability of this behavior while opening a second question about why the first program failed. That a failed change depends on something "developmental" yet to happen is sometimes falsifiable, because its alternative, that the change was always shapable with the proper program, is sometimes verifiable. When a child's failure in a training program is explained in ways that allow experimental analysis, the explanation is verifiable or falsifiable; when the child's failure is explained in any other way, the result can be nothing but invention, inference, and theory. Such unreal explanations increase in plausibility (and no more than plausibility) mainly through successive failures of sophisticated and varied training programs. Thus they depend for their survival on the absence of a single demonstration of their opposite— a demonstration that there does exist a training program that will accomplish this behavior right now. Concepts that can survive only in the absence of a counter-demonstration are inherently fragile concepts. We suggest that the traditional account of development is just that—nothing more than a theory awaiting its demise, piece by piece, because its pieces are not nearly as verifiable as they are falsifiable.

We find it better to invest our time in the study of propositions that are both verifiable and falsifiable. Behavior analysis offers us that, and so our curiosity about progressive, orderly changes in children's behavior has become a curiosity about the experimental analysis of behavior, and about how progressively and orderly are its typical applications to those children. Anyone not committed to verifiability and falsifiability as their first premise will probably go in another direction. It is indeed interesting that most developmental psychologists see behavior analysis as nondevelopmental. Is it that they are indeed committed to a different first criterion than verifiability, and thus are free to seek more thoroughly explanatory but correspondingly less accessible conceptualizations? Or have they simply not been shown enough behavior analysis beyond the introductory text's brief and most often inaccurate paragraphs on the topic?

References

(1971, September 20). Skinner's utopia: Panacea, or path to hell. *Time*, pp. 47-53.

Ausubel, D., & Sullivan, E. (1970). *Theory and problems of child development* (2nd ed.). New York: Grune & Straton, Inc.

Baer, D. M. (1970). An age-irrelevant concept of development. *Merril-Palmer Quarterly of Behavior and Development, 16* (3), 238-246.

Baer, D. M. (1985). Applied behavior analysis as a conceptually conservative view of childhood. In R. J. McMahon & R. D. V. Peters (Eds.), *Childhood disorders: Behavioral-developmental approaches.* New York: Brunner/Mazel.

Baldwin, J. M. (1902). *Development and evolution.* New York: MacMillan.

Baltes, P. B., & Goulet, L. R. (1970). Status and issues of a life-span developmental psychology. In P. B. Goulet and L. R. Goulet (Eds.), *Life-span developmental psychology: Theory and research*, (pp. 3-21). New York: Academic Press.

Baltes, P. B., & Goulet, L. R. (1971). Exploration of developmental variables by manipulation and simulation of age differences in behavior. *Human Development. 14*, 149-170.

Bijou, S. W. (1989). Behavior Analysis. In R. Vasta (Ed.), *Annals of child development: Six theories of child development: Revised formulations and current issues* (pp. 61-83). Greenwich, CT: JAI Press.

Bijou, S. W., & Baer, D. M. (1961). *Child Development I: A systematic and empirical theory.* New York: Appleton-Century-Crofts.

Bijou, S. W., & Baer, D. M. (1978). *Behavior analysis of child development.* Englewood Cliffs, NJ: Prentice-Hall.

Brainerd, C. J. (1978). The stage question in cognitive-developmental theory. *Behavioral and Brain Sciences, 2*, 173-213.

Bronfenbrenner, U. (1979). *The ecology of human development: Experiments by nature and design.* Chicago: University of Chicago Press.

Clark, E. V. (1973). What's in a word? On the child's acquisition of semantics in his first language. In T. Moore (Ed.), *Cognitive development and the acquisition of language.* New York: Academic Press.

Collins, W. A. (Ed.). (1982). *The concept of development: The Minnesota Symposia on Child Psychology.* Hillsdale, NJ: Erlbaum.

Costall, A. (1986). Evolutionary gradualism and the study of development. *Human Development, 29*, 4-11.

Daehler, M. W., & Bukatko, D. (1985). *Cognitive development.* New York: Knopf.

Damon, W. (1977). *The social world of the child.* San Francisco: Jossey-Bass.

Erikson, E. (1950). *Childhood and society.* Harmondsworth: Penguin.

Fisher, K. W. (1980). A theory of cognitive development: The control and construction of hierarchies of skills. *Psychological Review, 87*, 477-531.

Flavell, J. H. (1982). Structures, stages, and sequences in cognitive development. In W. A. Collins (Ed.), *The concept of development: The Minnesota symposia on child psychology* (pp. 1-28). Hillsdale, NJ: Erlbaum.

Freud (1905). *Three essays on the theory of sexuality.* London: Hogarth Press.

Gewirtz, J. L. (1969). Mechanisms of social learning: Some roles of stimulation and behavior in early human development. In D. A. Goslin (Ed.), *Handbook of socialization theory and research*, (pp. 57-212). Chicago: McNally.

Ghiselin, M. (1986). The assimilation of Darwinism in developmental psychology. *Human Development, 29*, 12-21.

Gleick, J. (1987). Chaos: Making a new science. New York: Viking.

Glick, J. A. (1992). Werner's relevance for contemporary developmental psychology. *Developmental Psychology, 28* (4), 558-565.

Gollin, E. (1981). Development and plasticity. In E. Gollin (Ed.), *Developmental plasticity: Behavioural and biological aspects of variations in development*. New York: Academic Press.

Harris, D. (1957). Problems in formulating a scientific concept of development. In D. B. Harris (Ed.), *The concept of development: An issue in the study of human behavior*. Minneapolis: University of Minnesota Press.

Holland, J. (1992, July). Genetic algorithms. *Scientific American, 267* (1), 66-72.

Kagan, J. (1983). Classifications of the child. In P. Mussen (Ed.), *Handbook of child psychology, vol. 1: History, theory, and methods*. New York: Wiley.

Kantor, J. R. (1959). *Interbehavioral Psychology*. Bloomington, IN: Principia Press.

Kaplan, B. (1967). Meditations on genesis. *Human development, 10*, 65-87.

Kessen, W. (1960). Research design in the study of developmental problems. In P. H. Mussen (Ed.), *Handbook of research methods in child development*. New York: John Wiley & Sons, Inc.

Kessen, W. (1962). "Stage" and "structure" in the study of children. *Monographs of the Society for Research in Child Development, 27* (2), 65-82.

Kohlberg, L., Levine, C., & Hewer, A. (1983). *Moral stages: A current formulation and a response to critics*. Basel: Karger.

Lerner, R. M. (1986). *Concepts and theories of human development* (2 ed.). New York: Random House.

Miller, P. H. (1983). *Theories of developmental psychology*. New York: Freeman.

Morss, J. R. (1990). *The biologising of childhood: Developmental psychology and the Darwinian myth*. Hillsdale, NJ: Erlbaum.

Overton, W., & Reese, H. (1973). Models of development: Methodological implications. In J. R. Nesselroade & H. W. Reese (Eds.), *Life-span developmental psychology: Methodological issues* (pp. 65-86). New York: Academic Press.

Pepper, S. (1942). *World hypotheses: A study on evidence*. Berkeley, CA: University of California Press.

Piaget, J. (1971). *Biology and knowledge*. Chicago: The University of Chicago Press.

Piaget, J., & Inhelder, B. (1969). *The psychology of the child*. New York: Basic Books.

Reese, H., & Overton, W. (1970). Models of development and theories of development. In L. R. Goulet & P. B. Baltes (Eds.), *Life-span developmental psychology: Research and theory* (pp. 115-145). New York: Academic Press.

Schoenfeld, W. N., & Farmer, J. (1970). Reinforcement schedules and the "behavior stream." In W. N. Schoenfeld (Ed.), *The theory of reinforcement schedules* (pp. 215-245). New York: Appleton-Century-Crofts.

Siegler, R. (1981). Developmental sequences within and between concepts. *Monographs of the Society for Research in Child Development, 46* (2), 1-13.

Skinner, B. F. (1953). *Science and human behavior*. New York: Free Press.

Skinner, B. F. (1969). *Contingencies of Reinforcement: A theoretical Analysis*. Englewood Cliffs, NJ: Prentice-Hall.

Skinner, B. F. (1981). Selection by consequences. *Science, 213*, 501-504.

Watson, J. B. (1919). *Psychology from the standpoint of a behaviorist*. Philadelphia: Lippincott.

Watson, J. B. (1926). What the nursery has to say about instincts. In C. Murchison (Ed.), *Psychologies of 1925* (pp. 1-35). Worcester, MA: Clark University Press.

Werner, H. (1940). *Comparative psychology of mental development*. Harper.

Werner, H. (1957). The concept of development from a comparative and organismic point of view. In D. B. Harris (Ed.), *The concept of development: An issue in the study of human behavior* (pp. 125-148). Minneapolis: University of Minnesota Press.

Wertheimer, M. (1982). The evolution of the concept of development in the history of psychology. In G. Eckardt, W. G. Bringmann, & L. Sprung (Eds.), *Contributions to a history of developmental psychology: International W. T. Preyer Symposium* (pp. 13-25). New York: Mouton.

Wohlwill, J. H. (1970). The age variable in psychological research. *Psychological Review. 77* (1), 49-64.

Wohlwill, J. H. (1973). *The study of behavioral development*. New York: Academic Press.

Zuriff, G. E. (1985). *Behaviorism: A conceptual reconstruction*. New York: Columbia University Press.

Footnote

[1] The authors are grateful to Irene Grote, Bryan Midgley, Charalambos Cleanthous, and Shahla Ala'i-Rosales for sympathetic, careful, competent, and usefully persistent argument; to John Wright for extraordinarily competent and challenging counter-arguments requiring answers which, when possible, improved this argument; and to the National Institute for Child Health and Human Development for research support (HD 18955).

Chapter 10

Child Psychology, Development, and the Patterning of Human Action: An Essay on Concepts and Issues

Peter Harzem
Auburn University

There are many ways of *understanding* and *having a knowledge* of human behavior, and the scientific understanding of it is only one of them. In the ordinary course of daily life, as we interact with each other, every one of us develops a knowledge of other humans and, indeed, of ourselves. However, as Sigmund Freud and many a scholar before and since has noted—Freud's observations on the matter have been the most influential of this century—the knowledge we thus acquire is almost always erroneous when judged against external, independent criteria. It is subject to deep rooted biases and desires, of which we may not be aware and which we cannot, therefore, eradicate even if we so wished. Of course, it is nevertheless the case that as we go about our daily lives such knowledge and understanding, despite their faults, serve us quite well most of the time. Without them interacting with others, and therefore our daily lives, would become impossible.

This "experiential knowledge" is not solely the result of each individual's own experience. Experiences of others, too, profoundly affect it in several ways. It gets strengthened and substantially enlarged through the experiences of others which we learn by various means: We are told about them, we are given advice, we draw impressions from variety of sources such as the daily news; and perhaps, most powerfully the arts—the novel, poetry, drama, music, and the like—provide rich insights into human nature and human action. In this way, within a culture, an individual's understanding of life cumulates across generations, building upon the prior experiences of others.

This important characteristic of being "cumulative" is, then, a universal feature of cultures and not confined to scientific knowledge. We turn to scientific knowledge, that is, we seek both to build it and to use it, for reasons different from those that are ordinarily entailed in our day-to-day actions although, of course, scientific knowledge enters into our lives through the many ways in which it is used to construct our environments. Scientific inquiry is one of several forms in which the fundamental human characteristic of curiosity, the never ceasing human desire to know, finds natural expression. There has not been a society in history where such inquiry, however primitive, did not take place. Sometimes it flourished even in the face of despotic prohibition.

There is another reason, a reason which has become overwhelming in this second half of the present century, for our collective desire to sustain scientific inquiry in our societies: We have learned through the centuries that scientific knowledge enables us to design and control our environments more effectively than we can without it --to build bridges, to navigate ships, to communicate rapidly in many forms, to cure diseases, to acquire riches; in short, in endless ways to make our lives more comfortable and more enjoyable. (As everyone knows, there is also the other, the dark, face of all this. We now know and put to awful use more than ever before the enormously destructive possibilities of scientific knowledge.)

In our time, as scientific knowledge and its uses have increased at an accelerating pace, we have turned to science all the more in search of remedies, improvements, solutions. And now, we seek in science ways of developing, improving and controlling not only our environment but also our own actions. The notion that just as we can control our environments through science we should, by the same means, also be able to understand and improve ourselves is an old one, going back to the writings of Thomas Hobbes in the sixteenth century and, no doubt, before. But as Psychology textbooks are wont to tell us, Psychology began its growth as a Science—with at least the capital "S"—in the latter part of the 19th century. Since then, this important discipline has grown and spread—some may say 'evolved'—like an untended garden, with its share of weeds and with no overall scheme to its subdivisions and specialties.

The areas of Psychology now constitute an enormous version of what Gilbert Ryle called a "category mistake." They overlap and criss cross in ways that defy logical classification. The result is a conceptual mess, regrettable not merely because of its untidiness but, more seriously, because it has led to the same sets of phenomena being studied under different names, each going its own way without benefiting from and building upon the others. For example, the areas traditionally termed "personality" and "individual differences" are concerned with aspects of the same cluster of phenomena and yet they have rarely paid heed to one another.

The matter gets even more complex when we come to consider the area termed "developmental." Developmental Psychology, too, is concerned with the development of "personality" as well as its aspects that fall under the head "individual differences;" yet these three "areas"—personality, individual differences, and developmental psychology—have tenuous interactions in the sorts of issues they pursue, in the ways they pause their research questions, in the sorts of scientific investigation they conduct to answer those questions, and in the formulation of their theories. This is one reason—and there are others—why, in the contemporary literature of Psychology, for every broad question there exist several different, often incompatible answers, each resting on some selected part of the total available evidence.

Developmental, Child and Life–Span Psychology

"Developmental Psychology" had its beginnings under the head, "Child Psychology." "Psychology," without that qualification, was taken to deal with adults. It is as reasonable now, as it was then, that the study of the psychology of children would constitute a distinct, cohesive area. As late as in the 1950s the statement, "children are not miniature adults," had impact and meaning in many contexts, although now, one would hope, the same statement would be regarded a self-evident truth, and it would raise eyebrows as to the necessity of asserting it. It is, therefore, yet another curious accident of history that in recent decades the term "Child Psychology" was to fall out of favor, to be replaced by "Developmental Psychology."

The reasons for the shift to "Developmental Psychology" are not persuasive. They seem to have arisen from the difficulty of locating by chronological age the end of childhood, and a wish to emphasize the focus of the area on "development" rather than on the child. However, this change carries with it the mistaken, though no doubt unintended, implication that development is a property of childhood. But, of course, behavioral development is a universal characteristic of an individual's life, even though it is more intense at some periods, particularly childhood, than others. Conversely, and even more importantly, there is far more to the psychology of childhood than development. In other words, just as there is more to development than what occurs in childhood, more occurs in childhood than what is conveyed by the term "development." "Development" places a demand to observe any *changes* that may occur *across* time in, for example, how an infant interacts with objects in his environment. Such a demand to focus on change is inessential, of course, if the research question at hand calls only for discovery of the essential features of such interactions. It is unwise to place restrictions on scientific inquiry merely by virtue of the name given to the general subject matter.

The next, most recent, shift in the name of the area has been to "life-span development." This serves to eliminate by implication the confinement of development to childhood, but in the process makes matters even worse. Through the intermediary of the term "development" ("child" to "development," and "development" to "life-span development") it breaks away from the original and perfectly reasonable focus on the psychology of children, and creates a new division between, on the one hand, the study of the *development* of action, and on the other hand, ... what? Does not all Psychology concern itself with the *development* of some pattern of acting, of solving a problem, of perceiving a situation, and so on, ad infinitum? Subdivisions of a discipline are helpful when they serve to draw distinctions; when no such distinction can be found they are unnecessary, and they cause arbitrary separation of cognate investigations that might otherwise be constructively related to each other.

It may be said that the developmental area, whether of the life-span variety or not, is distinguished from the other areas of Psychology by its focus on development that emerges *through the passage of time*, that is, by age. This will not stand up to scrutiny, however, for at least two reasons. First, note that here the passage of time is taken as an independent variable and also used as the criterion for identifying the area. But it is poor practice to divide a scientific discipline by independent variables. Independent variables are generally pervasive, and they cannot be confined into tidy bundles. Second, in any case, the changes that occur in development cannot be *attributed* to age. Chronological age is a measure in years, months, etc., of how much time has elapsed since the person was born. Causally attributing changes in psychological phenomena to elapsed time is like causally attributing the growth of a tree to inches and feet. The growth of the tree can be said to be so many inches long, but it cannot be said to have been brought about by the inches.

The Pervasiveness of Developmental Psychology

The argument presented this far is not, of course, a recommendation to overlook the obvious fact that the performance of an organism takes place within the limits of its anatomical and physiological possibilities. The behavior of children is constrained by these limits, just as are the behavior of adults and of older persons. The measure of age is, therefore, sometimes a helpful indicator of the physical and other capabilities an individual, whether child or adult. Moreover, there are abilities and behavioral dispositions that reach a peak at certain points in the individual's life; as, for instance, in the case of "imprinting" that has been found in some species of animals, and as in maternal bonding and, perhaps, first-language acquisition in humans. These too—but not the age range *in* which they are observed—determine in complex ways the interaction of the individual with the environment. There is good reason, therefore, for the research that has been conducted into the range and limits of actions that are available to an individual at a given point of growth, that growth most conveniently being *measured* by chronological age. However, the discoveries that emerge from such research do not merely end at a conclusion but, rather, they open up new and important lines of inquiry. They lead to questions as to what factors determine these limits and what changes such limits undergo across time. They do not answer them. For answers what is needed is extensive, programmatic, sustained inquiry of the kind that has previously been directed at, say, the discovery of critical periods as regards imprinting. The additional benefit here would be the re-emergence of Child Psychology in its own right. This, in turn, would give distinct—though related—emphasis to the generality of the important phenomenon of development. Development must be investigated and understood in every area of Psychology, and not carved out of Psychology as a free-standing subject-matter.

The Need to Study the Transitions of Behavior

In 1976 B.F. Skinner published a brief note in the *Journal of the Experimental Analysis of Behavior*, entitled "Farewell my lovely." His lovely, in that case, was the *cumulative record*, and the note expressed regret at its disappearance from the pages of that journal. Cumulative records show *transitions* of behavior, that is, the *development* of behavior from one form to another. By the time of Skinner's note, however, the so-called "steady-state method" had become pervasive in behavioral research, especially in behavior analysis. Steady-state data show State A, and perhaps,

State B, but not the changes that A undergoes as it is transformed into B. There is, of course, value to such data; but to be satisfied with them is not unlike in biology being satisfied with observing the caterpillar and the butterfly, and not worrying about how one changes into the other.

Generally psychological research has been limited in the attention given to the questions of how patterns of action develop and how they are maintained. Two main reasons appear to have resulted in this curious constriction. First, the methods of analytical statistics have dominated all of Psychology since mid-1930s. These methods have determined not merely how the data shall be analyzed once obtained, but also what sort of investigation shall be "designed" so that the data obtained will be suitable for analysis by these techniques. By the late 1930s it had become customary in Psychology to fit the question to the format dictated by the technique of data analysis that was to be used, instead of fitting the techniques to the question. As this practice became entrenched, it severely constrained the kinds of possible research questions that could be asked and therefore, in turn, the phenomena that were to be parts the subject matter of Psychology. (For a detailed discussion of these matters see Harzem, 1995.)

These methods of analysis—including their more recent versions—entail the comparison of sets of discrete data so as to discover continuities between them and, most often, whether they differ from each other such that the difference can be attributed to an identifiable factor. Where the question arises as to the changes—development—that took place between the sets of data, the answer is based on speculation, whether of a theoretical variety or not, even when observation and analysis of such transition are entirely within the reach of the investigator. What is not available is a technique of analysis from amongst the habitually established techniques. This is like comparing two or more snapshots of, say, a runner, and from that reconstructing the action that may have occurred between them. Now, this is a perfectly rational way of arriving at statements about the development of behavior, in the absence of methods such as video- and cine-recording, that might permit the researcher to record and analyze the stream of behavior in question. It does not, however, relieve the science from the necessity to search for better methods.

Second, in the areas of Psychology not confined to the use of analytical statistics, notably in operant research, the steady-state analyses have displaced the cumulative record. Yet the cumulative record stands out as the one method in Psychology that made possible the continuous tracking and accurately recording of changes in streams of behavior. Its development by Skinner was a singularly important departure from the established ways of research of the time, and it remains important now. Nevertheless, the cumulative record, too, has important limitations. In the first place it can be applied only to repeated occurrences of the same act, each instance occupying a brief period. These repeated acts are then recorded across long stretches of time; typically an hour or more. This repeatedly recorded act is deliberately brought about by the researcher, for the purposes of research, through "shaping," "autoshaping," and the like. Acts of the sort that can typically be recorded in cumulative records do not occur in nature, as in the case of bar pressing by the rat; or if they do, as in the case of pecking by the pigeon, they do not occur in extended repetitions. Consequently, the behavioral phenomena that are discovered through experiments involving such responses, whether by observing cumulative records or in steady-state research, lead to speculations and conclusions that remain ultimately to be confirmed -or not- by studies of the natural behavior of organisms, both within and across species. This requires that the corresponding research must be conducted into natural behavior when appropriate methods can be used.

Thus, implicitly, the patterning of behavior observed in a cumulative record is in *theory* taken to *represent* the sort of behavior that would be expected to occur generally in nature, when the behavior stream consists not of repetitions in monotony but varies in topography with no clear cut borders. It is good scientific strategy to work with the assumption that the relations observed in the former also occur, *with the same particulars*, in the latter. It is,however, erroneous, to forget the tentative characteristic of this assumption, and to assert it as if the matter were closed.

Difficulties in Studying Patterns in Human Behavior

The patterning of human behavior, from its emergence at or before birth through the continuity of its changes throughout life, has remained resistant to the kind of experimental analysis that, when conducted with laboratory animals, has been so distinguished in accuracy and detail. There are numerous reasons for this, and the most obvious of them is also the most persuasive: It is neither possible nor desirable experimentally to control the multitude of variables that determine human behavior. At best, therefore, there has to be a compromise between experimental rigor and the demands of civilized standards that apply when conducting research on human -and, for that matter, animal- subjects. This, by itself, is a powerful constraint. There are, however, other, fundamental reasons that arise from the particular nature of human behavior.

The principal difficulty is one of units. In the absence of well defined, readily identifiable units neither cumulative recording nor meaningful quantitative analysis is possible. There have been innumerable and valiant attempts at finding reasonable units by which human behavior might be quantified and which are amenable to mathematical treatment. Yet, the behavior stream we seek to *understand* has no such units. In psychological research attempts to overcome this problem of units have been of three kinds. First, there have been the approaches that generally take the terms of ordinary language as identifying rather large patterns of behavior. Here, terms such as "choosing," "deciding," "searching," "loving," and yes, "bonding" are implicitly assumed to relate to identifiable action patterns, and research is conducted to discover, for example, the conditions that determine the occurrence of such actions. This kind of research does not call for the recording of frequency. Furthermore, the patterning of sequences of such large units, across time, would hardly be informative. In fact this research represents the kind of compromise that was indicated above, between experimental rigor and the demands of civilized behavior. Unfortunately, however, in psychological literature this is not the view that has been taken. Instead, sustained effort has been made artificially to ascribe to the behavior under study a degree of precision that it does not possess. This is done through the device, "operational definition." Here the researcher does not in fact study, say, "bonding"–that is, what any reasonable speaker of the language would understand by that term. Instead, conversely, what is actually studied is claimed, *by the researcher*, to be "bonding." This linguistic trick is achieved by asserting that *for the purposes of that particular research* the term "bonding" is "operationally defined" to stand for what is being studied. In other words, instead of ensuring that the phenomenon of interest is what is studied, it is–falsely–claimed that what is studied is, merely by virtue of the idiosyncratic verbal manipulations of the researcher, the phenomenon of interest. This is a practice that violates the basic rationale of operational definitions, and yet it has been rampant in Psychology with substantial consequent damage to the discipline in general. (For more detailed discussions of this issue see Harzem, 1984, 1986, 1995; and also Bridgman, 1927.)

Second, in some research the different strategy is adopted of taking advantage of the fact that some psychological phenomena already have, by nature, small and readily identifiable units. Examples of these are words and sentences. It is not by accident that when Skinner and other behavior analysts were interested in showing the effectiveness of reinforcement upon verbal behavior, they turned for experimental evidence to counting the occurrence of given words and word sequences in speech. This too, however, has its limitations. In the first place, units of this kind naturally occur only in some parts of the broad range of phenomena that constitutes the subject matter of Psychology. Moreover, the frequency of occurrence of a word may be of some interest in connection with only a limited set of questions that may be asked about language. When people speak and write, how often they say the same thing, with what distribution in time, is seldom the issue of significance in scientific inquiry into language and verbal behavior. Of course, from observations of the effects of various experimental manipulations upon the frequency of the same utterance it may be possible to derive guesses (suggestions, hypotheses, etc.) as to how, for example, language ordinarily functions. However, no amount of further counting of occurrences will answer those questions; it is, rather, necessary to return the research attention to language as it naturally occurs.

Third, in the face of these limitations a particularly productive strategy has been the deliberate creation of one or more units of action, such as bar presses, that do not ordinarily exist in the behavioral repertoire of the subject, and if they do, they do not occur in prolonged sequences of repetitions. The frequency and temporal distribution of these *experimentally created* units can then be studied in relation to the variables manipulated by the researcher. Here, too, however, the advantages and the limitations of this strategy apply, as discussed above.

Developmental Behavior and the Patterning of Behavior

As early as in 1899 Bryan and Harter reported some of the complexities to be observed in the development of "habits." They noted that such development takes place not at a steady pace, but at varying rates of progress with interspersed plateaux. Since that time, the extensive data that have become available in psychological literature have provided evidence of the enormous complexity that is involved in the patterning of human behavior, as well as in the behavior of other species. This article started by noting that these complexities may be *understood* in a number of ways, and the scientific understanding of them is only one of those ways. As our societies become more complex, however, and thus the fitting of our actions to the demands of society become more difficult, our need for a *consistent*, systematic knowledge of behavior is rapidly increasing. We need a Psychology where there is a body of undisputed, empirically based knowledge, and where every assertion is not contradicted by rival theories so that only the devotees of doctrines are prone to be confident, wholly to their own satisfaction, about what is actually the case. If our cultures are to survive, we need a body of sound knowledge so as to enable us to control the technologies we have developed. We are living at an age where the consequences of a human error that may be minor in one context turn out to be vastly disastrous in another—as, for example, in the cases of the Chernobyl nuclear accident and the Texaco Valdez oil-spill. In those, and countless other cases, the failures were in human behavior and not, in comparison with the behavior of people in general, of great magnitude, but the consequences were vastly disastrous. Our societies now need means by which we can effectively and humanely control our own behavior, as effectively as we have come to control our environments. To meet that urgent need, we must in the first place discover the conditions under which new patterns of action develop, how they are sustained, and in what ways they are transmuted. In short, we need to understand the phenomena involved in the *development* of behavior. The development of behavior that we need so urgently to understand is ubiquitous, however, not confined to any one subdivision of Psychology.

In order to distinguish the concept of behavioral development as discussed here from what has traditionally been characterized as "developmental"—as in "Developmental Psychology"—I have occasionally used the term "patterning." I do not claim any particular value for this term but wish only to insist that for both scholarly reasons and in order to face up to social responsibilities, building a broad, dependable knowledge of the development—or patterning—of behavior is a demand that must be faced by all of Psychology.

General Observation

One of the less attractive features of contemporary Psychology is the chasm that apparently divides "soft Psychology" from "hard Psychology," the former laying claim to humane concerns and the latter, to scientific rigor. Now, this is an especially damaging separation which is unsound in its rationale—if such there is—and unwise in its posturings. On the one hand, self-righteousness and claims to humanistic concerns hardly go together; on the other hand, scientific extremism has shades of uncaring in the face of the social needs of our times. Our cultures are threatened from many directions. There is pressing need for a Psychology which is both rigorous in its science and informed by the issues and values of its times. It is relevant to note that there has been no distinguished scientist in the history of the sciences who were not also broadly cultured, with interest in the knowledge and achievements of their times.

A science confined within itself, oblivious to its context is like distilled water: it is colorless, tasteless, and odorless, and it is open to dissolve every contaminant that comes its way. Good water has taste which is subtly imparted to it by salts, just as good science is that which is subtly informed by its culture and intellectual heritage.

References

Bridgman, P.W. (1927). *The logic of modern physics*. New York: MacMillan Company.

Bryan, W.L. & Harter, N. (1899). Studies on the telegraphic language: The acquisition of hierarchy of habits. *Psychological Review*, 6, 345-375.

Harzem, P. (1984). Operationism, smuggled connotations, and the nothing-else clause. Comments on B. F. Skinner's article, "The operational analysis of psychological terms." *The Behavioral and Brain Sciences*, 7, 559.

Harzem, P. (1986). The language trap and the study of patterns in human action. In T. Thompson and M. D. Zeiler (Eds.) *Analysis and Integration of Behavioral Units*. Hillsdale, NJ: Erlbaum and Associates, pp. 45-53.

Harzem, P. (1995). Seven disasters that derailed psychology. (In press; preprint available from the author.)

Skinner, B.F. (1976). Farewell, my lovely. *Journal of the Experimental Analysis of Behavior*, 25, 218.

Other Books from CONTEXT PRESS